ʃ
M000231430

SHAMANIC
TRANSFORMATIONS

5, Wesselman — realm of transcendence

28 the invisible world of spirit

36, here to bring more beauty, healing &
an joy to the world

73 the awakening that must happen
in every person

178 — very similar to my experience

*92 celtic connections

* 111 Star beings - faith in all is one

117 Courage is embracing fear as teacher & friend

123 Spiritual psychotherapist

122 Ability to embrace path after vision
124 Spirit travel into other worlds

* 132 Jamie Sams Book, look @ PhD

138 Shamanic psychotherapist

SHAMANIC
TRANSFORMATIONS

True Stories of the
Moment of Awakening

EDITED BY ITZHAK BEERY

Destiny Books
Rochester, Vermont • Toronto, Canada

Destiny Books
One Park Street
Rochester, Vermont 05767
www.DestinyBooks.com

Text stock is SFI certified

Destiny Books is a division of Inner Traditions International

Copyright © 2015 by Itzhak Beery

All rights reserved. No part of this book may be reproduced or utilized in
any form or by any means, electronic or mechanical, including photocopying,
recording, or by any information storage and retrieval system, without permission
in writing from the publisher.

Library of Congress Cataloging-in-Publication Data
Shamanic transformations : true stories of the moment of awakening / edited by
Itzhak Beery.
    pages cm
   Summary: "Inspiring accounts from renowned contemporary working shamans
about their first moments of spiritual epiphany"— Provided by publisher.
   ISBN 978-1-62055-475-3 (pbk.) — ISBN 978-1-62055-476-0 (e-book)
   1. Shamanism. 2. Shamans. I. Beery, Itzhak, 1950– editor.
   BF1611.S525 2015
   201'.44—dc23
                                                        2015002948

Printed and bound in the United States by Lake Book Manufacturing, Inc.
The text stock is SFI certified. The Sustainable Forestry Initiative® program
promotes sustainable forest management.

10   9   8   7   6   5   4   3   2   1

Text design by Debbie Glogover and layout by Virginia Scott Bowman
This book was typeset in Garamond Premier Pro, Avenir, and Gill Sans with
Garamond Premier Pro used as the display typeface.

To send correspondence to the author of this book, mail a first-class letter to the
author c/o Inner Traditions • Bear & Company, One Park Street, Rochester, VT
05767, and we will forward the communication, or contact the author directly at
itzhakbeery.com.

Contents

Acknowledgments   ix

Introduction: The Relevance of Shamanism   1
By Itzhak Beery

1   The Three Stages of Spiritual Unfolding   5
    By Hank Wesselman

2   Shamanic Impact: From Child to Crone   11
    By Dana Jefferson

3   Urban Shamanism: Treating Depression Using   18
    Shamanic Healing Practices
    By Ellie Zarrabian

4   Shamanic Ecstasy   26
    By Alberto Villoldo

5   The Call to Service   37
    By Sandra Ingerman

6   Raptor Medicine: A Portal to Shamanic Beginnings   44
    By Thomas J. Mock

7   A Mountain's Light   51
    By Ginny Anderson

8   Journey about Love Doctoring   58
    By Katharine Weiser

9   A Most Extraordinary Vision on the Power Path   61
    By José Luis Stevens

10 Into the Red Path   67
    By Julián Katari

11 Mount Everest   74
    By Jan Engels-Smith

12 Rappers Don't Go on Meditation Retreats   81
    By Bezi

13 Moon Struck   88
    By Mama Donna Henes

14 A Lifetime of Awakenings   92
    By Tom Cowan

15 Encounters with an Ally Plant   96
    By Carol L. Parker

16 Call of the Ancestors   101
    By Phillip Scott

17 There's Been a Whole Lot of Grace   105
    By Reverend C. Ayla Joyce

18 An Experiential Journey toward Trust   111
    By Julie Dollman

19 Of Mountains and Men   116
    By Rebekah Brandon

20 Shamanism in the Amazon   119
    By Deborah Goleman Wolf

21 A Visit from Apó Lákay   124
    By Lane Wilcken

22 The Non-Dualism of Shamanic Psychotherapy 131
    By Joseph E. Doherty

23 Baby, I Was Born This Way 139
    By Linda Star Wolf

24 Shapeshifting: From Dying to Apprenticing 145
    By John Perkins

25 A Doorway Called Africa 149
    By Misha Hoo

26 Sacred Journey of a Lifetime 156
    By Holly Gray Schuck

27 A Pathway to Transformation 162
    By Raymond Nobriga

28 Shamanic Awakening 170
    By Nadiya Nottingham

29 A Luminous Re-Membering 178
    By don Oscar Manuel Miro-Quesada

30 My Shamanic Initiation: The Fire of Transformation 185
    By Mona Rain (Smith)

31 The Power Animal Experience 190
    By Debra Fentress

32 Pandora's Box 193
    By Wendy Whiteman

33 Sacred Place 200
    By Peter Brown

34 The Awakening of a Medicine Woman 208
    By Katherine Gomez

35 Warrior Wisdom 212
    By Colleen Deatsman

36 Spirit Chases Me 220
By Randall Sexton

37 Shamanic Impact 225
By Niramisa Weiss

38 Pine Spirit Medicine 229
By Rita Baruss

39 Communal Song and the Art of Healing 235
By Elizabeth Cosmos

40 Temples of the Earth 243
By Zacciah Blackburn

41 Direct Dialogue with Mother Earth 251
By Michele Gieselman

42 The Calling 257
By Michael Drake

43 The Gifts of Shamanism 265
By Pamela Albee

44 The Story of a Bear 273
By Leon Sproule

45 The Soul Union Community 279
By Johanna Lor Rain Parry

46 The Slow Build of a Shamanic Path 289
By Lewis Mehl-Madrona

47 Northern Lights 296
By Lynn Andrews

Epilogue: Back Where It All Began 303
By Itzhak Beery

To my grandchildren, Ayela and Abraham
May the Great Mystery guide you on an awe-inspiring life journey.

Acknowledgments

My deepest gratitude to all the shamanic teachers who came forward to share in this collection the most personal and intimate moment of their lives' transformations. Thank you for your trust and courage, and for believing in the importance of this book. I am in reverence to you and in awe of your journeys. I know they will inspire the readers as well.

This book could not have happened if it weren't for the vision and passion of my longtime pal and fellow traveler on the path Ariel Orr Jordan; I am indebted to you for your insights, continued generosity, and support. Special thanks to my friend and inspirational agent, Joe Kulin, who knows how to calm me down and get me to the finish line. Thank you, Ken Jordan of Reality Sandwich, who got the ball rolling over a Zen platter at one of our lunches. Thank you, Nora Logan, for assisting me with heralding the authors and entries. Thank you to my fellow New York Shamanic Circle's Core Members and community for your enthusiastic support. To my family who encourage me to continue to pursue my life passion, an endless thank you!

My profound thanks to Ehud Sperling and his Inner Traditions team for believing in the book's message, taking on this project, and making it happen so beautifully.

INTRODUCTION

The Relevance of Shamanism

Itzhak Beery

"You better make it absolutely relevant. Listen to me, rel-e-vant is the key word!" My longtime friend Ariel Orr Jordan, who is a talented film-maker, a prolific writer, and a shamanic soul himself, was fired up and animatedly repeating this over and over as we were speed-walking in circles around Washington Square Park. It was a beautiful early spring morning, and passersby glanced at us in amusement as we exchanged words in throaty Hebrew. "Ask them to send you their personal stories of how their shamanic experience forever changed their lives. The more personal it is, the more powerful and inspirational it will be for others," he added in growing excitement and passion.

I knew he was on to something, as he had been many times before. I had asked his opinion because I was searching for a big idea, something exciting that would make the new website I had just created in 2007, Shaman Portal, not just popular with our readers but also useful.

"Yes! You're right!" I agreed wholeheartedly, trying to catch up to him.

"Everyone must have had one single moment, a split second of a personal experience, an 'aha' moment, a eureka of unexpected realiza-tion, inspiration, insight, recognition, or comprehension, after which their world, as if by magic, changes lenses, like wearing a new pair of different, clearer eyeglasses, and a new consciousness emerges," he said in one long breath.

1

As we started our last lap around the park he continued decisively, "Listen to me. If you do that, your site will be a tremendous success."

Back at my office, I asked my webmaster to add a new section to the website. I called it "Shamanic Impact."

This was not the first time that Ariel had taken part in a moment of birthing ceremony. On the base of Cotopaxi—the snowcapped volcanic mountain in Ecuador, which reaches a height of 19,347 feet—Ariel, our friend Samuel, and I had stood frozen. We were part of a group of sixteen individuals who had traveled to South America in the spring of 1997 with John Perkins, the renowned author and shaman (who also is a contributor to this book), to learn and perform healing ceremonies with the Quechua and Shuar shamans. It was already late afternoon when we arrived at the base of Cotopaxi, and as the sun started to set we shivered from the cold temperature and the merciless strong blowing wind. The legendary symmetrical glacier cone we knew from pictures was all but gone, covered by a heavy blanket of gray clouds, and the fierce wind blew so hard it literally swept us off our feet.

For no apparent reason, I took a drum and started drumming, chanting, and calling on the spirit of Apu (the god who lives on the mountaintops) and began walking in a large circle. Soon Ariel and then Samuel joined me, and the others followed as if in a trance. Down below, a group of Andean geese looked at us in surprise from the puddle they were enjoying. Quickly and magically, a powerful ritual circle was formed. About twenty minutes later, suddenly, as if by the hand of Apu itself, the sky opened up above the mountaintop and massive rays of light poured down, revealing the magnificent snowcapped tip and with it a beautiful bright blue sky. The whole mountain came alive. I was mesmerized. "What just happened? Did we have anything to do with that?"

In this superb collection of stories you will have the opportunity to read accounts of people who have experienced such moments. Although most of them are now shamanic practitioners, they used to be just regular folks, just like you and me. There is no way to know how, where, and when that game-changing moment will occur. It can happen in strange places and situations. The experience can come in response to life challenges or illness, and/or just by "accident"—on mountaintops, in cities, by rivers and oceans, or even in one's kitchen. It sometimes happens as a spirit visitation, through dreams, or when one is walking in Nature or even just driving a car.

According to the now famous prophecies of the Inca and Maya (the two more well-known and well-documented ancient South American cultures), as well as other indigenous cultures around the world, we have entered a new period in mankind's conscious development. The Inca's Pachakuti (which means Earth/time correction—a period of five hundred years) began in 1993, five hundred years after the execution of the last Incan king and the fall of the empire. This was the beginning of the occupation of the white man, and on December 21, 2012, the thirteenth Baktun ended and a new time cycle began (marking the start of a new calendar).

The Inca and Maya prophesy that this will be a period of peace and cooperation between all races, and a time of knowledge-sharing between all people. It is the time of the return of feminine energies, a return to the heart-center and to a more just society.

Since 1993, shamans, medicine men, and wisdomkeepers from all over South America have come down from the mountains, out of the Amazon basin; they have heard their calling and started to spread their hidden and well-kept ancient wisdom to the people of the industrial world. The impact stories you are about to read are all part of that extraordinary change we are witnessing, which is happening ever more rapidly now. Lawyers, housewives, celebrities, auto mechanics, corporate executives, financiers—people from all walks of life are hearing that calling. Like mushrooms after a long-awaited rain, they are opening their hearts and listening, which is not always easy, as you will see from their accounts. The skeptic gatekeepers of our rational mind still stand guard.

And yet we are learning to unlearn. We are learning to re-remember the wisdom we have forgotten. We are learning to make room for the magic, the miracles, and to be in the awe of the unseen universe. We are learning to pay close attention to supposed "coincidences" and not to dismiss them as accidents. We are rediscovering our connection to our ancestors and beginning to see our lives as a continuum of our family trees. We are discovering our soul's life mission and purpose and truly paying attention to it—aware as we are of how important it is to embody it and make it manifest.

Each story in this book is the story of a unique personal journey of one individual. But its impact reverberates beyond that of one individual life. Its influence spreads close and far—to the storyteller's family, students, coworkers, immediate community, and the entire world. For as you change, so does the world around you.

Enjoy.

ITZHAK BEERY is an internationally recognized shamanic healer, teacher, and author. He was initiated into the Circle of Twenty-Four Yachaks by his Quechua teacher in Ecuador and by Amazonian Kanamari Pagè. He has also trained intensively with other elders from South and North America. The founder of ShamanPortal.org and cofounder of the New York Shamanic Circle, he is on the faculty of the New York Open Center. His work has been featured in the *New York Times*, films, TV, and webinars. An accomplished visual artist and owner of an award-winning advertising agency, he grew up on Kibbutz Beit Alfa in Israel and lives in New York. Itzhak's book *The Gift of Shamanism: Visionary Power, Ayahuasca Dreams, and Journeys to Other Realms* was published by Inner Traditions. His website is www.itzhakbeery.com.

1

The Three Stages
of Spiritual Unfolding

Hank Wesselman

In considering the initiatory experience of shamanic impact, many people are aware that my wife, Jill Kuykendall, and I were drawn into connection with a Hawaiian kahuna elder named Hale Makua; this occurred during the last eight years of his life. One of the things that Makua discussed with us during that time was our uniquely human experience of spiritual unfolding—a process in which we, as souls, grow and become more than we were, often through the experience of shamanic impact. His shared wisdom and our conversations with him have been published in my book *The Bowl of Light: Ancestral Wisdom from a Hawaiian Shaman*. Others such as Ken Wilber have addressed this phenomenon as well.

Allow me to now bring this topic up for consideration because when we understand fully what it is that we have stepped into—or as Makua was fond of saying, "what we have all signed up for"—the rest of our life may become increasingly clear.

THE FIRST STAGE:
BELIEF

The first stage of our personal spiritual unfolding is belief. There can be many different kinds of beliefs: magical beliefs, mythic beliefs, rational beliefs, scientific beliefs, and so forth. Magical beliefs include the notion that we can dramatically affect the physical world, as well as other people and their lives, through the power of our ego—in other words, through our intentionality. Kids' TV shows are filled with such beliefs—scenarios in which superheroes can leap tall buildings in a single bound, travel faster than a speeding bullet . . . or even heal others from life-threatening illness.

A couple of the latest New Age fads illustrate this nicely. The film called *The Secret* is an example of magical belief systems in action. It draws upon the "power of intention" and "the law of attraction" so that we can manifest the things that we want and bring them into our lives. If one's belief is strong enough, whatever one wants may magically appear. Through one's focused intentionality, wealth, the perfect relationship, and a new BMW may all be manifested.

Without casting judgment, allow me to observe that such efforts, though worthy, rarely result in effects that are measurable, and we eventually come to understand (and accept) that we are not all-powerful, that we cannot affect the world (let alone the universe) through our egoic intentionality. It is usually at this point that we begin to embrace mythic beliefs in which we delegate authority for manifesting our requests to God or to Jesus or to various other saints and sages, deities, and spirits—including those compassionate archetypal forces usually anthropomorphized as winged super-humans called angels.

At the onset, we find much support for these mythic beliefs in unending avalanches of well-intentioned metaphysical books, seminars, and workshops, as well as in our organized religions. Yet at this level we are still dealing with beliefs, in this case the belief that the deities, including "the Creator," have ultimate power over us and can be persuaded to serve us in various ways if our belief is strong enough, or we pray hard enough, or we do ritual and ceremony correctly or long enough.

Sound familiar? Here's the rub: While magical and mythic beliefs can be greatly sustaining in the short term, we eventually notice that not much changes in our lives in the long term. The problem with belief systems, whether magical or mythic, rational or scientific, is that they are at best mental phenomena—collective thoughtforms with strong emotional sentiments attached to them. And as such, we can continually embrace beliefs without ever changing our present level of consciousness in the least—in other words, no growth. Because of this, our beliefs usually fail to compel us in the end. We can believe in God or spirits or angels for decades, yet little to nothing may really change in our lives in response. This is usually when the second stage of spiritual unfolding occurs—faith.

THE SECOND STAGE:
FAITH

Faith soldiers on when our belief systems falter, and most people choose to remain at this level because faith is another great sustainer, another great supporter. Yet faith can take us in two quite different directions. In one direction, faith can and does spiral us backward into belief. This is what fundamentalism is, and this includes the whole "born-again" phenomenon.

Fundamentalism—whether Judaic, Christian, Islamic, Animistic/ Paganistic, or even Buddhist—is a trap of immense proportions on the spiritual path. This is because fundamentalism, despite all of its fervor and intention, ritual and rapture, proclamation and pontification, will not ultimately bring believers into connection with that which they are seeking. In truth, salvation lies in precisely the opposite direction.

When faith is doing its job correctly, our self-serving and self-limiting magical and mythic beliefs, including faith itself, are transcended. With this courageous act (of faith) we are drawn not back down the hill into narcissistic and egocentric belief systems once again, but forward and up the hill into the third stage of spiritual unfolding—direct experience.

THE THIRD STAGE:
DIRECT EXPERIENCE

Direct experience of the transpersonal realms of the spirits lies beyond both belief and faith. This is the shaman's realm. It is also completely and irreversibly life-changing, revealing why the shaman's path is of such interest to members of the transformational community. What we're talking about here is direct connection, but not with our culturally determined mental constructs of gods and goddesses and angels. Rather, at this stage we discover that each of us has the power to engage in authentic transpersonal experiences through which we may discover the real archetypes. . . . And because these forces are etheric in nature, they make take a form that is meaningful to the one with whom they have come into relationship . . . as Jesus or Athena or an angelic being, for instance. Or they may reveal themselves as they really are—as the light beyond the form, and the formless beyond the light.

Transpersonal in this sense implies that we are expanding beyond our personal self—and beyond those self-created mythical thought-forms that usually tell us just what we want to hear. In this we are talking about what the philosopher Ken Wilber and others refer to as the "deep psychic," through which our conscious awareness can expand exponentially, allowing us to directly experience the authentic spiritual worlds and the forces that reside within them.

In my small book *The Journey to the Sacred Garden*, it is revealed that most of us may be hardwired to be able to do this. When that genetic "program" on our inner hard drive (your DNA) is double-clicked with the right mouse, the deep psychic kicks in and true transpersonal experience then becomes available to us. The ability to do this is a learned skill that improves with practice, which is why a deep immersion experience in shamanic journeywork forms the experiential centerpiece of our hands-on Visionseeker workshops.*

---

*In Visionseeker workshops we examine the nature of the personal self, the self in service as a shamanic healer, and our immortal cosmic self—our Oversoul, a level that may bring us into connection with the Higher Organizing Intelligences.

Once learned, the shamanic method usually brings us into the experience of "Nature Mysticism." This is an authentic spiritual path with heart that many of us experienced spontaneously as children through our contact with Nature. This is a path that may bring us as adults into direct connection with the spirits of Nature as well as with the World Soul—the same multileveled archetypal matrix and intelligence that many call Gaia or, following the Gnostics, the Sophia.

Often, this connection may be sensed as an immanent and user-friendly presence that makes us feel good. Some of us experience this presence on the golf course, a fishing trip, a weekend camping expedition, or a trip to the beach. Through such experiences we may sense that Nature is aware of us, and that it may express itself through those archetypal forces the traditional peoples call "the spirits."

We're not talking about belief systems here. We have now gone beyond them and beyond faith as well. We're talking about the direct transpersonal connection with the sacred realms that define the mystic, and this is the realm of the shaman. As we mature spiritually, we are given more pieces of the puzzle to understand, and we eventually become aware that we have entered into communion with the Infinite.

This experience inevitably draws us into the fourth stage of our spiritual unfolding—personal transformation.

And nothing is ever the same after that.

ANTHROPOLOGIST HANK WESSELMAN, PH.D., received his doctoral degree from the University of California at Berkeley and has worked with an international group of scientists for much of the past forty years, exploring the fossil beds in Eastern Africa's Great Rift Valley in search of answers to the mystery of human origins. Born in New York, Dr. Wesselman served in the U.S. Peace Corps and has taught for Kiriji Memorial College and Adeola Odutola College in Nigeria, the University of California at San Diego, the West Hawaii branch of the University of Hawaii at Hilo, California State University at Sacramento, American River College, and Sierra College. He currently resides on Hawaii

Island with his family on their small organic farm. He offers experiential workshops and presentations in core shamanism at centers such as the Esalen Institute in California and the Omega Institute near New York. He is the author of nine books on shamanism, including his critically acclaimed Spiritwalker trilogy, the award-winning *Awakening to the Spirit World* (with Sandra Ingerman), and *The Bowl of Light*. His website is www.sharedwisdom.com.

2

Shamanic Impact
From Child to Crone

Dana Jefferson

My linear mind can point to one particular incident where my life was changed forever by a shamanic experience. Yet a nagging thought tells me that shamanism impacted and changed my life as far back as my Methodist childhood, when I had two professional educators for parents. I didn't know at the time, nor did my poor parents, that the snakes I saw at the bottom of my bed at night were not a nightmare but a glimpse into another realm where those same snakes—who would later be my allies and helpers—lived.

My childhood epilepsy was viewed as an unfortunate and scary disease resulting from a brain injury rather than a gateway to another world. Instead of hanging out with the kids in the neighborhood, I hung out with animals, birds, and all of Nature. Yes, perhaps the shamanic impact happened so far back that its starting point can't be remembered, or maybe, just maybe, its true impact is yet to come.

My gateway experience was simple but profound. I was struggling with my marriage, with my place on the church vestry, and with depression. I went to a very wise therapist who recognized a spiritual crisis when he saw one. He gave me books to read, such as *Way of the*

Peaceful Warrior, which opened my mind to new possibilities in the world. Then he gave me an Omega Institute catalog and told me to pick a workshop in that catalog, any workshop, and just go. I knew Omega to be a wonderful retreat center whose central base was in Rhinebeck, New York. It offered all manner of spiritual workshops, but I had never attended one.

During the same time period, I had my astrological chart read. The stars said that whatever was going to happen on a specific weekend in February would forever change the course of my life. "That's odd," I told the astrologer. "I signed up for an Omega workshop that weekend in Warrenton, Virginia. The course is 'The Way of the Shaman,' to be led by Michael Harner." The astrologer then told me that if this workshop had the full effect that had been predicted in my chart, he would give me the name of an acquaintance of his who was looking for shamanic apprentices.

From the very beginning, this workshop endeavor was to contain many initiations, and driving through the Washington, D.C., area on my own was the first. Having grown up in a small town that only had one stoplight and a mere five hundred people, I was terrified of driving in city traffic. When I had arrived successfully at my destination, I was therefore very proud of myself and fell immediately under the spell of Michael Harner (although going into the workshop I had no idea what shamanism was all about).

Although there were at least seventy people in attendance in the huge room that the workshop was being held in, the gathering felt small and intimate. The first day I was lucky enough to sit at the same lunch table with Michael Harner, and thus I could further enjoy his stories. That weekend I was introduced to journeying. What we were learning seemed to come easily to me, but I attributed this to the power of my extremely overactive imagination.

For the journeying exercise, we worked in pairs. One individual would pose a question that needed answering and the second person would try to intuit the answer. My partner was a woman I didn't know and hadn't spoken with her at all. The only thing I knew about her was her first name and her question, which was: "What should I do about conflict resolution?" Settling into the exercise, I had total performance anxiety, worrying that I wouldn't be able to adequately intuit the answer, especially because I had no idea what her question really *meant*.

I lay down on my blanket, eyes covered by a bandana, as the consistent drumming commenced. At this point in my mere hours-old shamanic career, I was only aware of one spirit helper—a crow that had spontaneously appeared in an earlier journey. (Much later I would learn that Crow would typically appear only when some sort of divination was required.)

I did receive a message, but it made no sense to me and because of this, before I even told her what I had intuited, I apologized for what I perceived to be my lapse. Then I told her what I had gleaned. I discussed how my newly discovered spirit helper, Crow, had spread his wings before showing me a picture of someone. Coupled with this, the message I received was, "Diversity will make all the difference."

At these words the woman turned ashen. She then asked me to describe the person I had seen. This was easy, for my vision had been very clear—like looking at a photograph. The woman seemed totally taken aback by my description of the person I had visualized and it was at this point that she explained the meaning of her question.

Her job involved training in conflict resolution. She had asked her question because she was trying to determine whether to stay with her old training partner or undertake an upcoming training with a new partner. She was Caucasian, as was her current partner. The new opportunity (if she so chose) would be with an African American male who exactly matched the description I had given her, thus illuminating Crow's message about diversity making the all the difference.

As this almost total stranger connected with the message of my journey, I felt chills run up and down my spine. I had just recently finished my doctorate in psychology and my world was filled with factor analyses and multiple regressions. My brain was prepared for insights gleaned from my subconscious, but it was *not* prepared for receiving specific information about a total stranger. In my world, this was just not possible.

I had spent the last couple of decades shutting down my anomalous early-childhood experiences, seeking to be a normal person in a normal world. In an instant, the nice, structured rational world I lived in—of control groups and random number generators—was breached. I was terrified and spent the next several months, with the help of my therapist, trying to make sense out of what hadn't made sense to me at all.

I knew I had to work this out and not turn my back on the distress that this turn of events was causing me. I used to ride horses and frequently fell off them. I knew that the only way to get rid of the fear of falling was to get right back up on the horse again. So that's what I did. I signed up for a one-week shamanic counseling course with Sandra Harner (Michael Harner's wife). In the meantime, I continued to practice the journeying technique I had been taught, and eventually most of my immediate fear subsided.

The shamanic counseling course was delightful. Coupled with Sandra Harner's gentle explanations of shamanism, and the reading I had done after taking that first workshop, it helped to reshape my entire worldview. By the end of the week I was hooked! Dr. Harner talked me into signing up for a three-year shamanic training program offered by the Foundation for Shamanic Studies. From the astrologer I had worked with previously, I obtained the name of the individual looking for shamanic apprentices and ended up working with her for several valuable years until mama bird kicked me out of the nest.

As the saying goes, when one door closes, another opens. At that point, I was introduced to a teacher who is still shaping my life today. He helped me to keep at least one foot on the spiritual path during the years where my main focus was on my energy-draining career as a high level government official. Now, as my path is moving forward once again, he is assisting me on it.

It's hard to believe that first shamanic workshop with Michael Harner happened twenty years ago. My spiritual path has since expanded beyond basic shamanism, but my spirit helpers and power animals (including a few additions) are always with me.

Sitting in my living room with my new husband (whom I call "new" even though we've been married for a decade), I look around and see I'm surrounded by drums, rattles, representations of my power animals, my kachina, and souvenirs from spiritual journeys to foreign countries. I have learned many things, including the power of living in gratitude, and I have greatly expanded my spiritual tool kit. After these many, many years, I can clearly say that my experiences with shamanism were not a phase I went through or representative of a particular period of my life (such as the years I raced sled dogs or the years in graduate school or the years working as a human resources professional). I no longer spend every weekend going to or teaching shamanic workshops, nor is journeying the only way I get information anymore.

However, that doesn't mean that the world of the shaman is ever far away.

A couple of months ago, I got a phone call informing me that my sister had been hospitalized. At the time, they hadn't diagnosed the problem, but she was very ill. Due to the fact that she was hundreds of miles away, I felt a sense of helplessness and I panicked. My husband, in a firm voice, said, "Stop it. You're a shaman. Do your shaman thing." When I heard these words, it was obvious what I needed to do. I sent one of my power animals, Wolf, to aid my sister, asking that the aid he delivered be for her "highest good." I then relaxed, knowing that everything would be fine—no matter what the outcome.

Wolf had helped my mom cross over into Spirit about nine months earlier. At that time, I had been on the other side of the country and thus the only way I could communicate with her was by phone. So I called the hospital room and my sister, who was there with my mother, held the cell phone to her ear while I spoke with her, even though Mom was unconscious.

The wolf I had sent to assist Mom looks very much like one of the huskies I used to own, whose name was Kolai. Mom's condition was critical and I sensed her time was limited. I told my sister that I had sent Wolf to help our mother recover or to assist her in moving to the next realm. At that, my sister asked Mom if she had seen Kolai, and though unconscious my mom squeezed my sister's hand, indicating that she had.

I can't imagine what Mom's passing would have felt like for me, being thousands of miles away from her as she lay dying, if shamanism had not by then become part of my DNA.

I'm also not sure what's next on my personal shamanic journey, given that this journey is always assuming different forms. What *is* clear to me is that, as I approach my second Saturn return, something new is ready to be birthed. (A Saturn return occurs when the planet Saturn returns to the point in the sky that it occupied at one's birth. Saturn returns occur at intervals of approximately twenty-nine and one-half years and are said to usher in another phase of that person's life.)

All I know for sure is that shamanism is no longer a separate thing, to be undertaken only when I have a chance to drum or journey. Spirit gave me the name "Winter's Joy." I add this to the many different names that I have gone by throughout my life. I've been called my given name, my chosen grandmother name (Taika), and other names by my loved ones. (I've also been called other things by those who don't like me quite so much!)

But all I truly know for sure is that when it's my time to transition to the next world, I'll still be Winter's Joy, and my spirit guides will be right there alongside me, showing me the way.

DANA JEFFERSON, Ph.D., was ordained as an interfaith minister in 2000 and has been trained in a variety of shamanic and medicine traditions. She is a 1998 graduate of the Foundation of Shamanic Studies' three-year program and has been trained as a Harner shamanic counselor.

Her doctorate is in psychology from the University of Delaware. After a thirty-year career, she retired in 2009 as the director of human resource management for the state of Delaware while president of the National Association of State Personnel Executives. She is lifetime certified as a senior professional in human resources. Since her state retirement, she has traveled extensively and worked part-time as a senior policy fellow at UMass Boston. She resides with her husband, Ed Tos, a black cat named Ouija, and two Silken Windhound dogs, Taymis and Apollo. Her son, Zachary Gordon, is married and a lawyer in Pittsburgh. She has two wonderful stepchildren and three amazing grandkids, Leah, Joseph, and Mia.

3
Urban Shamanism
Treating Depression
Using Shamanic Healing Practices

Ellie Zarrabian

Clinical depression is one of the most common mental illnesses, affecting more than nineteen million Americans each year. This includes major depressive disorder, as well as manic depression and dysthymia, which is a milder, longer-lasting form of depression.* Coupled with this is the fact that antidepressant drugs such as Prozac, Luvox, Paxil, Effexor, and Zoloft have become household names and obtaining them has become almost as easy as purchasing any over-the-counter drug.

Given such staggering statistics, as well as the side effects caused by these drugs and the tremendous amount of money that is spent by American consumers attempting to mitigate their mental health issues, it can be beneficial to look at alternative methods of treatment. These other methods may offer other avenues to health without being as chemically invasive, addictive, and/or financially costly. One such approach to treating depression is through the use of shamanic healing practices.

---

*For more on depression, visit the National Institute of Mental Health website at www.nimh.nih.gov/health/topics/depression/index.shtml.

WHAT IS SHAMANISM?

Shamanism is believed to have developed during the New Stone Age and the Bronze Age. The word "shaman" derives from the Manchu-Tungus word *šaman,* meaning "he who knows." Shamans can be found in all indigenous cultures of the world, from Southeast Asia to the Americas, Russia and the Balkans, and the Middle East, India, and Africa.

It is questionable whether or not shamans of all cultures can be seen in the same light. Although this question may remain unanswerable, there are certain commonalities that shamans all over the world do share, together with common ritualistic practices, that make some generalizations possible. For example, shamanism may be applied to all religious systems in which the central figure or the spiritual leader is believed to have direct exchange, through an ecstatic state, with the transcendent world. This permits the shaman to act as healer, diviner, or psychopomp (a guide who assists individuals in making their transition to the afterlife).

Shamans use ecstatic states for the purpose of helping to bring health and wholeness to affected individuals and communities. Once shamans enter these states, they are fully in control of their journeys to other realms and are conscious of everything that transpires. They are also able to invoke spirits and inner allies that will be protectors and givers of power.*

The belief system of the shamans and the rituals they use to perform the healings vary from culture to culture. For example, in her book *Shamanism,* Shirley Nicholson explains that Native American shamans hold the belief system that the universe has three levels—sky, earth, and underworld—that are connected by a central axis. These shamans use various techniques to journey from one of these regions to another in order to access the information they need to help the individual they are treating. Muslim Indian shamans, on the other hand, believe that there are three classes of living beings "higher" than

---

*For more on shamanic ecstatic states, please see Shirley Nicholson's *Shamanism* (Wheaton, Ill.: Quest Books, 1987).

men: *farishta* (angels), *shaitan* (satanic beings), and *jinn* (demons or spirits). They believe that it is the interference of the shaitan and the jinn that can cause chaos and disorder in a person's life, creating an overall state of imbalance.*

My own interest, or rather, my initiation into shamanism, began at an early age. As a third-generation shamanic healer born and raised in Iran, I recognized early on that herbalists, soothsayers, religious healers, and shamans had their own place in society. Tracing any disease or illness of the mind or body back to the evil eye and/or immediate family or generational curses was as valid as seeking the help of a medical doctor who had been trained in the West. Folk remedies for such ailments involved enlisting various healers to murmur prayers and generate potions and to enact healing rituals and ceremonies (including animal sacrifices).

Having been raised and educated in the West for the majority of my life, it was not until my mid-twenties that my own interest in shamanism resurfaced. It was then that I began uncovering memories of my paternal grandmother secretly engaging in such esoteric practices. Gradually, over the years, I began incorporating my ancestral teachings with my doctoral background in psychology to work with individuals who were seeking some deeper level of help.

Over time, I have witnessed enough transformative results with my clients to know that this powerful path to healing remains relatively open and uncharted. Thus, the goal of this article is to create an avenue whereby other practitioners and seekers interested in urban shamanism might explore alternative means of promoting mental, emotional, spiritual, and psychological health and the well-being that it offers.

---

*For more on this, see Sudhir Kakar's *Shamans, Mystics & Doctors: A Psychological Inquiry into India and Its Healing Traditions* (Chicago: University of Chicago Press, 1982).

MODERN-DAY OR URBAN SHAMANISM

Urban shamans are everyday healers who continue to practice the essence of traditional shamanism in today's modern society. In a sense, any individual working in the healing arts profession today is, to some degree, a modern-day shaman. These practitioners use a core belief system (such as cognitive/behavioral therapy, traditional psychoanalysis, dialectic behavior therapy, etc.) as well as techniques and rituals (a weekly visit to the therapist's office, sitting or lying on a couch, talking about life events or dreams, and so forth) in order to promote mental and emotional health.

A more traditional shaman, however, might induce and then access an altered state of consciousness within clients, as a way of obtaining more information about them and to accelerate the healing process. Sandra Ingerman, author, healer, and educator, is an urban shaman who utilizes altered states to promote healing. She uses a technique called "soul retrieval" as way to bring back an afflicted individual's lost vitality and essence. In *Soul Retrieval: Mending the Fragmented Self,* Ingerman explains, "Soul loss is a result of such traumas as incest, abuse, loss of a loved one, surgery, accident, illness, miscarriage, abortion, combat stress or addiction." She goes on to further explain, "Individuals who suffer from soul loss often carry with them a painful sense of incompleteness and disconnection . . . may spend years in therapy or self-help groups trying to uncover traumas and to become whole."

DOES IT ACTUALLY WORK?

Jeanne Achterberg, author and professor of psychology at Saybrook University, did experiments to see if in fact shamanic healing rituals are beneficial. Her experiments showed that *any* healing ritual has a significant impact on a person's physical and psychological well-being. She also demonstrated that incorporating ritual of any kind by healing practitioners is a way of encouraging hope in patients and reducing their depression and anxiety. She explained that it is the activity of the ritual—particularly if it prescribes a series of behaviors that has the critical psychological effect of pacing people through difficult times—that makes the difference. These rituals provide a road map for the unseen, unknown, and uncharted territory. In "Ritual: The Foundation for Transpersonal Medicine," Achterberg noted that these rituals can be but are not limited to acts such as "chants, songs, or prayers to quiet a troubled mind, making space for mental and spiritual clarity."*

Another study by Marlene Dobkin de Rios, a renowned medical anthropologist and psychotherapist, revealed that using shamanic healing practices with the U.S. Latino immigrant population suffering from psychological and emotional disorders was far more beneficial and productive than using straight insight or talk therapy. She believes that this is because most indigenous people are apt to feel more comfortable with shamanic rituals as opposed to the traditional Western model of healing.†

MY CLIENT LINDA AND HER STORY

Linda was referred to me by an ex-client of mine. Her initial reason for needing therapy was because she suffered from chronic depression. She mentioned that she had been receiving psychological counseling for a number of years and although her symptoms seemed to have improved significantly, her depression still lingered. She felt there were unresolved issues in her life that never seemed to get fully resolved. Not only had she been seeing a therapist for some time, but some years prior she had also gotten involved with occult practices. Although her spiritual practice had helped her initially, lately she felt it was compounding her depression. She had heard about my work from her friend and was curious to know whether or not I could help her.

---

*For Achterberg's complete article see *Revision* 14, no. 3 (1992): 158–65.
†For the complete article, "What We Can Learn from Shamanic Healing: Brief Psychotherapy with Latino Immigrant Clients," see the *American Journal of Public Health* website at http://ajph.aphapublications.org/doi/full/10.2105/AJPH.92.10.1576.

The next time Linda and I met, I checked in with my guides and was instructed to perform a shamanic healing. The session began with the same ritual I always practice at the beginning of every healing session. I had her lie down on my medicine table (similar to a massage table) face up as I stood beside her at the table's head. I then held my hands in a prayer position and allowed myself to enter into a quiet place within myself where I could invoke the presence of the spirit world to help guide me through the therapeutic process.

As I entered an altered state, I consciously began to surrender and let go of my will so that I would become an open channel for Linda. Once I was able to let go of my thoughts and ideas of what the session needed to look like or what I was expecting might take place, I knew the session was ready to begin.

What happens next is different with every individual. With some I may not need to talk but instead perform the healing in silence. With others, I may have a continuing dialogue. In Linda's case, I felt I needed to tell her what I was experiencing. While in an altered state, I began to see scenes rapidly flash by in front me. Each scene depicted a man with a young girl or an adolescent girl or a woman. Although each scene was different and took place in a different time period, the theme was always the same. Each one clearly depicted a man abusing, exploiting, or otherwise taking advantage of the child or the woman.

As I described each scene, something began to shift in Linda. First she began to quietly sob, and then gradually her sobs turned into cries. She began to resonate with the images and said she had always suspected that her father had abused her as a child but she could not confirm it. Despite her numerous attempts to have her father acknowledge the abuse, he continued to deny that he had done so. This left her paralyzed and unable to move on with her life.

As I continued to share the scenes with her, eventually something even more interesting began to happen. Linda began to see the same images I was describing. Pretty soon I would start describing a scene and she would finish telling me the rest of it. Each time she finished describing a scene, her body would relax more. It would appear that viewing the images helped her let go of the pain she had been holding on to for so long. We continued going back and forth for the next hour or so until there were no more images visible to either of us. Then I knew the session was over.

Linda and I continued to work together for the next several months, processing the events of the session. The images had opened up a doorway for her, enabling her to do the inner work necessary for her to gradually understand and let go of the deep hatred and resentment she felt toward her father.

As she continued to do this inner work, her sense of self became stronger. Her depression began to gradually lift, and each time I saw her she looked healthier and happier. She also became more confident in her own intuitive abilities and began relying on her intuition more frequently in her daily life. She no longer felt she needed an external source of affirmation for her spiritual beliefs and practices. Later, she used her gift to work with abandoned and abused animals. She was able to communicate with them and help them release their trauma . . . many of them were then adopted into loving homes.

In the shamanic work that I do, I am often reminded of this wonderful Chinese proverb that describes the essence of shamanic healing as it relates to the innate restorative power of the human mind and body:

> *When the winter is severe*
> *the pine trees in this ancient land*
> *stay green throughout the year.*
> *Is it because the Earth is warm and friendly?*
> *No, it is because the pine tree has within itself a life-*
> *restoring power.*

ELLIE ZARRABIAN, Ph.D., obtained her doctorate in psychology from Saybrook University in San Francisco in 2010, her master's degree in transpersonal psychology from John K. Kennedy University, and her bachelor's degree in psychobiology from UCLA. In 1992 she became a certified massage therapist and worked for a number of years treating trauma in the body. After receiving her master's degree in 1997, she became a drug and alcohol counselor and worked with individuals struggling with addiction. From 2001 to 2010 she held a teaching post at Santa Monica College in the department of behavioral studies teaching psychology and spirituality to young adults. A third-generation shamanic healer from the Sufi/Jewish tradition of Iran, she is the founder and spiritual director of Centerpeace Foundation (www.centeronpeace.com) and the Centerpeace Project (www.centerpeaceproject.com) in Los Angeles. She is also a member of the American Psychological Association, the Los Angeles County Psychological Association, the Society for Shamanic Practitioners, and the Association for Transpersonal Psychology. She is currently working as a counselor and shamanic healer in the L.A. area.

4

Shamanic Ecstasy

Alberto Villoldo

When I was in my late twenties, I was a medical anthropologist doing research among indigenous peoples in the Amazon rain forest. For one season I had a grant from a Swiss pharmaceutical giant hoping to find the bark or root that could become the next great cure for some of the top killers known to Western medicine. After all, the jungle is Nature's pharmacy, and at the time we knew less than 1 percent of the medicinal properties of the rainforest plants. I was fresh out of graduate school and penniless so I thought I would give it a try.

I spent months canoeing to remote villages in the Amazon. Some of the settlements were extremely isolated and the villagers had not seen many light-skinned people before. When I arrived the children would run up and brush my arm to see if the "white dirt" would rub off. Right from the start I knew I was undertaking an impossible mission, because the peoples in the Amazon rain forest did not have to deal with the illnesses I had been commissioned to find a cure for. In fact, they had no dementia, no Alzheimer's, no heart disease, and seldom did I encounter a case of cancer. These are the diseases of civilization, the maladies of the white man that no herb or root could cure.

I returned from the Amazon many weeks later empty-handed. My sponsor was disappointed that I hadn't brought back the plant ingredient for a blockbuster drug that would make all of us famous. However, I did return with the wisdom of the shamans who had taken me under their wing. I learned there *was* a secret ingredient to health that could be found in the rain forest, but it wouldn't fit in a backpack and couldn't be pressed into a pill. It was not a sprig or a root or a bark. It was One Spirit Medicine. It was, the shamans told me, the medicine that would allow a person to become like a jaguar and journey consciously to the realms beyond death to return with the practical wisdom that could heal them.

At the time I had difficulty understanding what the shamans were trying to explain to me. I had read about the B'alams, the jaguar priests of ancient Mexico, who thought themselves to be mystical jaguars. But I believed they were talking about ayahuasca, the legendary vine of the dead, which allows you to see your life-journey with stunning clarity and understand the workings of Nature. The protector spirit of this sacred plant is supposed to be a black jaguar that can grant you the gift of immortality. And it was reputed to show the practitioner the realms beyond death. In fact the word *aya* means "death" and *huasca* means "vine." It would be many years later, with dozens of ceremonies with the Mother plant under my belt, before I would be able to comprehend what they were talking about. One Spirit Medicine turned out to be a state of awareness in which people recognize their union with all of creation without losing the Self, the observer. It is a blissful state that allowed the shamans of old to discover the Mother plant and her psychedelic gifts as well as hundreds of other healing remedies. And the most powerful of these remedies was the experience of the journey beyond death.

Take curare, for example, a muscle relaxant that causes paralysis and is known as "arrow poison" in the rain forest. Curare is prepared by a combination of as many as fifteen different plants, carefully boiled for seventy-two hours. During the cooking process the brew produces a sickly sweet aroma that when inhaled by the person cooking can cause a painful death through paralysis. The muscles in your chest fail to respond and you are unable to breathe, remaining conscious as you observe yourself suffocating to death. Curare is used by many peoples in the rain forest for hunting by anointing the tip of the darts they use in their blowguns. When the animal they kill with curare is cooked, the cooking neutralizes the poison and the meat can be ingested safely. When you ask the shamans how they discovered curare (the odds of doing so by trial and error are nearly impossible), they respond, "The plants taught us."

I had a glimpse of One Spirit Medicine in that far-flung expedition to the upper Amazon. My epiphany came as I was paddling our canoe through a tributary of the Mother of God River. We had run out of gas in our *peke-peke,* the native river craft that are so called because of their noisy, two-stroke lawn-mower engines. My guide and I were paddling lazily and our canoe was drifting downstream on a gentle current while I muttered to myself that we should have brought an extra five-gallon fuel can with us.

Then, as I dipped my paddle into the water, the river became liquid gold, and the river, the canopy of the jungle, and I were a single breathing, pulsing organism. For an instant, all of creation was happening *inside* of me, and I had vanished, disappeared into the tides and eddies of the waterway. Yet I remained the witness of All and One with the forest at the same time. I comprehended the singing of the birds and the howling of the monkeys, and I heard a voice, or rather had a deep sense of a voice, that said to me that I belonged to the forest and in the forest, that I belonged in the primordial garden. And then the moment passed and I was again straddling the bow of the boat, gripping the paddle in my hands, my face wet with tears. When I looked at my watch, more than an hour had gone by in what had seemed like seconds.

As a result of this ecstatic experience I awakened to a reality that had been hidden from me: the invisible world of Spirit. Until that moment I believed that the shamans were the envoys that communicated with the supernatural world. After that experience, I understood there is no supernatural world; there is only the natural world with a visible and an invisible component. I understood that our more familiar visible world is born of and arises from the invisible domain we call

Spirit. And I belonged in that world, even more than in this one of matter and flesh. I had returned to the garden.

Westerners are the only people on the planet to have a mythology in which we were cast out of the Garden of Eden. Everyone else—from the Native Americans to the Aborigines of Australia to the sub-Saharan Africans—were given the Garden to be its caretakers. And that day, I had been welcomed back to Eden. For the shaman the natural outcome of such an epiphany is a commitment to the stewardship of all life on the Earth. The experience is seen as a calling. And I took it as such. The bliss that I felt that day drifting along the river was profoundly healing. I felt welcomed back by Mother Earth to her rain forest. All my life I had felt homeless, until that moment. Yet while wonderfully healing, these epiphanies are not the goal. Dreaming a world of healing and beauty into being becomes the mission for those who choose to remain in the Garden.

HACKING THE HUMAN BIOFIELD

One Spirit Medicine works by upgrading the quality of the luminous energy field (LEF) that surrounds the physical body and tells our molecules, cells, and genes what to do. The LEF is a blueprint of the body, our *field state* (in contrast with the flesh and bone body, which is the *particle state*). It can be thought of as the software that informs our DNA (the hardware) and can switch off the genes that create disease and switch on the genes that create health. In my years of travel and work in the Amazon, I learned that sorcerers could create disease as readily as shamans could create the conditions for health. They are able to shoot psychic "darts" at the LEF of their intended victim so that they express the genes for disease.

This was a terrifying discovery; I was interested in learning the healing techniques of the shamans, not how to hurt people. I learned that the practices could be misused in the hands of a novice or people who had not healed their anger or desire. It was the ethics and the intent of the shaman that made all the difference in the world. Upgrading the quality of the LEF brought order and healing; downgrading the quality of the field brought chaos and disease.

I am not a Native American, so I needed to understand the workings of One Spirit Medicine not only in the language of folklore but also in the language of science. I realized that certain shamanic practices could best be understood with the help of classical field theory, a concept in physics used to describe the effects of gravity and electromagnetism. A field extends through the vastness of space, even though in practice it may be limited to the region closest to the body that generates it. For example, the Earth's gravitational field extends to the farthest reaches of the universe. Newton explained that the strength of fields diminishes with distance to the point of being undetectable.

Fields occupy space, contain energy, and hold information. So for example the electromagnetic field from a radio tower (the signal) can contain information about a weather forecast. Fields influence the particles within them; thus your LEF organizes your physical body (and your psychological experiences) according to the instructions encoded within it. Most of these instructions (your beliefs, emotions, and prejudices) are inherited from your parents. Your LEF replicates the heart conditions, the breast conditions, and the psychological stories and dramas that cut across generations in your family.

Despite our longing to see ourselves as different, better, more enlightened than our parents, we continue to live out their poor health. Remember the day you looked in the mirror and realized you had become a spitting image of your mother or your father, despite vowing you would never become like them? In the end we live the way they lived and die the way they died because of the markings and imprints encoded in the LEF. In the East they call this karma; the shamans I worked with call it fate. As you upgrade the quality of your LEF you break free from the grip of fate—where your health and your happiness are predestined— and step into your destiny, which you can guide and direct.

The LEF comes preloaded with the software that ensures the longevity of the species. This software destines the individual for reproduction so that the species can enjoy a long life. Longevity of species seems

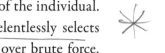

to be Nature's primary agenda more so than longevity of the individual. Yet the shamans of old observed that Nature also relentlessly selects for intelligence, preferring brain over brawn, wisdom over brute force. When we study evolution carefully, we see that it is the wisest, and not the fittest, that thrive. Mother Nature gave us the possibility of "hacking" our LEF, breaking into password-protected regions of the DNA code that would allow the wisest among us to express the genes for longevity of the individual. These ancient shamans were interested not only in healing the sick, in mending the body after it had broken down, but also in upgrading the quality of their LEF to ensure the longevity of the individual—creating a long and healthy life. They discovered that the LEF consists of light and vibration, so whatever you vibrate in your LEF, you create in your body and your health.

When you erase the imprints for disease in the LEF, you create the conditions for health—and then disease goes away. You can break out of the bell curve that says that you will die from heart disease or from cancer or suffer dementia. You not only heal disease, you prevent disease in the first place and create optimal health.

REPAIRING THE BRAIN

I learned this firsthand in the Amazon, but I also discovered that for modern people clearing the imprints for disease in the LEF is very hard to do. This is because our brains have been damaged by toxins, heavy metals, and stress. A person living one hundred years ago in America ate only free-range, grass-fed, organic foods. There were no pesticides and industrial chemicals, and the rivers and the air were largely unpolluted. We can no longer readily access the brain-mind states necessary to experience unity with all Creation and upgrade the quality of our LEF. No matter how long we meditate or how many times we chant OM, the invisible world of Spirit eludes us. But once we detox and upgrade the brain we can tap into One Spirit Medicine, and everything changes.

One Spirit Medicine awakens us to the invisible world of energy, where everything is intertwined in an entangled universe, and where every thought you have impacts every molecule in the cosmos, including every cell in your body. After you've experienced it, you cease to identify exclusively with your roles and the drama in the visible, material world. You are born into a new life, one in which you recognize your Christ-like, Buddha-like, illumined nature.

However, there's more: when you experience One Spirit Medicine, you recognize that you're not just *intertwined* with all of Creation; you and the Earth are inseparable. How can you not attend to your own well-being if you care about the Earth and your fellow beings? The idea that you have to look out for number one and damage the Earth or hurt others in order to survive becomes incomprehensible. This is the source of the Lakota greeting *mitakuye oyasin,* "all my relations," where we acknowledge our interdependence and connectedness.

When I experienced this awakening, it was deeply disturbing to that aspect of my Western education that didn't believe in the invisible world and was certain that the predatory world of mortals competing for limited planetary resources was all that existed.

One Spirit Medicine allowed me to realize that everything in my life is something I've chosen to dream into being—whether it's the emotional pain and suffering I may be experiencing or the sense that you and I are enemies or adversaries. Even the apparent schism between the visible world of the senses and the invisible world of Spirit is an illusion I have subscribed to. It's a helpful illusion when trying to operate in everyday life. It's not exactly easy to pay for your groceries at the cash register when you are in a state of timelessness, experiencing your oneness with the cosmos. (But this is only so because I believe it to be so.)

AWAKENING YOUR INVISIBLE SELF

After spending years in the Amazon, my body was exhausted. To get to the virgin rain forest I had to go by the last outposts of Western loggers and fortune seekers. And these were filth-laden river towns riddled with disease—curious how the white man is the only creature on the planet that fouls his own nest. In the process I had picked up far too many parasites and had suffered through too many courses of antibiotics. After all this I was determined to focus my research on the high Andes Mountains and its shamans.

Among the descendants of the Inca I discovered a flourishing community of practitioners of One Spirit Medicine. I was the first American anthropologist to have contact with the Q'ero Nation, a people that escaped to high mountain refuges at the time of the Spanish conquest, and whose practices and beliefs were untainted by Western religion and customs. Among the *paqos* (shamans) of the high Andes there is a belief that all life emerged from the Texemuyo, the One Source, and that the Texemuyo is not a place but a field of awareness that envelops us and creates the cosmos newly each moment. And in the same way that we exist in the world of time and form and shape, we have an invisible self, a self devoid of body or form, which resides outside of ordinary time. It is the invisible self that gives rise to our visible, manifest self. This invisible self is the LEF, our field state, and when our body passes away, the LEF will continue on its journey in realms that we visit only during dreams.

The visible and invisible realms always engage in a subtle dance between life and death, form and formlessness, time and infinity. These are topics that we in the West have associated with religion. Yet in my travels in the Amazon and in the Andes, I discovered that shamanism is not a religion. Shamanism is more concerned with Creation than with the Creator, with our ability to participate in creating beauty and healing through dreaming the world into being.

YOU ARE NOT YOUR GENES, YOU ARE YOUR DREAMS

My years with indigenous shamans showed me that my beliefs and assumptions about how the world works and what kind of health I would enjoy determined my personal mythology, which was buried in my unconscious mind. Let me give you an example. When I was in graduate school I worked as a psychologist for Head Start schools, specifically on a program for five- to seven-year-old children from disadvantaged families. On the first day of school, I would ask the kids to draw a house. They sketched the most amazing houses. Some were inside clouds or under the ocean—one was even inside a doughnut! At the end of the year I would ask them again to draw a house and almost to the last child they would draw a square with a triangular roof with two windows and a door. It was so disappointing to see how they had adopted the belief that all houses look like that. In later schooling these children would learn how to think alike, live alike, and die alike; they would become a statistic. A belief is about a single theme; it is like a cog in a wheel. A personal mythology is the entire wheel and can contain a hundred different beliefs. And these children were beginning to embrace a personal mythology that compelled them to become narrow-minded, obese, overfed, and undernourished adults who would find they had little to look forward to when they hit midlife.

A mythology is a road map, a way of organizing your experiences, values, and beliefs into a cohesive story. In the past our mythology was dictated by religion, whose priests spelled out the rules for our behavior in Ten Commandments, who told us that we were cast out of the Garden of Eden for eating the forbidden fruit of the Tree of Knowledge. The road to salvation lay in following the mandates of God's spokesmen, the priests or the divine kings who sent others to die on crusades or build cathedrals or pyramids.

Today knowledge is no longer in the hands of the few but available to all. Almost the entire body of scientific, philosophical, and literary wisdom of the past is only one mouse-click away. And today many of us have shed the mythology of religion for the myths offered by science.

Yet neither the explanations provided by religion nor those of science are entirely satisfactory because they don't tell me about my journey on this Earth. This is why each of us develops a personal mythology, which is the deepest beliefs you hold about who you really are, where you really came from, where you are really going, and how healthy you will be getting there. Our personal mythology can set the small acts and gestures of everyday life into a larger context infused with meaning and purpose. It's important to recognize your personal myth, because if yours isn't working for you, you may want to change your health or your life—these mythic stories become self-fulfilling prophecies. Whatever beliefs are embedded in your myths about your destiny and of your journey through this life, the Universe will prove you right. Whatever story you have crafted about yourself becomes the stage where the drama of your life unfolds. And for most of us this is a story we learned from our parents and our schooling. And it is a story in great need of revision. The popular life stories of victims that most of us have embraced and that our psychologies take such pleasure in dissecting and exploring have become stifling and boring.

Through One Spirit Medicine, your personal myth can become the story of a hero's journey—of sacrifice, facing challenges, overcoming tests, and working with the Divine to triumph over suffering and create beauty in the world. When our personal myths are not heroic, we remain disempowered victims, at the mercy of others and the whims of fate. And shamans know that you can change your personal mythology into a heroic story by picking up the metaphoric pen and putting it to paper.

Let me give you an example. On one of our expeditions to the American Southwest, I visited an old Navajo medicine woman whom I had befriended years before. On that occasion she asked me to tell her about myself. I was in my early thirties, and I explained that my father had left home when I was young, and I was still searching for a healthy wholesome image of what it was like to become a man. When I was done, I asked her the same question, and she replied, "The red-rock canyon walls am I; the desert wind am I; the child that did not eat today at the reservation am I." I was completely taken aback. What a better story than "boy looking for dad."

That very day I decided to change my story. On the flight home, the man sitting next to me inquired about me, making small talk. And I replied "The red-rock canyon walls am I . . ." and before I knew it he had moved to the empty seat in the row behind me, sure that I was deranged! And of course it was a lie, because every cell in my body still screamed "little boy looking for dad."

It wasn't until years later, when I had confronted my own failures as a father and as a man, found forgiveness and healing, and responded to my calling from Spirit, that I was able to exchange my mythic tale for that of a hero's journey. Today my personal mythology includes the idea that I am here to bring more beauty, more healing, and a little more joy to the world.

If your personal mythology—your road map through life—doesn't include a path that leads you to an experience of One Spirit, you will live life as a spectator. After you experience the Oneness of Spirit and how everything that you can observe in this world and in the invisible world is only Spirit, then you can become the author of your own story, the storyteller instead of the actor in the script written for you by your genetics or your family of origin. You will be able to grow a new body that heals and ages differently and at the end of your life make your journey back home, to the Spirit World, gracefully and fearlessly.

ALBERTO VILLOLDO, PH.D., has trained as a psychologist and medical anthropologist and has studied the healing practices of shamans of the Amazon and the Andes for more than thirty years. He directs the Four Winds Society, where he trains individuals in the United States and Europe in the practice of Shamanic Energy Medicine, with campuses in New York, California, and Germany. In addition, he directs the Center for Energy Medicine in Chile, where he investigates and practices the neuroscience of enlightenment. Dr. Villoldo has written numerous bestselling books, including *One Spirit Medicine: Ancient Ways to Ultimate Wellness; Shaman, Healer, Sage; The Four Insights; Courageous Dreaming;* and *Power Up Your Brain* (with David Perlmutter, M.D.). Dr. Villoldo is a member emeritus of the American Academy of Sciences, fellow of the Royal Anthropological Institute of Great Britain, and fellow of the Explorer's Club of New York. His website is www.thefourwinds.com.

5

The Call to Service

Sandra Ingerman

When I was a child, I had an extensive shamanic practice, even though I didn't have a name for my connection with the invisible realms. I also had my first near-death experience when I was little. It occurred when I was hit by lightning at the age of seven. I had two more near-death experiences later on in life. But even before that lightning strike, I was singing to the spirit of the trees outside my house and to the moon at night, and I was seeing spirits. Later, as a child of the 1960s, I experienced profound spiritual states of unity when I experimented with mind-altering substances.

In shamanic cultures, dismemberment marked an initiation that would be called "the shaman's death." There are no practices or exercises that can lead one to a shaman's death. Life brings this initiation to us, and if it occurs in a shamanic journey or a dream it happens spontaneously. An initiation such as this cannot be planned and has no safety nets. In such an initiation we lose the identity that we are attached to on an egoic and personality level. And then the "rememberment" takes place over time. In this, our previous identity is replaced with our authentic self.

Life circumstances that provide such a death experience can oftentimes be harsh. But in the end, once we surrender to what our new identity is, we emerge reborn and refreshed. Our ego has been truly sculpted, allowing our spirit to shine through. More specifically, after these initiations we typically stop being led by our ego and follow a path of Spirit instead. Going through an initiation is akin to a snake shedding its skin. We let go of the old and birth new aspects of ourselves.

I have been through many initiations in life. I remember once saying to my spiritual teacher Isis, while performing a shamanic journey, "I don't think I am going to live through this."

She looked at me and replied, "If you thought you were going to live through this, it would not be an initiation!"

As harrowing as a shaman's death may be, it can also bring beautiful experiences that teach us how precious life is. We can have blissful experiences after which we never perceive life in the same way again. I will share a couple of these joyful and life-changing revelations with you here.

I can still remember the day when I was just a young girl sitting on a couch in my house in Brooklyn. As I was letting my mind wander I had the deep revelation that as humans we came here to experience joy, but somehow we got our destiny wrong. At that moment I made a decision to dedicate my life to helping people remember that our destiny is to create joy. Our Creator, Source, the Divine, the creative force of the universe, created us from a true place of unconditional love. There is an inherent joy in manifesting Spirit into form, for this is how our world was created. Many shamans believe that everything we experience in this reality is a dream, and they have shared that understanding with us. They have also shared their belief that we are dreaming the wrong dream. This occurs because we are not focusing our daydreams on the life we want to live and what we would like to see for the Earth and all in the web of life. We tend to focus on what is not working instead of shaping our dreams in a positive way that creates healing for ourselves and the Earth.

In my moment of revelation I had an understanding of this. As a result, from that day forward I have been fascinated with this idea of manifestation, for all spiritual traditions teach that everything that exists in the physical realm is born from the invisible realms. We spin threads from the invisible into the tangible realms, weaving together our fabric of reality. I learned as an adult studying shamanism that <u>thoughts</u> <u>are things</u> and our thoughts become the fabric of reality that we end up dreaming into being. Words are seeds. When you speak words out loud, these words are <u>like plants</u> in a garden that <u>grow deep roots and</u> grow toward the light. If we want to change our personal world and the world we live in, we must learn how to plant different seeds in our garden. We must learn how to use our thoughts and words to create the world we wish to live in.

The phrase *abracadabra* that many of us said as a child is an Aramaic phrase, *abraq ad habra,* and means, "I create as I speak."

I also had the revelation that spirits don't get to enjoy the senses that we experience in a body. They don't get to see all the colors and beauty that surround us, hear the birds singing or the children laughing, or smell the beautiful fragrances such as that of a rose or the scent of lavender. They don't get to touch and experience all the wondrous sensations that come through our hands. Spirits don't get to taste chocolate! Being in a body is a gift. We came here to experience the world of the senses and also to manifest form from Spirit—through our thoughts and words—just as the Creator created this incredible planet in all its beauty—rich with many creatures who share the Earth with us.

All of these thoughts and observations, coupled with my revelation, thus set my intention: I devoted myself to learning about the world we wish to live in, and how to dream it into being. As a result, my life changed significantly.

An initiation into becoming a shaman might typically involve some type of life-threatening illness or a near-death experience where the initiate loses any sense of ego or separation from Source. In this numinous state it is remembered that we are one. In my own near-death experiences I only felt the deep unconditional love and accepting presence of God. In my early twenties I "drowned" while I was swimming in Mexico. An undertow pulled me beneath the surface of the sea and the last words I remember hearing were those of a friend who said, "Whatever happens, don't panic." As I found myself not being able to breathe, I kept hearing those words again and again. In what seemed like a second I felt an amazing peace, and I found myself going down a tunnel and then emerging into the light. As I did so, I was sitting on a stone bench in a garden. I cannot even describe the unearthly beauty of the garden I sat in while listening to music that I would never hear again in any experience on Earth. The unconditional love, peace, and beauty I experienced stay with me every second of my life.

In another experience that I had even earlier than my drowning in Mexico, I traveled to the heavens and experienced a being I called God. God had no form but was a brilliant light—an unearthly type of brilliance. I stood in front of this light. Right next to me was a man who, in his lifetime, was known for his heinous crimes; he was responsible for killing millions of innocent people.

God, as I experienced God, just beamed and embraced us both in unconditional love. There was no egoic recognition of our personalities or retribution for how we had lived our lives on Earth. We were simply embraced in objective, unconditional love.

When I returned from this experience I truly understood what oneness and unconditional love were all about. I do not condone people's violent behavior toward others and life itself. But this experience gave me a bodily sense that, when we transcend this world of separation and move into a place of unity consciousness, the state of true unconditional love is what we return to. Death is not an end but a doorway to the eternal.

In the experiences I have described I was able to experience the dissolution of the ego. In the Eastern tradition it is taught that our resurrection is only possible when we allow our attachment to our material nature to be destroyed. We sacrifice our identity, ego, and beliefs to the Divine. In the study of alchemy it is taught that the self-possessed man must die and a new one be born. Among shamans, initiation experiences often brought a feeling and vision of the body being renewed, and it was sometimes the case that the journeying shaman returned with magical and healing powers.

Knud Rasmussen, a Danish polar explorer and anthropologist known for his work with the Eskimo shamans, quoted an Eskimo shaman as saying, "Every real shaman has to feel *qaumaneg*, a light within the body, inside the head or brain, something that gleams like fire, that enables him to see in the dark, and with closed eyes see into things which are hidden, and also into the future."

When I experienced the luminosity of God, I understood myself to be divine light too. And when I did, I became passionate about learning more about this—and more about oneness. As a result, I have spent the last fifteen years teaching about the power of experiencing one's divine light, and how that can help to heal the planet. This led me deeper on my spiritual path—to understand the spirit within me and everyone else. I had, you see, learned that life is a dream and we have unlimited potential to fill it with joy, peace, and health.

However, as I looked around me I saw people drained and worn down by life. I did not see the light and joy shining from their eyes—as one would see in those who had been brought up with the understanding that joy, light, love, health, and wealth lie within. I did not meet people who understood that we must cultivate a rich and beautiful inner garden, which would be reflected back to us in our outer world. I did not see passion for life in the eyes of these people.

Even so, I did not want to give up on finding a new way to live. I had left Brooklyn when I was eighteen, feeling that there had to be more to life than the humdrum existence of going from a boring job to going home and watching TV. I tried to find communities where people lived in a spiritual way. I tried to find people who did not settle for what the collective taught: don't shine your light too brightly, behave, follow the rules and you will get by.

I can't say that in the 1970s I found healthy examples of people who were living in community and trying to create a new paradigm. That said, I did live in Haight-Ashbury for many years, searching for a more spiritual way of life, but it wasn't until 1980 that I was formally introduced to the practice of shamanism. What I had previously lacked was a form of practice; this was the gift that shamanism provided me with. This led me to a path on which I could learn how to work with and bridge the spiritual knowledge I had attained. Through working with the practice of shamanism I learned how to shift from feeling disempowered by life's circumstances to feeling empowered by performing daily spiritual practices and teaching others how to do the same. And I learned tools to help me ride the joyful and turbulent waves that are all part of the flow of life.

Through the practice of shamanic journeying I had the opportunity to meet helping spirits who could provide guidance and healing in my life. Through their unconditional love for me they taught me about my potential and helped me to reshape my life so that I could find inner joy and peace. I learned about the power of direct revelation and understood that I had access to all the guidance I needed.

My spirits taught me powerful ways of healing that would help the clients I worked with and led me to write books. I have been passionate about sharing what I have learned, for we have so much potential to create change in the world through the spiritual work and practices we engage in.

I learned how shamanism is a life path and I began to start each day with gratitude and giving honor and respect to earth, air, water, and fire (the sun), which give us what we need to thrive. I learned how to integrate what I learned in my shamanic journeys into my daily life to create a deep, rich inner world. That said, I will be the first to admit that I am definitely a work in progress, for life brings us both challenges and joyful experiences to facilitate our growth. How we react to what it brings shapes our physical, emotional, and spiritual health. I do not hold a victim stance during the difficult times. I stay present during the joyful times and understand that this state will change, too.

My only real desire is to continue to cultivate that rich inner garden where joy, love, and light shine through, no matter what is happening in the outer world. I am grateful for all that life brings me.

SANDRA INGERMAN, M.A., a world-renowned teacher of shamanism, is also an award-winning author of ten books, the presenter of seven audio programs produced by Sounds True, and the creator of the Transmutation app. For more than thirty years, Sandra has taught workshops internationally on shamanic journeying, healing, and the reversal of environmental pollution using spiritual methods. She is recognized for bridging ancient cross-cultural healing methods and our modern culture. Sandra is also a licensed marriage and family therapist, a professional mental health counselor, and a board-certified expert on traumatic stress. She was awarded the 2007 Peace Award from the Global Foundation for Integrative Medicines and in 2013 was chosen as one of the top ten spiritual leaders by *Spirituality and Health* magazine. Her website is www.sandraingerman.com.

6

Raptor Medicine
A Portal to Shamanic Beginnings

Thomas J. Mock

Driving home from work one evening, I began to have an unusual experience. There seemed to be static in the air and it felt literally charged—so much so that my body hairs were standing alert. While experiencing these sensations, I had a vision in my mind's eye. The vision was of a large dead bird of prey laying on an embankment approximately two miles ahead of me down the interstate. *What a wild imagination I have!* I mused to myself, and was about to dismiss the experience when I remembered a recent conversation with my spiritual teacher. I had asked her, "How does one differentiate between one's own imagination and real communication from the unseen spirit world?"

Her response had been, "There is no difference."

Pulling off to the side of the highway, I recall feeling amused and silly when there was no dead bird in sight. Remembering that this vision was of a bird over the bank and out of sight from the road, I decided to go with it. I walked down over the bank and there lay a great horned owl. As I touched the bird I could feel that its warmth had not yet dissipated from its lifeless body. As I knelt and held the bird to my chest, the static and the electricity in the air returned and I began to weep.

In retrospect, with that first bird encounter, I had figuratively

44

slipped down through the proverbial rabbit's hole into a world I previously thought was only written about in fairy tales or experienced by those consuming some type of mind-altering hallucinogen . . . a world where one can learn to commune with winged ones, communicate with them directly, and interpret their subtle yet very powerful messages.

Having regained my composure, I decided to drive with this beautiful creature to the home of my spiritual teacher. When I walked into her house with the bird wrapped in a towel, another wave of uncontrollable emotions struck me. This time, though, I had the awareness that something quite profound was unfolding. I understood it to be one of those life-changing events that, if you don't turn away from it, could alter your life forever. I would later come to understand that what I had sensed in that moment was true. Yet it would take much more convincing before I would come to a place of any significant surrender.

My teacher, who was trying to imagine what terrible event had befallen me, asked, "Has someone died?"

I opened the towel and showed her the owl. "Oh *that*," she said with a twinge of frustration and a look of impatience . . . a look she would sometimes give me when I was having an experience that rocked my world but to her was an everyday happenstance. She went on to say, "I wondered when and how this was going to occur for you. You know that you are a carrier of bird medicine, particularly birds of prey like owls and hawks."

Oh really? was my immediate internal response. Despite feeling confused and incredulous, I still retained my childlike sense of wonder and curiosity.

"Yes," she answered, responding to my unspoken question, and she began teaching me how to take and preserve the medicine from this bird. I was to pray with, commune with, and join with this bird. I was to sit with it in a tree in the forest in the middle of the night. After completing these initial instructions, I was to bring her two of the preserved owl wings.

Upon my return, my teacher performed a ceremony of initiation that utilized one of the wings. Once it was completed, I gifted her with one wing. (In time, the other wing would become an anchor, holding space on my Mesa in the Northwest.)

I "received" another twenty-eight birds of prey, mostly barred owls and red-tailed hawks. When I say "received," I mean that they came to me in the way that the first had. I would feel an energetic shift in the air around me and have either a clear vision of what I was about to see or a sense of an impending encounter to take place within the next few minutes. One of the many strange aspects of these ongoing encounters was that they all occurred within approximately three miles of my home.

During this same time period, I didn't have access to my spiritual teacher. Instead, the birds became my teachers. They showed me a great deal about their lives, their deaths, and their unique means of communicating. What they taught me specifically is perhaps best left between the winged ones and myself. (The initiation I was going through, while very relevant for me, may not carry the same significant meaning for another, or worse, might be misleading.)

To imply that this initiation was easy or enjoyable would be the opposite of my truth. I felt very confused. Although I wanted desperately to understand intellectually what was occurring, I had way too much ego to allow myself to get out of the way and just accept what was manifesting. I had no familial, cultural, religious, or spiritual references to ground me during this time. In fact, all of my reference points served to do just the opposite . . . causing me even more bewilderment and anxiety.

In time, when I felt I could no longer keep what was going on to myself, I went to a group of male friends and shared with them what had been taking place. I only did this out of sheer desperation because, as with many of the earlier spiritual experiences I had had growing up, there was a large part of me that thought I must be going crazy. These things just do not happen to "normal people." I was so afraid of being judged or treated as an outcast.

So I plucked up my courage and shared with my friends how I had gone to a local ornithologist and told him about a "friend" who had said he had seen as many as twenty-eight dead raptors in one small geographic area. The ornithologist's reply was, "Not possible. Even with a severe decline in their food chain up north, we still would not see that concentration of raptor activity in such a small area." Honestly, I already knew this was way outside the norm, but I wanted some rational expert opinion to help confirm my suspicions. The reaction from my circle of friends was so much better than I could have dreamed. Among the many helpful suggestions, two proved to be especially powerful. One man told me, "I have a friend in New York City who is a Peruvian shaman. He is coming up to visit me this summer and perhaps he could be of help to you."

Another spoke to a haunting thought that shook me to my core. Even though I had considered it myself, hearing another human speak the words made it real in a way that could no longer be denied. This friend suggested to me, "What if these birds are giving their lives to convey a message to you, and you're just not getting it?" This notion filled me guilt. I couldn't bear the thought that I might in some way be responsible for the deaths of these birds.

I went home that night and prayed out loud in my yard in the dark and told the universe that I was done with this and that I would not pick up another dead raptor even if it fell on me directly from the sky above. The next day, my wife returned home from some errands carrying two dead barred owls. She said to me, "I believe these are yours."

Okay, I know the universe has a great sense of humor, but *really*?

I did call the Peruvian shaman and that June he came to my home. When he arrived, in the short time between when he'd entered the house and I'd offered him something to drink he told me about three traumatic events in my life (all true) and how I had done a good job of resolving and healing two of the traumas, but there was still work to do on the third one.

He looked at me thoughtfully for a moment and then said, "Have you ever seen the Harry Potter movies?"

"Why, yes, I have," I replied, feeling baffled. He then said, "Do you recall the scene where the owls are trying to deliver the letter to Harry, inviting him to wizard school, and when their attempts are thwarted by his relatives, how the birds came to the house en masse?"

"Yes," I replied.

"Well then, there is really nothing more to say," he continued. "You are being invited to wizard school." He went on for some time telling me how, although this was a choice for me, it really wasn't a choice at all. He explained that while I could choose to turn away from it, during this life-time it was still my destiny and one I really could not escape in the next life or the next. This was now the third time that a two-legged whom I respected as a knowing spiritual being had told me about this destiny of mine.

He then performed a beautiful cleansing and energetically lifting ceremony on me, using wonderful fragrances, a staff, and a large con-dor feather. (By now, it's probably of no surprise to the reader that this condor feather resonated with my very soul in a most powerful way.) As our visit drew to an end, he told me that he and several other Pachakuti mesa carriers were attending a conference that fall in Washington, D.C., and that I should attend it and sit in their mesa lodge.*

To make a long story short, I made arrangements to attend the upcoming multicultural conference. I brought with me a suitcase full of raptor wings, tails, and claws. You see, among the many messages and teachings I received over the several months of my initiation was one that informed me that there were many other people who desperately needed the medicine of these winged ones. It was my job to see that they were in receipt of such medicine. Given that I was still "in the closet" about my budding spiritual life, no one knew to come to my front door, knocking and asking, "By the way, sir, do you have any rap-tor medicine for me?"

Sitting in the mesa lodge later that year, I told my story to the group of amazing practitioners assembled there. Later they would arrange a ceremony in which I could distribute the bird parts I had brought with me to the two hundred or so medicine people who had come to

---

*A mesa lodge is comprised of any number of Pachakuti Mesa Tradition practitioners with their individual mesas, or altars, arranged in precise geometric designs to maximize the flow of unseen energies to assist in healing work.

the conference from all corners of North and South America.

During the actual ceremony my heart was overwhelmed with emotion as I watched medicine workers and healers from many different nations take what they wanted and needed of this medicine gift. Tears flowed easily over the departure of these parts of my winged friends whom I had prayed over. There were also tears of joy and relief given for what now seemed the completion of a journey that had been full of self-doubt and wonderment. While attending that conference and the ceremony, I met some walking angels in the form of Iris Bolton, Bruce Pemberton, and Matt Magee, the author of an amazing book, *The Pachakuti Mesa*. These angels welcomed me, prayed over me, held me, laughed and cried with me, and touched my soul in a manner I shall never forget. They also all insisted that I needed to meet their spiritual teacher, don Oscar Miro-Quesada, a highly respected Peruvian *curandero*. Several months later, I did just that.

In a large Atlanta conference room with approximately eighty other seekers, I met don Oscar for the first time. We were all standing in a circle with our backs to the wall. Oscar walked into the center and began scanning the room. When his gaze fell upon me, he motioned me to come forward. As I approached he smiled and said, "I know you."

I responded, "I don't think so, at least not in this lifetime." He smiled his infectious smile, reached out and embraced me, and said in my ear, "Welcome home, brother, it is good to see you again."

That weekend turned out to forever change the course and the quality of my life. Among the many remarkable things that occurred that first weekend was the simple fact that don Oscar had me stand up three separate times and read the same quote from the Gospel of Saint Thomas. The quote states, "If you bring forth what is within you, what you bring forth will save you. If you do not bring forth what is within you, what you do not bring forth will destroy you." Let's just skip all the rational chatter here and say I began to get it. The winged ones had been teaching me all along what Oscar now began to teach me in earnest. As don Oscar is often heard to say, "Lose your mind and come to your senses."

So, was it by chance or synchronicity that the birds led me to don Oscar and my spiritual family? Regardless of the answer, my new spiritual family helped to anchor me within a community where I am fully embraced and loved in ways that have allowed my fears to melt into an ever-expanding awareness. They have enabled me to more fully embrace the universal matrix of life

As my path unfolded before me over the next few years, I completed a four-year intensive apprenticeship with don Oscar and became a sanctioned Pachakuti Mesa Tradition teacher. This training has allowed me to pass along these sacred traditions.

THOMAS MOCK, LICSW, has studied with don Oscar Miro-Quesada since 2000. He completed a four-year apprenticeship training in 2007 and is now a sanctioned teacher of the Pachakuti Mesa Tradition. Thomas was the first executive director at the Heart of the Healer Foundation. He maintained a private psychotherapy practice in Vermont for twenty years. He was the founding executive director of an HIV/AIDS nonprofit organization—AIDS Community Resource Network (ACORN)—and received the Robert Wood Johnson Foundation's National Community Health Leadership award in 2005 for his visionary work in the field of HIV/AIDS and hepatitis C. He is currently the chief of social work and geriatric services at the Providence Veterans' Administration Medical Center in Rhode Island. Thomas teaches the sacred Pachakuti Mesa Tradition throughout New England. For more information about the Pachakuti Mesa Tradition go to heartofthehealer.org.

7

A Mountain's Light

Ginny Anderson

Mt. Hood, in the Cascade Range, is the highest point in Oregon. Some fifty-five years ago, it was the site of my initiation—the turning point that provided an expansion of consciousness and an orientation ultimately leading to the spiritual practice of shamanism, which I pursue to this day.

Seeding the path that would unfold over my lifetime, the journey began with an adventure—my first mountaineering expedition. Of my climbing partners, two men were experienced climbers and the third a novice like me. Entering the impressive Timberline Lodge on the shoulder of Mt. Hood in Oregon, we signed the climbing register. In front of a roaring fire in the huge stone fireplace, we organized ice axes, ropes, crampons, food, and water. Even before we stepped onto the snow, I felt the enormity of what we were about to do. In the middle of the night, the lodge was deserted; our words echoed in the enormous space.

At 2:00 a.m. we set out, the crisp snow crunching underfoot. Our time frame was dictated by the need to get past a certain steep avalanche-prone area close to the summit before the sun altered the snow conditions. Crisp snow crunched underfoot. Initially my focus was on getting accustomed to the equipment we were using—handling the ice ax and feeling the pleasure of finding a pace and a movement of limbs that came into a workable rhythm.

The night was crisp and clear and the inky canopy overhead focused our close attention on the terrain directly in front of us. The snow was illuminated by the moon and the stars; I'd never seen such a stellar spread. From the moment of our first steps, my heart was wide open to the expanding beauty surrounding us. The spaciousness of the night sky, the enormous vista, the wonder of our surroundings played no small part in what happened for me that night. I was naive about the world of Spirit at that point, but the opportunities that were to come to me many years later through shamanism had their first expression in what took place that first evening on the mountain.

The early hours of our journey under the stars had led us through benign snowfields, but then the sky began to take on another quality of light and I paused as I realized that something quite magical was taking place. I could see farther now and everywhere I looked the violet light of the sky seemed to be spreading wings, illuminating and enfolding the undulations of the valleys, the peaks in the distance, and the fascinating shapes of distant fir trees emerging into view. I looked up toward the mountain's summit and felt myself being drawn *into* the lavender light that now totally surrounded me. A physical sensation of expanding beyond my body seemed to erase distinctions between my surroundings and me. The snow was lavender, the peak far ahead was lavender, and even my own body was encompassed by this beauty. The cluster of other climbers, as well as the stars overhead, were being swallowed into this beautiful color, and I envisioned them adding their illuminating power to the unusual violet light.

I was spellbound. We were one—the mountain, the snow, the forests, the sky, the stars, the climbers. We were not different, one life-form from another, but united. As the stars disappeared into the coming dawn, the quality of light changed—but I felt infused with its power, and I truly danced up that mountain.

Every sense was activated—every cell felt alive, receptive to the energy of the mountain, of the other climbers, of everything around me. I could only account for the energy that came into me for the climb from this sensation of fully participating in it. I was part of the mountain, part of everything. Because I was not separate, there was no effort—nothing to overcome. Even as the quality of light faded, the sensation of joy and full participation in the moment continued.

Completely present in that moment, I didn't think past it. I couldn't have imagined the significance this occurrence would hold for me as I journeyed forward in my life, or that a time would come when similar experiences could be learned and purposely practiced. But before that would come about, my life would unfold over the decades—through college and graduate school, marriage and motherhood, wild travels on several continents, exposure to meditation and mind-expanding experiences. Whether or not the sensation of light itself has been present, I've often recognized the power of the moment—in the sense of expansion past the separate self—as well as a focused awareness. My destiny is shaped by knowing that the potential exists to become one, cellularly and emotionally, with All That Is. Like beads on a precious necklace, ordinary life has been punctuated by enough experiences of this kind to bring the reminder that anything is possible.

Over and over again, when peak experiences have come to me through yoga, through qigong, through physical adventures, through the survival of life-threatening experiences, the sensations that accompanied the lavender light blanket me again. This proffers upon me an instant knowing, a familiar acknowledgment of an expanded mind-body state without label or categorization. It's simply a privilege to experience the reminder again and again.

Once, when I was in graduate school, raising and supporting five children on my own, I felt very overwhelmed and sought out and worked with a yoga teacher in the tradition of the great yogi Dessica Char. During a breath meditation with Craig Wilson, my teacher, I suddenly felt the shift into that same expanded space. I rested in it, feeling the immediate peace of the moment, and surrendered into it. I was left with the tranquility to deal with the overload of my life without the attendant stress. This was a precious gift.

When the meditation ended, Craig knew without words what had happened. He, after all, had also been immersed in the expanded space. Without pressuring me, he intimated that I could delve more deeply into yoga and with that might come an amplification of the power I felt in these transcendent moments. At that point, however, I was only able to cope with what was already on my plate, and I set aside a deep immersion in yoga. But that moment, which I recognized as akin to the moment when the lavender light had united everything on Mt. Hood, was a gift of Spirit that helped me deal with the challenges I'd created for myself. Deep immersion in spiritual practice would come later.

Other moments of profound intensity accompanied by enveloping light have come to me a number of times, under quite different circumstances. An aura that may be characterized by lavender or golden light typically attends these moments. One of them occurred when I was traveling home in the fast lane of a busy California freeway. I was returning from a session with a shaman, which seemed to have left me no more at peace than when we'd begun. But suddenly on that freeway, I felt myself enveloped in golden light.

Alarmed, I initially wondered if I was having a heart attack, and I looked for a break in the traffic so I could safely pull over to the side of the highway. Cars zoomed forward next to me, and I couldn't change lanes. I sped forward with the flow of traffic in the fast lane, and my fear turned to wonder as I continued safely forward, with the light beginning to extend to everything around me. The freeway, the cars, the dividers, and the buildings I sped past—all were bathed in light. The aura continued as I drove home, some thirty minutes away, and I felt empowered—as filled with joy and wonder by the radiance as I had been that day on the snowfields of Mt. Hood.

At home, I went into my garden, where I sat and marveled at the light and presence that surrounded me, and the sense of tranquility and peace that enveloped me. The issue I'd been concerned with simply disappeared in the sense of this greater well-being that permeated everything. I recognized the state of mind as that which had been brought on by the beauty of the lavender light on the mountain: all was one.

On other occasions, at times of great danger or threat of death, the light has arrived, together with an acceptance of the fullness of the moment and the sense of assurance of ultimate rightness. This sense of being fully present in the moment is complete unto itself, and from me it elicits an appropriate response that I could not have conjured or thought of on my own. Without doing anything to incur this other than spontaneously being open to the totality of the instant, my full self is invariably called into play. It seems that, when in this state, all the cells of my body become totally available to one another, resulting in a sense of effortless response that carries me toward the highest and best possible state of being. These experiences of light and total presence hold out reminders of ways to move forward through challenging times.

Some thirty years ago, a sense of feminist spirituality was emerging strongly in the Bay Area of California. When a life-threatening experience of violence (not the first) shook the form of my existence, a group of my friends assembled; they would become an important circle of fellow explorers. A framework of creating sacred space, and how to work with it, became the field in which we experimented for over twenty-five leaderless years, utilizing research, music, art, joy, and creativity in the process. Our experimental approach shaped many aspects of my personal work, as well as my work as a psychotherapist.

Later, overlapping this time frame, the threat of another dangerous circumstance brought out a need that was different from what could be provided in our circle. I sought out a shamanic teacher whose book I had recently read, and after searching all over the country for his whereabouts, I discovered that Alberto Villoldo lived two miles from my home. Over time, I began a spiritual journey with several shamanic teachers that led me to one of the primary forms of my work in the world. It returned me more definitively to the original source of my spiritual experience of Nature. The Peruvian shaman Americo Yabar and Ruth Inge-Heinze were among these mentors.

Shamanism's approach, at once ancient and also new to many, brought me into deep and direct contact with Nature. My first spiritual opening had been a direct experience without the framework of a specific spiritual practice. Through shamanism, I now had that missing link; I realized that the experiences of union with the natural world that had begun for me on Mt. Hood could be fostered through shamanic practices. I returned again and again to the Andes, absorbing spiritual perspectives regarding how life is viewed on our planet, whether that life be stones, plants, animals, or the spirit of place itself.

I began to see clearly the relationship between human actions and their consequences, and I understood that time seemed to be racing forward toward a culmination of life on our planet. These insights made me want to participate in the transformation of consciousness necessary for the continuation of all life on Earth.

The concept of *ayni,* or reciprocity, is deeply embedded in the shamanic wisdom of the Incas. I began to consider how and what I might reciprocate, or give back, in gratitude for the many gifts of presence that have come to me over time. The shamanic approach to the natural world provides a means to do that.

The Bay Area, my home territory, is encompassed by the energy of six mountains. A group of friends and I searched out a series of sacred sites on these mountains, identifying places that could help people develop a better understanding of our connections to the complex web of life. One such traveler was Sandy Miranda, the producer of a world music radio program. She called these mountains "the pillars of our paradise," and indeed, they frame the space of one of the most sacred places on Earth.

An upshot of these explorations was that I began to develop a project called Circling the Bay, which offers a series of journeys to the sacred places that encircle our communities. After more than two decades of journeying in the territories of these mountains, the award-winning book *Circling San Francisco Bay: A Pilgrimage to Wild and Sacred Places* was published in 2006. The processes of relating to the natural world described in this book are adaptable everywhere. They've been used to expand connections to the natural world in Russia, Canada, Alaska, and elsewhere in the United States. Wherever we are, the intent to relate to the land on which we stand can help us enrich our bonds with the natural world.

Returning to the beauty and power of Nature is a constant affirmation of the simple yet profound importance of returning to right relationship with the powers that sustain our very lives. Without direct experience of the natural world, it is much more difficult for people to comprehend that Nature's power to support or destroy our lives will be shaped through our own reciprocity.

GINNY ANDERSON, PH.D., is an ecopsychologist who works with individuals and groups in outdoor settings to help them develop and expand relationships with each other and the natural world. A licensed psychologist with a doctorate from Stanford, she maintains her practice in the San Francisco Bay Area. She has worked at Stanford, UC Davis, and the Institute of Transpersonal Psychology (now Sofia University). Ginny is the author of the award-winning book *Circling San Francisco Bay: A Pilgrimage to Wild and Sacred Places*. Her long life experience with feminist spirituality, shamanism, Buddhism, pilgrimages, and hospice all contribute to her practice. As world community evolves, she pays particular attention to the transforming role of women elders, weaving threads of lineage through traditional stories and their connection to nature's wisdom. You can visit her website at www.eco-psychology.com and find her therapist listing through *Psychology Today* at www.psychologytoday.com.

8

Journey about Love Doctoring

Katharine Weiser

Several years ago, I was invited to do a series of shamanic healings for an animal (named Po) that had been severely abused and traumatized. This journey that I am about to relate was one of the last journeys I undertook with Po.

We found Po outside, looking well. He seemed relaxed and happy. His ancestor spirits were there, and so was his power animal, the Eagle, circling overhead. We stood in front of him, and my helping spirit assessed him, regarding him deeply.

Then something shifted and I suddenly realized that Po wanted to share his gift of doctoring with us—that he was offering to doctor *us*! I couldn't believe it! And I couldn't imagine how/why he would doctor the helping spirits.

But my helping spirit immediately knelt in front of him and touched his forehead to the ground in a gesture of deep respect, and we did the same. "He is offering a gratitude round," he said, "a round of honoring what has been done for him, and his gratitude for that." We stood up and joined hands with Po's ancestors, forming a circle around him; his power animal circled above him at the apex.

I could feel and see the love and light radiating out from Po's heart, and into the hearts of each one of us in the circle—which we received and then radiated back to him, magnified. The circle became a beautiful starlike structure, made of interwoven beams of love and light.

"Yes," my helping spirit said. "This is one of the highest forms of doctoring—to receive love from one another and to magnify it back."

And then I saw multiple images from all over the world—tiny impulses of love being offered to each of us in our lives, thousands every day. And I saw how often we ignore them—perhaps because they are so small we don't notice them, or because they are buried under so many other emotions, or because we have judged a person negatively and are not open to him or her, or for a million other reasons.

And I also saw that being open to receiving these gestures of love from others and nurturing that love and returning it tenfold or a hundredfold is the gateway to all kinds of healing for everyone involved—an amazing and beautiful form of doctoring.

I was moved to tears to receive doctoring in this way—especially from a being who had been so brutally hurt by cruelty.

This journey touched me deeply. I have become much more aware of all the ways that love is being expressed—or trying to be expressed—all around me.

And I love the practice of noticing that love and magnifying it back. I'm not great at it, but even *trying* to do it has changed my life for the better . . . and probably the lives of those around me too!

Although I am grateful for my training as a medical doctor, I am even more grateful to have been shown this new way of doctoring—and its medicine of love.

KATHARINE WEISER, M.D., is a retired physician, now in apprenticeship with medicine people around the world and with life itself—and thoroughly enjoying deepening into this mystery. Her background includes a bachelor's degree in comparative religion from Harvard followed by medical school and then training in family medicine, psychiatry, and holistic medicine. She recently completed her qigong teacher training and is also a certified Reiki practitioner. For the past fifteen years, Katharine has had the great blessing of studying with medicine people from many traditions, including in Mongolia, Zimbabwe, Siberia, Peru, and the United States. She frequently visits Peru and Brazil and is a graduate of both the Winds of Change two-year program in Andean shamanism and the Foundation for Shamanic Studies' three-year program in advanced shamanism and shamanic healing. Her heart's great joy is to be in communion with all of life and to love and serve it well.

9

A Most Extraordinary
Vision on the Power Path

José Luis Stevens

Some individuals walking the shamanic path have experienced a single, sudden opening that forever changed their perspective of reality. That has not been my experience. For me there have been many smaller awakenings, experiences that have opened my perception gradually, a little here and a little there. In some ways I have been very fortunate because these smaller openings have afforded me the opportunity to adjust little by little to a shift in my reality, unlike those who have been blown open suddenly and overwhelmingly.

While I was attending university in California in the 1960s, I had some eye-popping adventures in consciousness with the help of psilocybin mushrooms, LSD, and mescaline, accompanied by my voracious reading of the Carlos Castaneda books, the Seth books,* and Aldous Huxley. I saw that the world I had been taught to see by my conservative Catholic education was not by any means the world available to me through these deeply altered states. I would say that through these

---

*The Seth books are a channeled body of work by the medium Jane Roberts, the most famous of which is *Seth Speaks*.

powerful journeys I had my first spiritual awakening and it had nothing to do with organized religion.

In graduate school at UC Berkeley I signed up for a special Werner Erhard EST training, which was designed specifically for psychotherapists. As it was meant to do, it completely and radically altered my perception of reality. For the first time I was able to see that I was totally responsible for my experience and that everything I perceived was the result of collective agreements, and that I truly was creating my own reality.

In my late twenties, after working in a state mental hospital for a couple of years, I took an extended four-month solo trip through India and Nepal, on a journey that absolutely turned my world upside down. I met people who could do things that I had previously thought were impossible: people could read my mind, bend steel with their mind, and exhibit energy levels that could only be described as miraculous. I spent a month in Kathmandu studying with a Tibetan Buddhist lama and learned the fundamentals of Buddhist philosophy. I came back from this trip an entirely changed man.

Upon returning, I entered a doctoral program at CIIS (California Institute of Integral Studies) and began to formally apprentice with a Huichol *maracame* (shaman) in Mexico. Over the course of the next ten years, he showed me what my life's work on the shamanic path would be; it is something I have never veered away from since. But this was just the beginning of my transformation as a human being. Eventually, with his blessing, I was to travel to Peru over forty times to train with Shipibo *ayahuasqeros* and Andean paqos in their respective shamanic traditions.

It was during one of these trips that I had the life-changing experience I want to relate here.

During the early 1990s I was traveling to the Peruvian Amazon with regularity to work with an ayahuasqero whom I shall call Juan, a man I had met previously. My wife, Lena, and I had taken a good-size group to visit Cusco, the Sacred Valley, Machu Picchu, and a number of other sacred sights in the Andes. When the first part of this trip ended, a pared-down group flew to Pucalpa, a hard-core Peruvian jungle town in the Amazon, to work with Juan. We were scheduled to do a two-night ceremony in his ceremonial *maloka* (hut), which nested within beautiful botanical gardens that he had cultivated himself.

I don't remember much about the first evening ceremony, it being many years ago now, but I do remember the second one as if it were yesterday. Late in the evening, at approximately 10:00 p.m., we got started. Juan liked to start late because he felt that there would be less interference from local people, given that, at that time of night, most of them would no doubt be asleep in their beds. The evening was a warm one and there were just a few pesky mosquitos around.

We sat in a circle and took the bitter ayahuasca brew and then sat back to wait for the visions to begin. Although I was always excited about these ceremonies, I had no inkling how the evening would unfold. Taking ayahuasca can be like rolling the dice. Sometimes with this medicine the experience would be rough, with lots of purging and dissociation, and at other times it could be blissful and sublime.

On this particular evening, I had many colorful and pleasant visions that lasted for several hours. At about three in the morning, or even later, I thought the experience was winding down. Suddenly I found myself in a visionary state approaching a temple, where I saw a mysterious but beautiful light emanating from the windows and doors. Upon arriving at the temple I discovered that it was packed with people. The people all had their hands raised up, reaching for a most extraordinary light that seemed to be streaming down from the great dome above. Somehow I knew that this was Christforce light pouring down, and I felt more motivated than I have ever been in my life to reach up and receive it. The problem was that there were so many people crushed together in the temple that it seemed almost impossible to get in. I squeezed in as hard as I could and all I could do was get my right arm and shoulder inside. Reaching my hand upward as hard as I could, I felt the extraordinary light streaming into it.

I have never felt any sensation like that ever in my life, before or since. It was an indescribable state of bliss—but I only felt it on the part of my body that was subjected to the light. The rest of me was out in the cold, so to speak. I stayed there for I don't know how long, marveling in the exquisite sensations flowing through my arm and shoulder. I wanted so badly to push on in and let my whole body experience the light, but it was simply not possible. You could say that it was, at the same moment, the most wonderful experience I had ever had and the worst torture at not being able to subject myself to it wholly.

It began to dawn on me that this experience was designed to offer me only a taste of what could be. I don't know how long I strained and basked in the light, but little by little the medicine began to fade and with it went the visionary experience of the temple. And then just like that it was over. But it wasn't over for me in the sense that I had tasted something so compelling that I could never be satisfied to be without it.

Unable to sleep, I sat in the warm damp night of the jungle listening to the dripping trees and the murmuring of the geckos until the sky began to lighten and a new day dawned. The experience was so personal, so unique, that I could not adequately share it with the other group members. It was an experience that just wouldn't translate in a way that would do it justice. Later I was able to discuss it with some very trusted friends whom I knew had had similar experiences. One of them, a very wise man, listened carefully and then after a pause said, "You are very fortunate that you had that experience. You may never have one like it again in your life. Or maybe you will. Just don't try to chase it. It was a gift." A part of me did not want to hear that, but I recognized the truth of his words. Although I found that I could reproduce the event very well in my mind, I could not quite reexperience the degree of intensity I felt that night.

It has been about twenty years since that vision and I have never forgotten the power of it, the beauty of it, the intensity of that light, and most importantly, I am aware of how much I would like to experience it again. That night I discovered what it was like to be in the absolute ecstasy of the light of the Christforce, and although I have not had such a direct experience of it since, I know what is possible, and that has changed my life indelibly.

For me it is very clear. This was no religious experience—not a conversion or anything associated with that. Yes, it was definitely a spiritual experience, but what I experienced was an extremely high frequency that is available to each one of us at any time whatsoever. This is a state of being that can only be described as a great blessing—a state that fulfills every desire, every wish, every yearning. In a word, it is a frequency that ends the state of separation, and yet interestingly I felt the light on my right side, the side that is typically associated with the male—the doing and the thinking. This is the part of me that is most dominated by what the Toltecs call the parasite, the ego, the false personality, which leads to feelings of separation. In this sense it was a great healing, for this is the side of me that needed this frequency the most. Since that time I have made much better friends with my feminine side (and yes, there is more work to do).

So, do I want to have that experience again? Of course I do, but I am not looking for it anymore. It will come when it comes, when it is right. I have learned some patience from that vision so many years ago. Since then I have had many indescribable, extraordinary experiences, and I truly feel like a most fortunate human being, extraordinarily blessed. I see now that the temple was too small to fit me entirely into it because I could not yet envision a temple large enough to hold me and everyone else. I now know that the temple can be as big as I need it to be and there is no shortage of space. Perhaps one day I will walk into a temple and although there will be millions of my brothers and sisters in there with me, there will be plenty of room for us. In fact, I now know that is not just a possibility, it is inevitable.

José Luis Stevens, LCSW, Ph.D., is the president and cofounder of the Power Path Inc., a center for the cross-cultural study of shamanism based in Santa Fe, New Mexico. An international lecturer, organizational consultant, executive coach, and teacher of shamanic practice, he uses his knowledge of shamanism and indigenous wisdom with corporate leaders and individuals from all walks of life. José and his wife, Lena, completed a ten-year apprenticeship with a Huichol maracame in the Sierras of central Mexico and are currently studying with the Huichols, the Shipibo healers in the Peruvian Amazon, and Incan paqos in the Andes. He is a licensed psychotherapist in New Mexico and California with an active consulting practice. The author of twenty books, manuals, and numerous MP3s, José often speaks on the subject of the indigenous wisdom of shamans and how it applies to the modern-day world. He is currently on the board of the nonprofit Society for Shamanic Practice and contributes regularly to the *Journal of Contemporary Shamanism*. His website is www.thepowerpath.com.

10

Into the Red Path

Julián Katari

This is the story of my initiation. It is ironic that something previously invisible to you can become something you seek to learn and experience. Irrefutable proof of the nonexistent, of the ignored, of the occult, presents itself when knowledge, the Spirit, a living being, comes to you and reveals your first out-of-this-world, miraculous experience—which is designed to prove to you the existence of "it."

That's when "it" becomes the only real thing you can seek in life.

That is how I felt. That is how strong my first shamanic experiences were. They proved to me what my true destiny was. Let me tell you, friends, how it was that the sacred Spirit presented itself to me. My ordinary life changed, and my walk on the sacred path began.

When I was eleven years old my mom and I decided to leave Mexico City for better opportunities in the United States. My mother had reestablished an old relationship and married an ex-boyfriend now living in Eugene, Oregon.

I set out on this adventure with my mother, only to find the unexpected. For four years I tried to adapt to a culture and society that, to me, was never very welcoming. My mother, on the other hand, was content with the more polished social system available in the United States. But we found no real tranquility. A painful story of verbal aggression, treason, and cheating developed in our small family.

After a few years I became unable to deal with such a painful situation at home and with a system that was so unfriendly to me. In the United States, a teenager is more or less forced to fit into a stereotypical group. As a Latino, I fit into the black and Latino group at school, adopting the behavior of my peers. Predictably, I began to skip school, drink socially, and smoke marijuana. I had no idea that the system creates these situations intentionally to hook people into different patterns of dependence. What was different for me is that the experience really became a catalyst for me to escape the prison of my life.

But I had to live the experience of escaping first. I had a friend who lived with the same experience that I did (that of an aggressive stepfather). Together we developed an almost perfect escape plan, with Mexico City as our final destination. We were able to slip away, unnoticed, from our homes and reach the Mexican border, where the authorities finally caught us and put an end to our plans. My friend returned home, and although my plan to escape the system had failed, at least I was able to return to Mexico City and live there with my ex-stepfather.

The system in Mexico turned out to be more bearable, although living with my other stepfather wasn't quite what I wanted either. In Mexico City I met friends who told me that if you were to drink a bottle of cough syrup, you'd get very high. I followed my curiosity and tried this powerful hallucinogen a couple of times. These experiences, though they might seem negative, had their positive effects: I began to develop a feeling that something wasn't quite right in the world. I wouldn't learn anything more insightful than this until I drank cough syrup for the third time.

I had returned to the United States by then and was hopelessly trying to finish school. Coincidentally, my stepfather there had been "fond" of cough syrup also and would drink small gulps a few times a day. Because he was drinking it, I thought to myself, *Why not try it one more time?* But this time everything was different and my life changed. The syrup my stepfather used had twice the psychoactive compound concentration of the ones I had indulged in before. I overdosed and very quickly became very ill.

The illness turned into pain, and the pain knocked me to the ground. I couldn't stand up. I continued crawling on the ground trying to reach the phone to call 911, but I was unable to do it. I felt I was going to die and my last recourse was to—almost involuntarily—pray.

Somebody please help me, were the words that I formulated within my deepest self.

In the same instant that—in my mind and most especially in my heart—I had formulated that thought, I felt immediate relief. I opened my eyes and felt baffled by the sudden response to my prayer: I no longer felt ill. I could still feel the presence of the hallucinogenic substance in my bloodstream, but I no longer felt sick and dying. I felt as if someone had put a healing hand on my stomach and soothed me. I rose and looked at where I had the warm sensation, and there were three tiny colored feathers—one blue, one yellow, and one red.

I looked up, trying to imagine how a bird could have dropped its feathers on me, but I was inside the house. I quickly thought of the colored feather dusters that are used to dust household furniture; they are very prevalent in Mexico. I searched the house looking for one such duster, but I found none. Still doubting the validity of the feathers, I put them in a container and looked at them every day for the following months.

I was sixteen years old when this experience unleashed a neverending journey of discovery and self-transformation that fifteen years later is still happening. It was those feathers that began the quest for answers to the mystery of that miraculous experience.

A place called the Saturday Market became my new school. People from every walk of life offered their various goods and services here. You could find organic produce, crafts, alternative healing services, and other curiosities in this interesting, lighthearted, alternative street market. I was there every week, looking for and finding people with answers. My newborn sense of seeing guided me to people who had some higher knowledge and an advanced state of perception. One of them was a weird-looking man who hung around the market in the area where the bad-boy teenagers gathered. He stood out from the others and I felt the call to speak to him.

He was a Native American of the Lakota tribe and I soon discovered that this young but quickly aging man was a dedicated drunk—not your ideal Native teacher! But in spite of his drinking problem, his dark affect, and the fact that he hung out with the "bad guys," he retained some of the wisdom and spirit of his ancestors, and this is what drew me to him. In my newly developed state of perception and spiritual openness, I approached him. My presence quickly took him out of his common state of being into a more sensitive and spiritually connected place. He looked at my soul and heard what I had to say. When I told him my story he said, "The Spirit listens when the soul knows how to ask."

This man, whom I had just met, understood perfectly what had happened to me—I even felt he knew who I was. He quickly confirmed that when he grabbed my arm and took me over to another man: a tall, thin, aged man who sat on the edge of a short wall. He wore a dark leather suit and dark glasses and had long, straight white hair and extremely pale white skin. The man was quite the sight.

"Show him," said my new teacher.

Calmly this white man (who looked Native American) opened his leather jacket to reveal a precious pendant that hung around his neck. It was a white silver wolf with emerald eyes. I saw myself as the wolf and felt that these men knew that to be true as well.

The next thing I knew, my Native friend instructed me, "Now you have seen. I must teach you how to heal." He paused and continued, "Go to the Native American store and buy either one or two bundles of sage, or sweet grass braids, whatever you choose. You must also buy a red string. Bring these things back to me."

I did as he told me to do. I went to the nearby Native American store and bought two braids of the greenest sweet grass I had ever seen, as well as a red-and-black shoelace, and brought them back to where he was.

"You have passed the test," he told me upon my return. "You have chosen two, not one, and sweet grass instead of sage. If you had chosen otherwise, it would mean I must not teach you, but you have passed; now I will teach you."

He showed me how a sacred bundle must be made. This was done by tying one of the braids in a circle to the thick end of the other braid with the shoelace. Then he showed me how to use it—holding it and burning it to the four directions. Once I learned this he further instructed me: "You must now go to the top of that mountain and do what I just taught you. You must look for two women to help you and you must heal this city."

Straightaway I hopped on a bus and went to Spencer's Butte Park, a park shot through with trails, overlooking the town. I spent more than an hour in the parking lot, talking to various women, attempting to have them accompany me to the summit for the ceremony I would perform there, but everyone refused. It was getting late and many people where leaving, so I made the difficult decision to continue on by myself. To save time I climbed directly to the summit through the forest, rather than taking the more time-consuming trails.

As I arrived at the summit, which was a large rounded rock outcropping, so did two women, each of whom had come up a different side of the mountain. The three of us arrived at the summit at exactly the same time. We looked at each other calmly and then I said: "You know what we are here to do." Both women nodded their heads in assent.

We three carried on with a brief, powerful, tranquil, and silent ceremony, burning sweet grass to the four directions. I continued waving the sweet grass over each of the women, cleansing them, and then I allowed them to cleanse me. After that, we hiked back to the parking lot in a very peaceful fashion. The women had a car and gave me a ride back into town. As soon as I got out of the car, a homeless black woman saw me and shouted, "It's you," and then she ran over to me.

"Give me what you have," she said as I pulled out my sweet grass and cleansed her. She gave me a hug and continued on. Seconds later another person felt immediately attracted to what I had to offer and approached me, and then another and another.

My life was never the same after that seminal day when I began healing others, plunging into the sea of wisdom inherited by the Natives of this continent. That day I learned the meaning of the red-and-black shoelace. It represents the red path—the path of the people of this continent that today is called North and South America by its invaders, the white man. I prefer to call the continent its true name: Abya Yala.

This path I have followed is exponentially richer than the imposed path that modern people walk on. My life before that moment was a terrible, invisible prison with no way of escape. After my encounter in the market, a light showed me the way to freedom. Freedom didn't come easily, and it still hasn't completely arrived; the first years were tangled in an intense magic incomparable to the more experienced, softer magic I experienced later on.

Those initial days were an exciting time for me in that I had firmly decided to permanently remove the evil that had been subconsciously planted in my mind and body. It was a time when miracles happened so frequently that they became my new normal, and "warrior" was the best word I could think of to describe what I did. During this time, I met with many healers, sorcerers, wise men and women, and shamans who taught me and guided me. They helped me develop my newly learned capacity to listen to the sacred Spirit. I began to receive constant teachings from the Spirit as manifested in the elements of Nature.

My journey has since continued through many places in Mexico, Guatemala, Chile, and Bolivia. At times I have lived with different indigenous peoples, but always I have followed the sacred Spirit and the red path. With many ups and downs, I have made more than one attempt to leave this path, for the shamanic life of spiritual enlightenment is not one of play; it is one of real work. And although it might seem easier to sleepwalk through life in a spiritually unawakened state, in reality it's not, for the modern life is one that is empty and hollow.

On some level I knew this, and thus my attempts to leave the red path weren't successful.

But learning has a price. When you are spiritually called, you, as a warrior, must answer the call. I have received many callings, and as a warrior I have always accepted the challenge at hand. It used to be that this type of learning was a privilege. Now it is an obligation. Today we have arrived at a point in time when everyone must choose this path, because it's the only path. It is the path of the heart, of Mother Earth and Father Sky. My experience is just a mirror of the awakening that must happen in every person—it is happening with the universe as a whole.

We are all one with the universe and with Mother Earth, for whatever happens to you, to me, and to the Earth happens to everyone. We must choose whether we desire to continue on the path of life or remain in a dying state.

JULIÁN KATARI began following a path of Native American wisdom at the age of sixteen. Over sixteen years he lived in five North and South American countries learning arts and sciences from what he identifies as his five main cultures: Chichimec, Toltec, Maya, Andean, and Amazonian-Arawak. He is fluent in Spanish, English, French, and Portuguese and has knowledge of five Native languages. He is firstly a Native, then a farmer, a philosopher, a father, a medicine man, an architect, an artist, a musician, and a conservationist in both the ecological and cultural sense. Julián is working in the deepest and most biodiverse region of the southern Amazon, in Bolivia, to create a self-sustainable community that lives in harmony with nature and to build a university of North and South American Native wisdom and sciences. His website is shamanamautakatari.blogspot.com.

11

Mount Everest

Jan Engels-Smith

In 1992, I went to Nepal on a trekking adventure. Although the trip itself was exciting, I was more intrigued with the possibilities of spiritual enlightenment in this most spiritual place. Nepal, like Tibet, is known for its high level of spiritual connectedness. Upon my arrival, however, these dreams rapidly dissipated. This happened for a number of reasons. I was traveling with four other women and felt as if I was the only one who was taking the trip for spiritual reasons. Conversations about spiritual topics were difficult, and to them, most of my thoughts probably seemed obscure and indistinct.

The real hardship, however, was physical. I immediately found that the sheer challenge of surviving took most of my energy. I realized that my all-encompassing spiritual attitudes, so present in my daily life, are facilitated by a comfortable American lifestyle. In Nepal, quite to the contrary, I was more concerned with basic needs: Could I manage the grueling terrain? Where was my next meal coming from? What would my sleeping conditions be? Would I be warm enough? Would I make it across the next wobbly bridge? Would I experience breathing difficulties at higher altitudes? As life began to present difficulties with which I had very little experience, my focus changed from a grandiose spiritual high to matters of everyday survival.

I did retain one spiritual aspiration, though: I wanted a close view of Mt. Everest.

Even though Mt. Everest is the highest peak on Earth, it is sandwiched between other extremely high peaks, making it difficult to see. As well, there is only one real vantage point from which to see Everest well, and that is from the top of Kala Patar, a peak close to Everest. From there, Everest can be viewed in all of her splendor.

Climbing Kala Patar, however, is a test of endurance. One's skill level doesn't need to be advanced to attempt this climb; however, the rugged crag rock and the altitude of 19,500 feet put much strain on the body. I had been training for months before this trip, running eight to twelve miles a day just to make sure my endurance levels were high and my lungs strong. I always kept the destination of Kala Patar in mind, for I believed it would be the highlight of my trip.

We spent two weeks trekking and finally we were only one day away from Kala Patar.

The weather had been cloudy for several days. The few people that we met who were descending the trail from Kala Patar were disappointed. There was zero visibility of Mt. Everest because of the massive cloud cover. Still, we maintained our enthusiasm and plodded ahead. I kept thinking, *Within twenty-four hours I will be there.*

I slept restlessly the last night, knowing that we would have to make an early start. In order to make it to the top of Kala Patar and back down to camp we needed to begin our day at about 3:30 a.m. We would start the climb with flashlights. I woke at 2:30 and tried to center myself. In my backpack I carried a book called *A Course in Miracles*—a spiritual text with a series of 365 lessons and meditations, one for each day of the year. I had been a dedicated student of this material and was continuing my commitment even in Nepal.

I snuggled down in my sleeping bag with my flashlight, trying desperately to concentrate despite my excitement, to read the lesson for this particular day. The lesson was titled, "Step Aside and Let Me Lead the Way." The "me" in this sentence referred to God. I read diligently, trying to absorb the words and waiting for time to pass.

Finally, at 3:00 a.m., we got ready to go. We all were very quiet packing our packs, arranging our gear, and heading out. It was totally dark, given that the clouds prevented any moonlight or starlight from illuminating our way. We forged ahead, watching our step, and tripping at times on the uneven rock surface. At this altitude the landscape reminded me of moonscape. Nothing grew here, not even moss or lichen. All was barren gray rock. We were lucky there was no snow; it was late March and much of the heavy winter snow was gone. The air was exceedingly dry due to the fact that the evaporation process, at such a high altitude, is very rapid.

By 5:00 a.m., the sky was beginning to lighten, making us more aware of the thickness of the cloud cover. By 5:30, our party stopped to talk. There was much discomfort. The air was thin, making breathing difficult; some in our group were experiencing feelings of light-headedness and headache. One woman was experiencing extreme nausea. Everyone, except for me, was hurting in some way. As a group, they decided it was wise to turn around. I stood mute as I listened to my friends make these decisions, my mind blank. They turned and began to walk back down.

I heard myself say, "I'm going on."

They all stopped and looked at me compassionately, understanding my desire to reach Kala Patar. I scanned their faces. Although they understood, along with the compassion were some expressions of disbelief. I know that my voice must have come from the pit of my soul because no one argued with me; I had declared my intention with conviction. We then discussed options for my continued journey and made a decision as to how to split up the gear. I would take our Sherpa guide with me. We also discussed where we would meet up again, for all of us were unsure just when that might be.

As I stood watching my travel companions walk away I thought, *Jan, you must be nuts!* I was standing in the middle of the Himalayan Mountains with a guide who spoke very little English. I was committing to a climb that would tax my body, just to see Mt. Everest, which was currently completely hidden by cloud cover, and we were facing the likelihood of a storm rolling in.

Still I chose to continue.

My guide's name was Nima and he was an experienced Sherpa. Like most of the Sherpas in Nepal, he was in outstanding physical condition and able to maintain incredible ascent speed regardless of rocky uneven terrain and thin air. Needless to say, I couldn't possibly keep up with him. Once we started off, I kept yelling for him to slow down but he paid no heed to my request, probably because he didn't understand all of my English words and he was impatient with me. I must have seemed extremely slow compared to his Native travel companions and I often lost sight of him as he scampered ahead of me.

In any event, initially I was fine; my destination was clear and I was determined to complete the climb. Even though there was no path, I knew which direction to go—up the mountain in front of me. I didn't need Nima to show me the way! My need of him was more to curb the fear I felt in the pit of my stomach—my fear of being alone in such an isolated place. It now was a matter of endurance and sheer will.

There were two moments of near collapse for me, times when I thought I just couldn't go on. The first time this happened, I dropped to my knees, put my head down on the ground, and tried to clear my mind. I happened to look at my watch and noticed the date. It was March 24, my sister's birthday. I knew it was close to the end of March, but I hadn't been conscious of the date for several days. The thought of my sister's birthday gave me incentive to continue. The day became special, which transferred into energy for me. This newfound energy put me back on my quest.

Several hours later, I once again suffered a near collapse and contemplated turning back. To my amazement, my shadow appeared in front of me. It was as though a spotlight had illuminated my figure, although the sun was nowhere to be found. I didn't even know which direction I was headed. Yet still my shadow loomed ahead, up the mountain before me. As I watched this ghostly image of myself, my thoughts turned to my morning lesson in *A Course in Miracles:* "Step aside and let me lead the way."

At that point I knew the will and determination I was experiencing wasn't me, but Spirit. Spirit was behind all of this, pushing me, urging me, helping me. If I would simply concede to the climb wholeheartedly, it would be much easier. I was creating such difficulty because of my fears. I was worried about being alone, not being able to see Nima, about whether the weather would hold, or if I would be able to find my friends later that day. This worry was stealing my energy and blocking me from Spirit's incessant urging. I then understood the lesson of stepping aside and letting him lead the way. I let go of the control and mentally walked through the doors of opportunity. From that point on, I knew I would make it. Doubt vanished and new sense of vitality surged through me.

As I neared the top, the terrain became much steeper and the rocks and boulders farther apart. I had to climb on all fours. I was concentrating on every movement. I heard Nima, who had undoubtedly been waiting for hours, call down to me from the top. "Look, clouds," he said, making a gesture with his hands to indicate that the clouds were moving apart. "Hurry, hurry," he motioned.

I turned to look where he was pointing. Sure enough, the clouds were splitting like the parting of the Red Sea. Everest was exposed in all of her glory. He kept repeating, "Hurry, hurry."

With tears starting to roll down my cheeks, I yelled back to Nima, "I see, I see, but I don't need to hurry, Nima. I think they are parting for me." I knew at that moment that this particular event had been divinely intended. This is what the trip was all about. I was experiencing a miracle designed especially for me.

I pulled out my camera, capturing this spiritual event in a time-lapse sequence. As I completed the last few yards of the climb, my body felt disconnected from itself. I was overwhelmed with emotion, sobbing with such intensity that my entire body swayed from my laborious breathing, and gasping for breath between sobs. Poor Nima must have thought I was truly losing it. He actually came over and patted my shoulder lovingly. It is unheard of for a Nepali man to do this, for it is a social taboo to touch women publicly. He was trying to help in a loving way that bridged our language barrier.

My eyes were fixed on Everest. I stared at it in disbelief. How could this be happening? Why? In the shadow of the world's tallest mountain,

I sat down. I was overwhelmed, but still able to clear my head somewhat. Finally the tears stopped and my vision focused.

I noticed that a red-billed chough had landed about four feet from me. A red-billed chough is a bird that resembles a raven. It is large, black, and strong. The chough is striking in appearance, with its massive black body and scarlet red bill. I kept glancing over at the bird, slightly aware of the oddity of its closeness, but then I would float back to blissfully gazing at the magnificent Everest.

It was several minutes before I questioned why the bird was at this altitude and so close to me. There was no animal or plant life noticeable in any direction. Just rocks, glaciers, and mountain peaks . . . seemingly not the natural environment of a bird. In fact, the bird was the only other life-form besides Nima and me.

I turned my head and focused intently on the chough. When I did so, everything became surreal. My head throbbed from the lack of oxygen; I was exhausted from the climb and I was still stunned by the miracle of Everest's sudden and glorious appearance. I sat motionless watching the bird—so out of place in this bleak environment, and close enough to touch.

Finally, I said out loud, "What do you want? What do you need to say to me?"

I didn't know the source of my questions. They seemed to emanate from someplace deep within me. Until that moment, I had never spoken a question directly to any animal, and certainly not with the expectation of communication with it. Yet some part of me, some cellular memory tucked away in my core, knew to ask and to expect an answer. The bird told me that I had been brought to this place by Spirit to help me understand my purpose and my worth. Much of the dialogue I had with this bird was extremely personal and I do not choose to divulge the details. However, the epiphany led me to dedicate myself to following Spirit's call. After the bird finished speaking, he spread his massive wings and flew away.

I sat for a long time. I clutched my camera like it was my lifeline back to reality. I was glad that I had taken pictures of the parting clouds, as though I needed future reassurance of this miraculous and mystical event.

Here I was, in a country on the other side of the world from my home, having a personal viewing of the highest mountain on the planet. I was being given direction concerning my worth and life's purpose. I was engulfed in a pure and holistic love. How could I have ever felt unworthy in my life? I knew that Spirit was showing me my value. If that meant having a personal showing of the greatest mountain on Earth, as well as a personal experience with a talking red-billed chough, and a personal message of love, then so be it. It was like Spirit was saying, "Do you get it now, dear one?"

"Yes I do, I do."

This moment had been divinely planned to prove this love to me, so that no matter what obstacles I encountered in my daily life, I could refer back to this moment and remember—remember the feelings, the awe, and the immensity of this miraculous time.

Thus began my life of trust—knowing that I can trust my experiences, knowing that I am guided and loved, knowing that I have allies that will appear and communicate with me. This is a trust that surpasses all understanding and propels me into a world of unlimited possibilities.

❖❖❖❖

Jan Engels-Smith, LPC, M.Ed., Sh.D., is the founder of LightSong Healing Center and LightSong School of 21st Century Shamanism and Energy Medicine. Jan's mission is to provide excellence in shamanic healing and education and to support personal growth for well-being by applying ancient healing techniques to contemporary life in the twenty-first century. Jan has developed the first shamanic energy medicine curriculum of its kind for those who would like to obtain a doctorate in it (Sh.D.). In her personal healing practice she has performed over 3,500 soul retrievals. She has also authored two books: *Through the Rabbit Hole: Explore and Experience the Shamanic Journey & Energy Medicine* and *Becoming Yourself: The Journey from Head to Heart*. She writes for numerous journals, magazines, and publications. Her websites are www.janengelssmith.com and www.lightsong.net.

12

Rappers Don't Go on Meditation Retreats

Bezi

Born and raised in Roxbury, Boston's equivalent of the South Bronx, or South Central Los Angeles, I thought of myself as carrying on the city's tradition of producing iconic black men along the lines of Crispus Attucks, David Walker, and Malcolm X. Having a dad who was a field organizer for the Student Nonviolent Coordinating Committee during the time they were organizing into the Black Panthers helped. He, as well as my mother and my aunts and uncles and their peers, was also involved in various singing groups and musical bands. Coming of age and becoming politicized in the 1980s (Reaganomics, apartheid, crack cocaine, etc.), it seemed destined for me to become a participant in the confrontational do-it-yourself subculture of hip-hop. In the winter of 2002, on the eve of the most decisive moment of my life, I was nothing less than thoroughly identified with my persona: *Sounds like fun, but* some *of us are too invested in the hard slog of dismantling the institutional superstructure, fighting the power. I'm a gate stormer, a social reformer . . . or, in a time of momentous upheaval, a potential martyr.*

As an inquisitor of apparent reality I was not averse to deep contemplation and intense inner work, so long as it yielded instantly obvious, practical, real-world results; to my mind, action and conflict generated meaningful change. A meditation retreat felt a bit too much like New Age, psychological escapism: white, middle-class, indulgent, privileged, and indifferent to the cries of the suffering masses. What did sitting on a mat have to do with "the struggle"?

I advance, not retreat . . .

But my ol' lady, a demonstrably psychic jewelry designer and daughter of classical Greek scholars, insisted that I begin to meditate with her. And since I'd courted her (which was completely out of character), on an intuitive hunch that she'd fling open peculiar and thrilling new doors of discovery and possibility for me, it didn't take a strenuous effort on her part to convince me to join her.

The meditation, situated in the high desert town of Joshua Tree in Southern California, is known by its Sanskrit name of Vipassana. Roughly translated, Vipassana means "things as they really are"—in other words, an immaculately clear perception of what is true at the deepest level. At the time of my arrival on the chilly compound, I hadn't a clue as to what the implications or consequences of "things as they really are" might be and whether or not the ol' lady had intuited anything she never said. As it turned out, ignorance or, more charitably, "beginner's mind" (in the words of the great teacher and Zen monk Shunryu Suzuki) was probably my strongest suit going into it. Being very goal oriented then, knowing there was a specific kind of favored outcome, would have caused me to seek it instead of simply experiencing what came up naturally, which seems paramount to the exercise.

Learning the *silas,* the virtuous codes of conduct to be observed over the course of the meditation, was scarcely a concern. No killing, smoking, lying, or stealing? Hey, I don't do any of those things anyway! The instructions for Vipassana were in fact deceptively simple: meditate, eat, sleep, repeat. No television, no reading, no electronic communication, no talking? No problem! *These ten days will be a cakewalk,* I thought to myself.

The first two days were a languid dream in spite of a fairly rigorous schedule that consisted of hours spent sitting perfectly still and silent, watching the breath as it entered and exited my nose—"treels," as the honorable instructor S. N. Goenkaji called them, in his thick Burmese accent. With typical Capricorn conscientiousness, I attended every sitting, beginning at 5:00 a.m. in the morning, pushing through back and leg pain, boredom, sleepiness, ringing ears, discomfort from the cold, and periodic bouts of severe self-doubt. I was doggedly determined to give whatever was being offered a chance to manifest.

The first effect was a subtle shift in my sensitivity to time. Meditations, meals, meandering aimlessly across the arid, stunning desert grounds and back to my cabin at night felt less like planned, discrete activities and more like a single flowing event. By the third and fourth days, bizarre things were happening with my body. Certain thoughts, mostly memories, would cause me to go into violent and, in the beginning, terrifying convulsions. Invariably these were visions of various women I'd had unrequited sexual feelings toward; some I'd known and some not. A puzzling pattern emerged: I'd recall a certain woman and immediately be wracked by involuntary spasms that I knew instinctively were related to past arousal, but which were not at all arousing in the moment.

Years later, I would come to understand that these were "karmic knots"—energy blobs of sorts that get lodged in the body as a result of unfulfilled desires, causing unconscious suffering. As disquieting as these were, I resolved to redouble my efforts; something powerful was definitely happening. Concurrently, the dusty wind on my skin had a new tactile presence; narrow bands of golden midday heat felt . . . intentional, benevolent. Stars in the crystalline midnight sky seemed closer than I ever remembered them being. Every taste, sound, and touch was more densely packed with sensation, with exquisiteness . . .

I spent the fifth and sixth days confronting the absolute loss of my sanity. After crouching behind a bush to avoid a helper banging a small gong summoning us to the meditation hall—fearing an instinctual urge to lunge at his throat like a cornered animal—I thought to myself, *Well now I've done it. I've gone and driven myself mad.* When I finally did drag myself back into the hall, we were collectively instructed to mentally "scan" our entire body from the top of our head to the tips of our toes and back up again.

Doing this, I discovered that the panging sensations had localized in the bottom half of my body, while enigmatic, tickling, swirling plasmas of sensation coursed through my torso and upper limbs. When Goenkaji predicted in his prerecorded remarks that "by now, you may be experiencing gross random sensations in one part of the body, together with subtle sensations in another . . . ," my imaginative capacity was driven to its outer limits. *What is this?* I wondered. *What's going on here? And how does he know?*

On the eighth day, I took my place in the meditation hall exactly as before, fussed myself into an agreeable position for my back and legs, took some deep breaths, and began to scan my body. As if ignited by the turn of a key, the gross and subtle sensations began. And then, in the midst of these (which I'd fully come to expect), Goenkaji remarked: "At this point, you better pay attention to the spine . . ." Funny, I had not thought about my spine at all. When I did, all tactile experience as a distinct physical entity was sucked into my spine and ejected from the top of my head as if pushed from below and pulled from above by unseen forces.

Okay.

If I lived seventeen more lifetimes I don't suppose I could summon the words to adequately articulate the state of awareness this particular set of circumstances left me in. But if I must make some poor two-dimensional overture to a sort of description, and my assumption is that one would be useful, I'd say that it was complete unmitigated liberation, a seamless merging with the Ineffable, Immeasurable Substratum of Being Itself. All distinction between me as a perceiver and an external objective reality disappeared. There wasn't a single passing millisecond that registered to my consciousness anything less than absolutely interconnected Oneness with All.

As above, so below.

Accordingly, I spent the rest of the day in a state of blubbering incoherent bliss, a newborn infant tossed before the overwhelming grandeur and sublimity of it all. Every character artifact of the distinct, separate "I" that I had carefully constructed over the decades, all of my labels—"black," "male," "Bostonian," "rapper," "intellectual," "radical," "Capricorn"—fell away like colorful but lifeless leaves. "Bezi" per se had left the building . . . and couldn't be more pleased. In his absence the distant mountains breathed for the first time. The scramble of life under the parched desert floor resonated. Each element—wind, sky, and earth—embraced as if greeting a long-estranged brother. Undulating tree branches pantomimed "Hi."

Nineteenth-century scientist and writer Johann Wolfgang von Goethe coined a phrase that seems apropos here: "delicate empiricism." Attunement to the ecology generates profound sensitivity. *How could the implicate order have been this premeditated, this sacredly and tenderly designed, this baldly obvious the whole time?* Apperceiving myself the hapless fool for missing truths explicit in every minute, I laughed aloud at myself. *What a misunderstanding that was!*

In the long run, this experience upended every conceivable dimension of my existence. When I've attempted to have others help me define what I experienced, whether it was nirvana, *samadhi,* satori, *jnana,* kundalini rising, or some such, I've had no luck. Thus I'll just call it an *awakening,* albeit one that has provided a fully substantiated master narrative for my life. Everything I've been through thus far hangs together in a coherent chronicle. My suspicion is that a "good story," as it were (and I realize now that that's *all* it really is), is pivotal in matters of self-actualization, of finding one's true purpose. I've tried several times to build a manuscript recounting this narrative but I always feel like I'm leaving out critical details of a still unfolding plot.

Stages and events in my life now fall into two basic categories: pre-Vipassana and post-Vipassana. Before Vipassana I was moving for certain in the direction of edification but hadn't yet found my "X factor," to use a hackneyed but concise meme. I had what seemed to be vague inklings on where to search, although looking back in hindsight, these were actually pretty exact. When an opportunity presented itself to me, that of participating in something that felt important but guaranteed no concrete outcomes, I took a risk and, trusting my inner promptings and the integrity of the company I was keeping, pushed past my comfort zone. In the midst of riotous psychophysical reactions I stayed calm and redoubled my efforts, trusting again that there was an intelligible, benevolent logic at work. The payoff absolutely surpassed anything my imagination could generate.

My post-Vipassana lifestyle could be summarized as what philosopher Ken Wilber called "transcending and including"—simultaneously being whole and part of a greater cosmic whole, yet also being very much integral to the natural world and grounded in basic animal physicality. All the ethno-cultural affinity remained, but it was mediated by wisdom revealed through the prophetic visions of seers and saints. How fortunate it is that these have been passed down to shepherd our enlightenment in this moment when they're desperately needed! And who knew? After years of trying fruitlessly to reconcile to Christianity and Islam, it turned out I was Buddhist the whole time! No other religion/philosophy/way of life speaks to me so convincingly, so forcefully; no other strikes me as being as empirically reliable as Buddhism. The new name my ol' lady contrived for me— the black bodhisattva—feels apt.

Though this was *my* formula for transformation, I know it's hardly the only one. I'm fond of the axiom "many base camps, one summit." A bodhisattva employs whatever means s/he has at hand to assist the awakening of others, always tracking that each of us is as unique and indivisible as we are interconnected and familial.

Coincidentally, the similarity between a bodhisattva and a shaman is that both have powerful medicine gained in victory over some dire existential challenge (often internal) that they bring back to their communities. And as I ponder unprecedented drought, shrinking glaciers, disappearing forests, structural racism, child, sexual, and elder abuse, geopolitical turmoil, religious fanaticism, disappearing species, and beyond, it's manifestly clear that wisdom gained in both the healing of the shaman's core wound and the bodhisattva's tending to the cries of the world will be indispensible in ameliorating the grim global situation we currently face.

In the final analysis, sitting on a mat had *everything* to do with the struggle, for it raised my personal ecology of meaningful change above anything that could be called "struggle" in the first place.

BEZI is a cofounder of the hip-hop groups Exile Society and The Subterraneanz. He is a multi-instrumentalist, singer/songwriter, producer/composer, documentarian, urban philosopher, strategist, activist, Vipassana practitioner, Zen student, and aspiring author. He was the filmmaker and editor for the short documentary *You Are Your Own Guru,* which can be found on YouTube. He launched a dharma-influenced political third party and was a Bernard Osher scholar at Berkeley City College. Bezi is certified by Master Stephen Co as a pranic healer. You can find Bezi's music at soundcloud.com/donmusic-2, and music from the group The Subterraneanz on YouTube.

13

Moon Struck

Mama Donna Henes

I was ten years old when I received my first compelling message from the universe delivered by Mother Moon. My cosmic call came in the guise of a homework assignment. Miss Lusk, my much-loved fourth-grade teacher, told us one propitious day to go home and compose a poem. Even as she was speaking, it came to me in a flash—a lunar illumination, if you will—that I would not be *writing* a poem that night but, rather, *waiting* for one to enter my soul.

It was perfectly clear to me that if I were to go outside alone in the middle of the night, my poem would come and it would be completely composed, sent special delivery directly to me. I *knew* this to be true. No doubt about it. This imperative mandate from the moon to me was completely irrefutable. Besides, the prospect was tantalizing, at once a promise and a dare.

I did all of my homework that evening except for writing a poem. It was thrilling to ignore an assignment. This was completely new, naughty girl territory for me. What fun to flaunt the expectation that I would do as I was told! It was hard for me to refrain from composing, as writing was my favorite subject and I adored Miss Lusk. But an assignment from the universe was not to be ignored, after all.

And I understood what I must do. I would stay awake until everyone was asleep, then sneak outside to find my poem. This might sound simple, but it was absolutely stunning in its implications. This was 1955 and nice little girls—the tribe of which I was a member in good standing—simply didn't let themselves secretly out of the house into the dark night to meditate in the moonlight.

Despite the daunting odds imposed by personality and convention, I did just that. For the first time in the life of this shy, painfully obedient child, my own inner prompting asserted its will. And I was impelled to follow, consequences notwithstanding. I was possessed with a completely primal compulsion that was beyond thought or reason or experience, propelled forward by some ancient instinct of spirit survival. I was buoyed by a sense of absolute rightness.

I itched all evening with the anticipation of my intended rebellion. I had much resolve and no reservation about the plan. My only concern was getting caught. But no matter—the moon is bigger than my mother, I realized, and She obviously had something very important to tell me. I recognized the beckoning song of my lunar muse and was honored that my heavenly siren was singing to me. My job was to listen and learn. I didn't once doubt that this was for my own good.

So, at 2:00 a.m., in my inaugural action as a consciously spiritual seeker, I tiptoed down the stairs and through the sleeping house. I opened the back door and stepped outside into the unknown, forbidden night . . . into the moonlight and the radiant magic of the moment, into my newly found self—scared, but triumphant.

The backlit clouds . . . the silvery mist . . . the billion stars . . . the sacred silence. There I was, totally solitary and aglow, surrounded by the vast emptiness, the electric fullness, the complex choreographed swing of all time and space. I was completely safe, embraced by the energy of the entire universe. Such a karmic calling carries with it a sense of assurance, of protection and conviction. That one small step for a young girl was every bit as phenomenal as Neil Armstrong's footfall on the moon. We both crossed the same crucial threshold toward cosmic consciousness.

It was my premier epiphany. The moon was my temptress, calling me out to play, and I trusted the impulse to follow. That alone, was a miracle—a bounding leap of faith. Had nothing further occurred, the elevation of trust and the development of confidence in my own understanding of the way Spirit moves would have been empowering in and of itself. As the Jewish Passover song "Dayenu" says, "It would have been enough."

But naturally, the poem did arrive, intact and unbidden. Today, I can only remember the first line: "As I lie beneath the sky, I look above and wonder why . . ." This was a perfectly respectable philosophical speculation in the time-honored tradition of sincere human contemplation—a frank and simple expression of overwhelming wonder and awe.

I snuck back inside, smug with victory. Afraid to turn on the lights, I couldn't see to put the poem on paper until morning. So I laid awake for the duration of the night committing it to memory. Reciting it in a reverent whisper, I chanted my first power song.

Of course the poem was completely beside the point. What I received that night was a heady taste of personal response-ability and a newly discovered sense of inner knowing and determined compliance that stands me in good stead to this day. That long-ago experience cemented my connection to the cosmic cycles of the universe and led me to my shamanic soul path.

My childhood lunar engagement was the first of thousands of personal and public ceremonies—*celestially auspicious occasions*—that I would come to celebrate during my four decades (and counting) as an active urban shaman.

What a profound and indelibly life-changing experience—Donna Susan's consecration ceremony—convened by the moon and enacted in full faith. Lady Luna whispered in my ear just what I needed to hear: "Come out, come out, wherever you are!"

I complied, and have been in Her thrall ever since.

> *I cannot sleep*
> *For the blaze of the full moon.*
> *I thought I heard here and there*

A voice calling.
Hopelessly I answer "Yes."
To the empty air.

Lady Tzu Yeh,
third-century Chinese poet

Mama Donna Henes is an internationally acclaimed spiritual teacher, popular speaker, and award-winning writer specializing in multicultural ritual celebrations of the cycles of the seasons and the seasons of our lives. Her joyful celebration of celestial events has introduced ancient traditional rituals and contemporary ceremonies to millions of people in more than one hundred cities for thirty-three years. Queen Mama Donna is the author of four books, a CD, and an acclaimed quarterly journal. She has been a recipient of four fellowships from the New York Foundation for the Arts and the National Endowment for the Arts, as well as numerous project grants from municipalities, corporations, and foundations. Her listings include *Who's Who in America; Who's Who in American Art; Who's Who in Entertainment; Who's Who in American Writers, Editors, and Poets;* and *The World's Who's Who of Women.* Her website is donnahenes.net.

14

A Lifetime of Awakenings

Tom Cowan

I don't think I had one particular "aha" moment. In some ways my entire life has been a slow, unfolding aha.

There has never been a time that I did not believe in God. And for some reason my life has had the right people and the right places at the right times to teach me about God and help me see, deepen, and strengthen my trust in this unknowable, unfathomable Godhead behind the visible universe. Even before I discovered shamanism I knew that this Divine Presence was interwoven throughout the natural world. And so I spent a lot of time outside in places where beauty or mystery or the thinness of time and space revealed a spirit of power that was everywhere, of course, but more intensely felt in those special places outdoors. I was (and still am) one of those people who can spend enormous amounts of time alone outside, in the woods, hiking across fields, or sitting along riverbanks day and night in order to feel held, protected, and directed by some intelligent and loving consciousness.

Shamanism helped me understand this all the more.

In 1983 I signed up for a basic training course in shamanism with Michael Harner, not really sure what it would be or what it would do to me. I only knew that the word "shaman" held some strange resonance for me and I knew that people who encountered shamans or were shamans had some understanding of the world that was different from other people's understanding. It was an understanding that I too held, if not consciously, at least close enough to consciousness for it to haunt my prayers, devotions, and spiritual reveries. "Shaman" seemed like a word that I would come to understand; it would have great significance for me. And it did.

That initial training in shamanism and the other teachings that followed unfolded the aha in a big way. The deeper I delved into shamanic ways of living, the more I knew that this ancient form of spirituality and healing made great sense out of my life and filled out the "picture" of the Godhead that had hovered over me since I was a young child. It also helped me understand the world, people, and events in ways that enriched not only me but (I hoped) others as well.

From the start I saw shamanism as a spiritual practice that would support and complement many of my previous beliefs and practices. I think what astounded me the most in those early years was the ability shamanism gave me to live a mystical life, that is, a life in which the mystery of the universe became clearer and more present to me. I don't mean that I understand this mystery, not completely, because I think it will always remain mysteriously unknown to us until perhaps after death—and maybe won't be revealed to us even then. But shamanism gave me the tools and the community to indulge in explorations of the universe that would slowly satisfy more and more of my yearnings to know what this great and amazing world we live in is all about. I mention community intentionally because shamanism has not been just a collection of practices to encourage the silence and solitude that I have always found congenial to a rich spiritual life. To the contrary, it has also acquainted me with others on the shamanic path who would become my community, tribe, and family of fellow searchers.

I am often asked why I practice shamanism, and like many practitioners I have a bagful of answers to that question, picking the ones that seem appropriate for the time and the person asking it. But I think the most basic answer that underlies them all is that I love shamanism because it helps me find God. Even though we work with various spirits, gods, goddesses, and other powers, the seamless web of consciousness that shamanism shows us reveals that everything in the universe is what Joseph Campbell called the "masks of God." For me, the spirits and other deities are manifestations of the Godhead.

I also explain my practice of shamanism in terms of its antiquity. Sometimes I like to flippantly say that Christianity (which was the religion of my childhood) is too new. It's only a couple thousand years old. It hasn't proven itself yet! Shamanism, on the other hand, has been around in some form or other for thirty to forty thousand years or even longer. Its staying power attests to its utility. It survives because it satisfies some deep instinctual need in the human psyche. I believe we all have some need to find God in some form or other, and shamanism emerged to satisfy that need among indigenous peoples who lived lives deeply interwoven with the spiritual mysteries of the universe. They lived close to the Divine Presence, and that closeness evolved into the spiritual practices that define shamanism. This closeness to God is what I wanted as a child, and what I still long for as an adult.

So I think that in discovering shamanism, the "eureka" moment emerged in me as a response to a lifelong craving that I was seeking to satisfy. The eureka moment said, "Here is the way!" And nothing since then has satisfied that craving as completely as this age-old practice.

As I embraced it, I began to see the parallels it had with indigenous Celtic spirituality. In time I was able to place my shamanic practice into the ancient spirituality of my Celtic ancestors, even into some of the beliefs and practices that were blended into what became Celtic Christianity.

Did my life change? Yes and no. Yes, in that I had new tools for pursuing a spiritual life in the physical world. Yes, in that I discovered spiritual worlds hiding behind, under, and over the physical world. Yes, in that I acquired spiritual helpers from the realms of animals, elementals, ancestors, and landscapes. Yes, in that I learned to journey through realms that, prior to my practicing shamanism, had only been accessible to me in dreams and reveries. Yes, in that when I am confronted with pain and suffering, I do not have to feel helpless, but know that there are sources of power available for healing. Yes, in that I found communities of like-minded shamanic practitioners to support, teach, and guide me in my yearnings for closer relationships with the world of Spirit.

But in some ways my life has not changed on a very fundamental level. I still seek God and want deeper and clearer ways to understand God. And in some crazy way I continue to structure my life very much as I did forty years ago. I still read spiritual books voraciously, although what I consider "spiritual" today is broader than years ago, and now includes books on consciousness, ecology, anthropology, and indigenous lifestyles. I still make time for morning prayers to begin the day. I still give thanks for my life to a Divine Power upon which I feel tremendous dependence. I still roam the woods and fields, sit by rivers, and watch the change of seasons consciously. I still need times of silence and solitude. I still go to others for spiritual direction when I need it.

So my spiritual life has broadened and deepened with shamanism, and the wonderful thing about shamanic practice is that it continually presents moments of aha. Thus, the aha of my life continues to unfold.

A statement about shamanism that continually inspires me is from Don Jose Matsuwa: "The shaman's path is unending. I am an old man and a baby, standing before the mystery of the world, filled with awe."

If I can live like that, as he did, the aha moments will never cease.

TOM COWAN, PH.D., is an internationally respected shamanic teacher, author, lecturer, and tour leader specializing in Celtic visionary and healing techniques. His practice combines universal core shamanism with traditional European spirit lore, and he has taught training programs in Canada, England, Wales, Austria, Germany, Switzerland, Italy, and Slovakia. Tom grew up in Missouri and received a doctorate in history from St. Louis University. He has studied with Michael Harner at his Foundation for Shamanic Studies and other teachers of shamanism and spirituality. From 1996 to 1998 Tom taught Celtic shamanism for the foundation. He is a minister in the Circle of the Sacred Earth, a church of animism dedicated to shamanic principles and practices. Today he lives in New York's Hudson River Valley, where he offers training workshops, spiritual retreats, and healing sessions. His website is wp.riverdrum.com.

15

Encounters with an Ally Plant

Carol L. Parker

About ten years ago, while leading one of my first vision quest ceremonies in a remote location in Death Valley, I was shocked when a young woman named Ricki returned from her solo site laden with three-foot-long stalks of wild tobacco. I had no idea tobacco could grow in such a bone-dry environment. Ricki is an accomplished herbalist, and she explained to our group that she had found a spring about two miles from base camp, in a hidden canyon, and near the spring were thick stands of this sacred plant. She planned to dry them and use the dried tobacco in ceremony.

A few months later, Ricki called from her home in southern New Mexico and asked me to go with her and some friends on a "plant walk" in the Chiricahua Mountains near the Mexican border. She wanted to teach us how to identify various desert herbs. She casually mentioned that we might be lucky enough to find some wild tobacco out there. I found myself immediately drawn to this adventure, especially after she mentioned tobacco!

Prior to the quest in Death Valley, I had given little thought to the role of plants in North American indigenous traditions and ceremonies, although I had learned from various shamanic teachers to make small offerings of tobacco and cornmeal in order to connect with Mother

Earth. After Ricki's incredible discovery that tobacco was growing in that remote desert of Death Valley, I found myself waking up a bit more to our relatives in the plant kingdom. Tobacco, however, carried connotations of addiction and ill health for me. Still, when Ricki issued the plant walk invitation, I noticed I was feeling drawn to the idea of finding tobacco in the Chiricahuas!

We met in Silver City, New Mexico, and caravanned to our campsite, which was in a lovely red rock canyon in the desert mountain landscape—about thirty miles from the nearest town or ranch house. Ricki knew this part of New Mexico very well from many prior herbal walks with her teacher.

No other campers or hikers were in the area, so we wandered freely for hours the first day, looking for desert herbs and enjoying the discovery of arrowheads and other evidence of prior wanderers, probably Apache hunters and gatherers from a century or more ago.

Ricki disappeared for a while and then returned, breathless, to announce that she had spotted some wild tobacco. I quickly volunteered to return to the area with her, and as we hiked through the sandstone spires and dry riverbeds, I found myself very excited that we might run into a stand of tobacco. As I came around a stone outcropping in a sandy arroyo, I suddenly saw a plant with large green leaves, standing about two feet tall. The plant seemed almost to jump out at me, and it was glowing, with a golden light all around it.

I don't usually see auras, so I was taken aback by this very clear visual experience. As I stood there entranced by this vibrating glowing plant, I suddenly knew exactly what it was trying to convey to me. Its message was, "I am your ally plant."

Stunned, I walked away in silence and later told Ricki about the encounter. She had fallen behind me in the canyon and had not seen this particular tobacco plant. She wanted to go back and harvest some of it, but I asked her to leave it there. That night, wide awake in my sleeping bag, my prejudices about tobacco slipped away as I wondered, with excitement, what it might mean to have an "ally plant" and how this relationship might develop over time. I remembered stories of shamans and curanderas who spent years wandering in the jungle or desert, sitting ceremonially with various plants in order to learn their medicinal uses from the plants themselves. I wondered why the tobacco plant had called me, and what I was supposed to do about it.

A few months later, I decided to drive up to North Dakota to support a sun dance on the Cheyenne River Sioux Reservation. A Lakota elder had issued the invitation to me and a couple of my friends, and we were thrilled to have the opportunity to learn more about this amazing ceremony and to participate in it. The sun dance chief said we needed to each have a ceremonial pipe, so he carved the pipestone himself and fashioned traditional Lakota pipes for us to carry during the ceremony. He also taught us the proper way to fill them with tobacco and red willow, as well as the correct way to make the prayers, smoke the pipe, and clean it afterward.

I was all thumbs. I seemed to be doing everything backward. The chief was not particularly pleased and told me so! I have since learned that the Lakotas often teach in a rather abrupt way, which can sound harsh or punitive to non-Native people. Because this was my first teaching from the Lakota tradition, I felt embarrassed by my mistakes and ineptness and didn't recover my confidence for many months. I put my pipe away, thinking that perhaps one day I would learn to use it correctly. At that time I had no desire to smoke it. I kept it in my car in a pipe bag, along with some tobacco and red willow, but soon forgot it was there.

One spring day about nine months after the sun dance, I drove to Taos, New Mexico, to see a friend who was housesitting there. I walked into the old adobe structure and was instantly bowled over by the heavy dark energies in the place. "Eliza, how can you sleep in here?" I asked my friend. She said she, too, had felt the negativity and had to camp outside each night.

Suddenly I remembered my pipe. Driven by the powerful sense of needing to do something to clear the house, I asked her if she would be willing to do a pipe ceremony with me and pray for the negative entities to be released and move to a better place.

She agreed, so I filled the pipe as best I could remember, and we made our prayers and smoked. The tobacco and red willow smoke soon filled the room. In about five minutes, we both felt the shift as the heavy energies departed. Amazed and grateful, we slept inside the house that night!

Since then, I have consciously developed my relationship with my ally plant, the wild tobacco. It has become a source of knowledge and wisdom for me. I use my Lakota pipe often and have begun taking it with me when I lead vision quests so that with it I can pray for healing and transformation of the people who are questing. I also have started taking the pipe with me when exploring new wilderness areas. Recently, for example, my partner Frank and I stumbled accidently into an ancient chalcedony quarry on Cerro Pedernal in northern New Mexico. Clearly this lovely translucent multicolored stone that lay in large chunks and small chips all over the hillsides had been used for centuries by the local Puebloan people for arrowheads, ax heads, and other tools. The energies were so strong there that we felt uncomfortable and a little sick. I had the "hit" that the ancestors felt invaded. The quarry was well off any trail and hidden in an arroyo, so likely it was rarely visited. We decided to do a pipe ceremony for the guardian spirits of the quarry. Instantly the energies felt more harmonious and we had a feeling of being welcomed to this magical place.

I have come to understand that one of the esoteric functions of tobacco is to create a pathway through the veils to help us access our helping spirits more powerfully. It also is a very strong cleansing agent (as in the house clearing Eliza and I did). Whenever I smoke tobacco in a pipe ceremony, or even in a cigarette, I immediately feel the connection with the ancestors and other helping spirits. This clears my mind and grounds my energy. I have also expanded my relationship with this ally by making the acquaintance of *mapacho,* a type of tobacco used in healings in the Amazon. Whenever I travel to Peru I scour the Cusco Witches Market looking for cigarettes made with mapacho to incorporate in various healing ceremonies, to ask for blessings, and to help cleanse energies.

I have also been shown by Navajo elders some simple ways to use Navajo "tobacco" for blessings and prayers. Navajo tobacco is composed of several plants gathered in a sacred way on the San Francisco Peaks and other parts of the Navajo Nation. These plants, though not actually related to wild tobacco, are smoked in cigarettes or Navajo-style pipes. They have cleansing and healing properties and help calm the mind during stressful times. I am so grateful to my Navajo friends for showing me these things and I am grateful to make the acquaintance of new friends in the plant world.

Since that day in the Chiricahuas when the wild tobacco made itself known to me in a very personal and obvious way, I have been blessed with many opportunities to strengthen my relationship with this ally. I now know it as a friend, a way shower, and a magical healer. Indeed, my ally has helped me see that my deepening relationship with it and my intentions to make use of it in a good way for the benefit of others are far more important than whether or not I do a ceremony exactly right.

With all gratitude to the elders who have shared their knowledge freely with me, the plant itself has been my most important teacher.

Carol L. Parker, Ph.D., is the director of the transformational ecopsychology program at Southwestern College in Santa Fe, New Mexico, where she also teaches. Carol received her Ph.D. in counseling psychology from Washington State University. She has been leading vision quests and pilgrimages to sacred sites for many years. She is an initiate in the lineage of *altomisayoqs* in the Peruvian Andes and takes students there annually. She helped found the Paqo School of Santa Fe in 2013 and regularly teaches ceremonial ways of the Andean spiritual cosmology. Carol has recently created special volunteer projects in Maras, Peru, to help the children of this rural impoverished Andean village. She is also a board member of the Andean Research Institute.

16

Call of the Ancestors

Phillip Scott

They arrived when I was six years of age: Big Medicine Dreams, as the Traditional Elders refer to them.

Though I am not at liberty to disclose the details, the very first Dream at that sensitive and receptive time was powerful and profound beyond measure. It allowed me to experience and realize that the Dreamtime in our nocturnal forays is equally if not more real than the dream of our diurnal, waking life. For nearly a year after that introduction and initial epiphany, I began to deliberately cultivate relationships and forged alliances with the Spirits and Ancestors of those realms. I also became a sleepwalker—dancing between the worlds—capable of negotiating and moving through the physical world while seeing and navigating other Dream worlds simultaneously. This was merely a prelude and preparation for what was in store.

As a consequence of an invitation for employment, my parents packed up the family and relocated us from the West Coast to the East Coast. It was there, in upstate New York, that the aforementioned Dreams and sleepwalking commenced. At the age of seven, my father and I joined Indian Guides. Far less about indigenous people, it was an organization that afforded an opportunity for fathers and sons to bond through sharing various adventures together. A sledding excursion was planned. It was my first exposure to snow, my very first actual winter.

Excited by the activity and energy, I desired to travel down the steep hill alone, just as the other boys. My father was reluctant, yet at my insistence, he finally acquiesced. Not in possession of our own equipment, we borrowed an old-style Radio Flyer with the wooden platform and two metal runners underneath. Not having tested it in advance, my father did not realize the joints were rusty. I laid my belly on the sled and pushed off. Careening down the hill, the sled was soon heading directly for a large conifer. Unable to steer, fearful of rolling off and unskilled at stopping by driving my boots into the snow, I shielded my head with my arms right before I struck the tree at high velocity.

Upon impact, I was immediately jettisoned from my body into absolute darkness, yet I was fully awake and aware. A black viscous substance surrounded and suspended me. There was a palpable sensation of movement, of slowly traveling upon an unknown trajectory toward an uncertain destination. I heard the muffled sound of my name being desperately called from somewhere behind me. It was my father's voice.

Suddenly, a tentacle of energy wrapped around my waist from behind and literally yanked me back into my lifeless body. As I slowly opened my eyes, a circle of panic-stricken, blurry faces appeared and hovered overhead. I drifted in and out of awareness as I was hoisted up the hill, swaying in a makeshift gurney, and then carefully slid into the back of a station wagon . . . my father making demands of a nurse behind a counter at the hospital, pointing at me while blood dripped from my face, pooling onto my lap . . . finally fully waking to the tug of a cold steel needle and thread through my right cheek, which had been lacerated by the bark of the pine tree.

Bedridden for months afterward, I was unable to walk, my equilibrium having been adversely affected by the disruption to the delicate structures within the inner ears involved in maintaining balance, alignment, and direction. Nor was I capable of forming and articulating words properly. My father, a neuroscientist, having observed the bright red blood that had flowed from every orifice of my head—eyes, nose, ears, and mouth—at the time of the incident, feared the worst: namely, that I had sustained neurological damage. Multiple tests were conducted to ascertain if this was true.

More disconcerting for me was the sheer madness I was enduring (and unable to communicate or escape), for I was now seeing and hearing all manner of apparitions and Spirits during the day, in ordinary space and time. It was a form of insanity. Their overwhelming numbers coupled with the cacophony of their voices was utterly terrifying and impaired my ability to function in all areas of my life.

Eventually, after regaining the ability to walk and speak, I returned to school. However, I found it exceedingly difficult to concentrate. I was constantly disoriented, unable to locate and return to my classrooms, confused by the presence and echoes of ghosts and Spirits in the halls. My physical performance and aptitude diminished significantly and I became isolated and withdrawn from others. As a result of my scholastic, athletic, and social decline, my parents considered keeping me back to repeat a grade. During their consultation with me regarding their concerns and sentiments, I pleaded with them to allow me to progress, assuring them I would improve. Encouraging the cultivation of my confidence and often supportive of my decisions and desires, they relented, granting me a chance.

Comprehending the gravity and urgency of my situation and aware of what was required, I requested the assistance of the Spirits and Ancestors with whom I had initially established alliances the year before. They availed me in sifting through the noise, chaos, and confusion—warding and sending off the Spirits who were tormenting me while introducing me to those in the throng who would (along with them) be of further guidance and service. Regaining balance and clarity, I began to excel in my life again, with an even greater appreciation and connection to the Dreamtime and its formidable denizens—Big Medicine and Sacred relationships that continue to this very day.

On my global excursions, when I meet with traditional Medicine People from various indigenous cultures, they frequently relate stories of their calling to the Path of Selfless Service. Often they have endured a harrowing initiatory crisis usually involving a near-fatal illness, injury, or tragedy, which intimately acquaints and familiarizes them with death and fosters a deeper lifelong association with their helping Spirits.

This is true in my case and story as well—a literal impact that inexorably transformed my life and catapulted me onto the Medicine Path.

Of mixed ancestry, Phillip Scott has walked the Native Path for over thirty years, learning from and sanctioned by Traditional Medicine/Holy People, Tribal Spiritual Leaders, Wisdomkeepers, and Elders from several indigenous cultures. Annually Sundancing in the Lakota tradition for over two decades, he is a Ceremonial Leader entrusted with sharing indigenous wisdom and traditional healing practices with the contemporary world. He has been interviewed both nationally and internationally on radio and television and for newspapers, and his life and experience have been featured in journals and books. In addition to directing and teaching the programs at the Ancestral Voice Center for Indigenous Lifeways in northern California, which he founded in 1994, he maintains a private healing practice, performs Ceremonies, conducts intensives, gives lectures, and leads pilgrimages worldwide. He is skilled in survival and primitive technologies, has received a master's degree from Naropa University, and is also a licensed EMT. His website is www.AncestralVoice.org, and he can be reached at info@AncestralVoice.org.

17

There's Been
a Whole Lot of Grace

Reverend C. Ayla Joyce

In the beginning
there was light.
It split me open and
showed me my plight.
Shocked I was, horrified at best,
Stinking thinking—words that came to mind,
You must be crazy,
sick in the head, imagining such dreadful thoughts as these.
I know.
I agreed.
You're right, I must be.

But if I am, what an awful child I really must be.
Well, you are, your name is S-I-N-T-H-E-A, after all.
Remember you are bad and evil too?
To imagine such things
could happen to you. Your poor parents, you've never stopped
pushing them, hurting them, hammering away.

And for what?
You want them to pay?

To pay for what?

No, I don't want them to pay. I want them to play . . .
Play what?

The game of truth—I tell, they listen.

But things happened—God got in the way
many, many times. Really
it's more than I can say.

The one big time
which was a turning key
happened
when my doctor said to me, on my nineteenth birthday,
"You have scar tissue
thick as a wall. You've got two holes—who did this to you?"
I had no memory beyond a recent D&C.
"Could that be it?"

"No," he said emphatically, "this is way too thick, and old."

He continued, "To let the fetus pass through I have to
      remove this wall
surgically, carefully. Oh and by the way, I've never seen this
      before."

"Okay, Doc Petrie, do whatcha gotta do!"

"Oh and by the way, surrounding the surgical stadium
there will be many eyes looking at you."
He goes on to say,
"You're at a teaching hospital here, at MCV, and a vaginal
      septum removal
we've never done before."

"Go for it, Doc Petrie, do whatcha gotta do."

Thirty-eight years later—in a hut made of bamboo, I
      visited a shaman
hoping to heal this deep, ingrained taboo.
Can't love God—can't love the church—can't love the cross,
that all crucified you.

Can't love me,
most certainly not.
Can't love me.

Mother ayahuasca running through my veins
bring me back home
to the place of my first grace.
Sitting alone—shivering to the bone,
I sat naked—topless—in a circle
They all sat around a pile of burning coal.
Warmth . . .
it offered,
but hardly enough.

Eyes once again, surrounding me—in the circle-shaped hut.
In front, I sat alone—shivering to the bone.
Teeth chattering,
was an altar made
not of stone
And before my eyes, was a crucifix—not meant to go
      inside of me.

The shaman was a priest,
he wore feathers instead of robes.
Musical bells replaced the buzzing drone,
love songs serenaded, my heart
raw and open, by disciples meshed through their tinkling
      bells,

weaving their very magical spells.
All wearing all white, replacing the men in black,
with hoods,
whose music sounded like angry drones.

Crucifix plunging in and out,
"take away the innocence"—incense burning—
"bury the Light—woman—child—girl of delight.
You are the cause of the human plight and carry the reason
    why we
must fight," happened fifty years ago.

In front of the altar—not made of stone—
was a crucifix, beautiful, encased in glass.
Small and delicate to my sight
and leaves called *chappas* feathered my body
with incense of Palo Santo
burning—burning—burning
around my body, so beautiful.

Where the power of the crucifix before was used
to hurt,
now a gentle shaman—priest with feathers on his head—
made the sign of the cross.
Gentle fingers touched my head, my shoulders, my heart,
    forehead, chest, navel, back and head, my shoulders, my
    heart, forehead, chest, navel, back and head, over and
    over again.
Clucking purrs softly filled my head.

Gaping holes torn before
now are filled with tenderness.
Smoke is blown, gentle words are spoken—welcome
    home—welcome home—welcome home,
shadows
you are free to go.

Loving purrs—tender touches—naked body upper,
    shivering to the bone,
chappas clearing, disciples singing love songs serenaded my
    soul back home.
A plant with thorns is whacking me . . .
wake up—wake up—wake up—wake up, little one, it's safe
    to come home!
Wake up nervous system,
wake up and come back home.
Spiraling down my spine, searing through my brain,
erasing all the evil spell
I heard the angels singing!
Welcome home, my little one.
A joyful welcome home
back to my birth, back to my worth, back to the joyful
    place of mirth
through
my birth and the loving that brought me to this Earth.

I am home again, home again,
jig-it-ty-jig.
I am not of this Earth, but a star being at birth!
A star being,
on Earth.

REVEREND C. AYLA JOYCE lives in reciprocity bringing sacredness to the pro-fane. She is highly skilled at tracking family lineage patterns that disturb the harmony within family systems. She is known as a "contemporary shaman" in her community at large. Her experience with indigenous medicine people began at age eighteen in Ecuador and has continued with the Lakota Sioux, the Qero and Shipibo of the Amazon jungle, and La Iglesia Episcopal as well as in Ecuador and Colombia, where she used the plant medicine ayahuasca. She is a Reiki master, certified massage therapist, sound healer, and creative. She is a channel for the presence of Christ and is humbled by the power that flows through her, opening the Way to our authentic Self and our sacred place within the web of life. She is a proud mother of two amazing young adults and a ya-ya to two special grandbabies. Through her children the path of LOVE awakened! Her website is www.aylajoyce.com.

18

An Experiential Journey toward Trust

Julie Dollman

How many times in life have you heard the words, "You only have to trust"? What does trusting actually mean, anyway?

I was a mother, wife, and working criminal analyst, among many other adopted roles, in her late forties, studying shamanism in the middle of Ireland in the early "noughties" (2000s). Each full-on training week was often challenging, profound, exhausting, and healing. During the times spent in class I remember holding the belief that anything was possible, even the ability to throw myself into the arena of "trusting." Until, that was, I arrived home and everyday working life took me to its plentiful bosom once again.

The daily grind of a self-built reality held me tightly gripped in its icy fingers. I was working eight to ten hours a day in a job where I often battled with my own conscience. I was partnered with my husband as we worked to pay the endless bills so that we could live under the same roof in this somewhat civilized twentieth-century world. We were among thousands of others all doing the same.

One day in mid-2006 I decided to create a new reality for myself. I left a well-paying salaried job to step into the unknown realm of spiritual service. I aligned with what I believed to be part of my soul's purpose, to become a shamanic healer and—boy oh boy—often during those early days did the "trust" word nip at my heels like the proverbial black dog! It seemed to want to constantly remind me that surely I must have ideas above my station, because does someone like me *really* leave a safe job to make a new life for herself? Many times my decision challenged my belief system, and its mantra that "It's going to be alright" would be hung out like wet laundry to dry. If I am honest, did I believe that things would actually be okay? No, not really . . .

Life took on a momentum of its own within a couple of months of my departure from mainstream society; my husband, who is also on the shamanic path, became ill. Succumbing to his own life's journey, he encountered the world of a breakdown, one that was to be both a challenging and life-changing path for him. Reality struck like a well-oiled bell and we both knew that the company he worked for wouldn't support his illness in the long term. We sold our home of nineteen years and rented a home in rural Oxfordshire in England so that he could regroup for a while.

During that time I became the first shamanic practitioner on the high street in Henley-on-Thames. I came out of the broom closet and stood blatantly naked before all who wondered what I was up to. People, though curious, came to me to be healed from a lifetime of separation and woundings. Within eighteen months the building that housed the clinic was sold and we decided to move back to my ancestral home for a while. After a somewhat tense year we bought a thirty-six-foot, secondhand American RV, and like a boomerang, my old friend "trust" came nipping at my heels again. We placed most of our belongings in storage and, one early morning in November 2008, left the UK to travel to Ireland. We were welcomed by a farmer who bred racehorses and allowed us to park up on his land indefinitely.

What followed was what I can only describe as a time of pure magic and awakening. We lived happily in the RV with our Labrador retriever; we experienced what it felt like to really live "off grid"—we were almost untraceable. It was the closest we had ever come to real freedom. I offered my healing services and we managed to always keep warm, well fed, and well cared for.

We walked the ever-changing scenery of the wild beaches in all weather. My husband calls these rugged and beautiful beaches "the organizing principles of life and beyond." His reason for saying this was because the beach and the ocean are never the same from day to day, which is just like life and the experiences we have requested in order to grow. We accepted the fact that we were both healing our own shadows, and we knew we had to be welcomed and accepted by the land of Ireland on her terms, not ours. It was during this time that we went through a baptism of inner fire, while coming to grips with an understanding of what it really meant to fully immerse oneself in a life lived in trust.

Our simple existence allowed even more magic to show itself to us. Often during the early hours of the morning one or both of us would awaken from a deep slumber to see what I could only describe as an entity that looked like a "green abyss" hovering above us. Neither of us could tell you what it was or what it required from us. These visions went on for months, and even when we had moved into a cottage one particularly cold winter, we still experienced visitations of energy. Sometimes it was the green abyss, and sometimes it was symbols and words written out in the blackness of the ether. Very soon images of people, or cartoonlike characters, would appear in what I can only describe as a TV screen in the dead of night. It was weird! I would catalog the visits to try and make some sense of them all.

Eventually we bought a home in Ireland, and still the nightly visitations would appear. By this time, however, the interactions progressed a notch. The images had continued to appear as if on a flat-screen TV, sometimes weird, sometimes wonderful. But all of a sudden this changed as the entities that visited began interacting with *me*. All of this occurred while I was awake; they were not part of a dream! This wasn't all: My husband was having separate visitations. One night a woman dressed in ancient clothing whom he called the "star weaver" came to visit him. She was weaving colored energetic strands around the bed. Another night he saw a fairylike child laying flowers over my sleeping body.

This is when the aha moment finally came rushing in like a tsunami. We both now fully understood that the universe was responding and interacting with us in unusual ways. This did not make us fearful; instead we were grateful that what came to us came in a language that we could understand. What was this communication for? I believe it was to convey the truth of human and off-planet human existence. Our star brothers and sisters wanted to show themselves to us in order to reveal a bigger picture, to help us fully come to grips with the idea that anything is possible. My husband and I both had to leave the veils of "normal" society, its stresses and materialistic ways, in order to cleanse ourselves of the old way of life so that we would be accepting of the magic of other dimensions and realms.

I know I have learnt and experienced so much from these visitations. I wrote *Living Shamanism* during this time period and I have started writing a second book about our origins. What do I now think of the word "trust"?

I say to you, hand on heart, it isn't just about trusting. No, it's much deeper than that. I prefer the word "faith," because one must have complete and utter faith in one's soul path and how we draw experiences to us that align with our soul path. We all have to understand that there is a larger reason for our Earth-walk at this time. Faith allows us the ability to know that we are always guided and being cared for as we learn and live out our soul's purpose. Faith is a knowing, a heartfelt wisdom that we are one with the Great Spirit, the All That Is. There isn't any suffering or pain in this secret knowledge; it feels like blissful joy, as though we are an integral part of the expansiveness of the web of life.

Ah ho!

JULIE DOLLMAN is a shamanic healer who trained with Dr. Alberto Villoldo at the Four Winds Society, where she graduated in 2005. She received the

Karpay transmissions from Dr. Alberto Villoldo, Don Sebastian, and Dona Maria. She now works as a full-time shamanic practitioner in rural Ireland and has done so since leaving her job as a crime analyst in England in 2006. She is the author of *Living Shamanism, Unveiling the Mystery,* and *The Constant Healer.* In addition, she writes for several esoteric magazines and conducts alternative sacred ceremonies for weddings and baby-naming and transformational ceremonies. Her website is www.aynishamanichealing.eu.

19

Of Mountains and Men

Rebekah Brandon

Ausangate, a prominent mountain of southern Peru pushing upward of twenty-one thousand feet, is a majestic being to behold. Balanced by the *nusta* or feminine mountain spirit Kayangate,* Ausangate beckons to adventurer and mystic alike. It is a holy Apu or mountain spirit, sacred and powerful, and a place of pilgrimage and initiation for those called to the Andean spiritual path.

Several months before my first initiation, Ausangate called to me. I had thought that receiving a vision of this mountain was a metaphor for looking at the mountain within myself. But the message kept coming. Soon I discovered that it was an actual mountain, a *real* place in the physical plane. So I went to it.

Less than a year has passed since my heart first opened to the wisdom and love of this mighty Apu. And now Ausangate has visited me again, this time in a dream. In it, Ausangate spoke to me, calling me to come back to the mountain for a purification. When I arrived, however, there were no paqos, no healers or teachers to perform the ceremony. I questioned Ausangate, "How will I receive a purification? There is no one here to help."

---

*Kayangate is a feminine Apu connected to Ausangate. For the Andean people, this is a powerful union of the masculine and feminine energies of the Earth.

Ausangate, in a commanding yet soothing voice, replied, "Do not worry. I will show you how." And the holy mountain led me to the glacial waters and showed me how.

After it had finished, groups of people began passing by. Ausangate called to me, saying, "I need you to help me give these people cleansings."

I was fearful and thought to myself, *These people are not going to trust me. Who am I to them? How can I possibly help?*

Sternly, yet with patience, Ausangate addressed my fear, saying again, "I will show you how."

After each person had received a purification from the Apu, they bowed and offered gratitude and love for the spirit of the mountain. Then silently they continued on their way. Not a single person noticed or acknowledged me. A lightness overcame me as all of the fear and worry that I felt about performing the ceremony lifted. I thought to myself, *This is how it should be. My ego does not need to worry about how others might perceive me or how well I can perform ceremony, because it really has nothing to do with me. It is about Pachamama (Mother Earth) and the Apus. It is connection and ceremony, getting out of the way to allow divine energy to flow.*

When Spirit calls me to show up, to do ceremony or to go to the mountain, I do not hesitate. But when Spirit calls me to connect with others in ceremony or to perform a purification on them, I generally freeze. Ego manifests in different forms. My ego dictates that I only do ceremony when and how I want, rather than when and how Pachamama calls me to. Swallowing this realization has brought me to a crossroads. Do I take a path that is comfortable, still focused on a relationship with Pachamama and the Apus, but checked out from the real work I am being called to do? Or do I take the path of true service, potentially one that leads me to face my fears?

True humility is knowing my place, neither running when I am called to show up nor cowering beneath my fears. And courage is embracing fear as a teacher and friend. Being on the Andean spiritual path requires me to constantly check in with my fears, to see where my ego keeps me from moving forward and seeking the mountains within.

I do not see the ego or fear as an enemy. It is simply a guidepost, letting me know where I am on this path—a guidepost reminding me to access the courage and humility its lessons have to offer.

In a night sky surrounding Apu Ausangate is an *allyu* (community) of twelve stars. Whenever I wonder where to go, how to serve Pachamama, how to show up on this path, I look to these stars. The answer is always the same: "Look within and find your own star." And when I ask the allyu how, a peace and love radiates outward as if echoing the benevolence of the Apu: "I will show you how."

REBEKAH BRANDON lives in Santa Fe, New Mexico, and manages a nonprofit community health program. She has a master's degree in counseling from Southwestern College, with an emphasis in ecopsychology. After studying Andean spiritual cosmology for several years with healers in Peru, she co-created the Paqo School of Santa Fe with Carol Parker, Ph.D, and Niccole Toral, LPCC. This school brings monthly teachings of the Andean paqos (healers) to other healers and spiritualists in the Southwest. Donations to the school are given to the paqos to support their communities and the sharing of the Andean spiritual wisdom.

20

Shamanism in the Amazon

Deborah Goleman Wolf

As I raise the thick glass of the powerful substance from which every-one before me has eagerly drunk to toast Pachamama, the Mother, I feel the pulse of the jungle in the darkness around me. I look around at the twenty-one people dressed in white. We all sit quietly, waiting, on the wooden benches that line the walls of the open-air, thatched-roof temple. My body begins to tremble in sheer terror. I know this is a sacred ceremony, that we all have come so far to participate, that we have spent months preparing ourselves for the enormity of this—and yet deep within me there is strong revulsion. Even if I do overcome my fear and drink, I'm not sure I'll be able to keep the ayahuasca down long enough for the Vine of the Soul to take effect and give me the guidance that I have yearned for, for such a long time.

After years of searching and doubt, I have come here to find out what I have been born into this lifetime to be and to do. I have come to get the kind of guidance I can really trust, so that I may then discover if I am truly "on the path." I certainly am not alone in this quest, nor do I think I am particularly special; most of my friends are far more gifted than I am. But I have a deep spiritual hunger and want to know how and where I fit in. I so hope that this time I can find the answers. If you focus on your intent and do the right kind of preparation, ayahuasca is said to show you what you ask for. Shamans have used the drink for thousands of years to induce visions, for divination, and for healing. It can change you, they say, down to the DNA level.

On the days leading up to the ceremony, we fast and rest and focus on the ritual to come. This is a time in my life when I still feel that I carry darkness inside and a lot of negative self-judgment. During one of the periods of contemplation in the jungle, I see my heart as though it is enclosed in hard dark clay, much like the huge termite nest in the burnt tree trunk on the way up to the temple. As I meditate on it, going into my hardened protected heart with compassion, the clay slowly cracks open and a large, beautiful blue butterfly flies out. I feel more hopeful.

In the late afternoon before the ceremony, we bathe in the river and dress in clean white clothes as the day becomes hushed around us. When we reach the temple, we sit quietly waiting for dark, which comes quickly so close to the equator.

As darkness falls, the ceremony begins. Augustin, the ayahuaqero who is leading the ceremony, has made the sacred mixture the day before by offering tobacco and prayers to the spirit of the vine before boiling it down ritually with datura and *chacruna* leaves.

These are not ceremonies to be taken lightly. We are told that the powerful spirits of the jungle are watching to see how we behave. They can be dangerous.

Augustin begins the ceremony by invoking a prayer to the sun. He prays to the jungle beings and the Mother and blows jungle tobacco smoke around the room to keep bad spirits away during the time we'll be deep in our visions and the most vulnerable. We are expected to sit quietly, open to Spirit, and then come in turn to salute the Mother, state our intention, and drink.

Although it seems almost physically impossible, when my turn comes all too soon, I, too, raise the thick glass and salute. "Please Pachamama," I pray, "please show me what I came into this lifetime to be and to do." I finally force myself to drink the thick liquid. I immediately feel nauseated and don't understand how people smack their lips and declare that the mixture tastes like honey. They imply that the way it tastes reflects their inner state, but I find that impossible to believe.

I am successfully able to keep the medicine down. I can tell it's taking effect because I begin to get restless, which is my standard reaction to the datura in it. As I watch the rest of our group get up and raise the glass and drink, I try to settle in for the remainder of the ceremony. When the last person has finished, Augustin blows out the one candle and we wait contemplatively in complete darkness. I hear the occasional jaguar outside but it is calm in the temple.

It seems as though nothing is going to happen for the longest time and then I gradually begin to see/sense geometric patterns whizzing into my consciousness, almost too fast to get them clearly. They last for several minutes and then I see beautiful incandescent light patterns not of this world.

Out of one corner of my mind I become aware that there is music accompanying my visions. Augustin is playing pipes and other wind instruments, singing ayahuasca songs, and whistling patterns that have been given to him in visions to help guide our journeys.

Finally the visions slow down, but I keep fidgeting, trying to find a comfortable position. To distract myself, I experiment with becoming various life-forms. I successfully merge with a grassy slope and then become, quickly in and out, a jaguar. At this point, I notice my tall, quiet friend Steve, lying next to me, absolutely still, wrapped in his blanket. I wonder what it would feel like to be able to take ayahuasca and be that still and to go quietly, deeply into one's visions. Actually I wonder what it would be like to *be* Steve. So I start to creep into his being with my heightened consciousness—but very respectfully, of course.

Suddenly, a wooden cartoon sign, like one you would see in a comic book, appears with the words, "Stop! It is forbidden! Go back!!" Chastened, I quickly bring my consciousness back to myself, knowing I'd never know what it felt like to be Steve and, furthermore, that I wasn't supposed to know.

Next I ask to see my Higher Self. Equally suddenly, a little red cartoon demon appears, smoking a cigar, playing poker, and drinking whiskey. "Are *you* my higher Self?" I ask incredulously.

He shrugs, acknowledges that it is true, and that he is as surprised as me.

I shrug back and ask to be shown my soul purpose, but by now I don't expect much. If I'm lucky, I might get a sense of the next step I'm supposed to take. But suddenly I see a huge, rickety, old-fashioned computer, again a cartoon. It has a message in bright lights running around the top of it: SOUL HEALER.

I am astonished. Soul healer?! Me?! That seems far too grand, too "spiritual," for who and what I think I am. After all, I'm still trying to integrate my lack of sufficient spirituality with my hunger to know, be, and *live* a spiritual life.

Gradually, however, these words that appeared to me in the Amazon—Soul Healer—begin to guide me, although it would be many years before any kind of real integration took place. It would take quite a long time for me to realize that what I was doing and what life was molding me into was technically "soul healing," and that, in fact, most of us perform soul healing in different ways every day—teachers, doctors, people who are sensitive to others and are kind. Almost all of us, when we are conscious of how interconnected we all are and honor each other, are doing soul healing.

Because of this vision, I eventually left the corporate world; learned more about using shamanism for healing; studied a form of integrative therapy that drew on the connections between the mind, body, and spirit; worked on purifying myself; and finally set up a practice as a spiritual psychotherapist. If this was "soul healing," then I was going to learn as much as I could about it in order to be a guide for those who came to me for help. I learned to pray and listen to my intuition more and more as I realized that I was being asked to become increasingly sensitive and tune into the unsaid—into the soul level of the person I was seeking to heal or to help. Without that vision in the jungle, I never would have dared to embrace this sacred path.

DEBORAH GOLEMAN WOLF, PH.D., developed an early interest in healing and spirituality. This passion led her to a master's degree in folklore at Berkeley, a doctorate in psychological anthropology, and a post-doctoral fellowship in medical anthropology in San Francisco, during which she was part of a team teaching medical students about ethnic healing practices. She moved to New York City, where she became part of a ceremonial pipe circle. She worked with Native elders and was elected to the board of the Native American Cultural Foundation. Completing the integrative therapy training at the New York Open Center, she opened a private practice as a spiritual therapist, adding regression therapy and hypnotherapy to her repertoire. She used these skills as a volunteer with people facing life-challenging illnesses. She is a spiritual psychotherapist in private practice in New York City, continuing to learn from her clients and pass on the wisdom she has acquired over a lifetime. You can find her at www.deborahwolfphd.com.

21

A Visit from Apó Lákay

Lane Wilcken

I am of Filipino, English, and Scandinavian descent. On my maternal Filipino side, my family has been blessed with many gifted individuals whose practices would be classified as shamanistic. My maternal grandmother, Catalina Coloma Rivera, was a well-known *mangngilut*, or traditional midwife in the Tarlac Province of Luzon Island of the Philippines. In her lifetime she delivered thousands of babies, but her practice also included healing with herbs, the properties of which were revealed to her through communication with the spirit world. My great-great-grandmother Apo Honorata Eslabra was a *manganito* or spirit medium who also experienced spirit travel into other worlds. My own mother is gifted with insight, primarily through dreams, which we paid special attention to growing up.

My parents were good enough to raise me with an understanding of prayer and the nature of spirits, and to recognize when I was having a spiritual experience, and whether I was sensing a good or bad spirit. I grew up in the United States, however, and despite this blessed lineage and upbringing, I adhered to Western ways, rooted in rational thought. I prided myself on my intellectual prowess. I fancied that all things could be explained through scientific and logical thought.

As I look back on my life, I see that I was guided through a step-by-step preparation to a greater understanding and acceptance of what most would call shamanic practice. When I was nineteen, I moved from California to Hawaii. When the plane touched down on the island, I felt what I can only describe as a familiar spirit about the island, its people, and the culture there. I felt an immediate kinship with the Hawaiian people, although I couldn't explain this. I simply *felt* it.

While I lived there I found there were many correlations between the Hawaiian culture and my Filipino heritage. As a hobby, I started making note of the cultural similarities, all motivated by this feeling of familiarity. Eventually, I moved back to the U.S. mainland, but I continued the hobby of researching cultural similarities between the Hawaiian culture and my own people. That research and the collection of cultural similarities became the basis of what would later become my first book, *Filipino Tattoos: Ancient to Modern.*

When I finally made the decision to write the book, I struggled to find scraps of indigenous knowledge that had been scattered by nearly four hundred years of Spanish colonialism. Frequently I found myself frustrated, stuck at a dead end. It was during one of these frustrating moments that I discovered the shamanic world. It was in the early spring of 2000 when I had my first powerful paradigm-changing experience.

I had gone to bed feeling thwarted in my research efforts to uncover the meaning of certain tattoo symbols. That night I had a dream that I was in the Philippines at some time in the past. I was wearing a *ba'ag* (loincloth) and was standing in a forest. I was greeted by a *lákay* (honorable old man) who wore a short white ba'ag; he beckoned me to follow him. We walked through the forest along a narrow winding trail until we came to a huge tree that had been felled, as if by a giant chain saw. I sat down with my back against the giant trunk of the fallen tree and the old lákay took my hand.

As he pulled it toward him, I saw that my arm was covered with tattoos! He then explained to me what each of the symbols meant. This was so vivid that I quickly realized that not only was I dreaming, but something supernatural was occurring.

I awoke with a start, fully conscious and alert. I immediately wrote down the information I remembered from the dream. The next evening a similar experience occurred. Again I was in the Philippine forest and the lesson with Apó Lákay was repeated. I recognized that this was my ancestor and one of the last of his lineage who understood the meanings of the tattoos, which had eventually been banned by the long arm of the Catholic Church.

Once again, when I awoke I jotted down what I had learned about the tattoo symbols in my dream. Throughout the day I pondered the possible meaning of the repeated dream, all the while remaining amazed at the experience. However, the following night I did not see Apó Lákay. So the next day doubt began to creep into my thoughts as my rational mind began to assert itself. I thought that perhaps the dreams were products of my subconscious, which no doubt was desperately trying to solve the impasse I was having in my research.

That next night, as if in a response to these doubting thoughts, I dreamt of Apó Lákay again, but this time I dreamed that I awoke in my bed to see him *standing in my bedroom!* There he stood next to my bed in my darkened room, clad in his white ba'ag, with a slightly disappointed look on his face. His demeanor was now quite serious.

I got up out of my bed and he ushered me to the bathroom mirror. As I looked into it, I saw that my face was covered with tattoos! Again he explained the symbols to me and I felt a great gratitude toward him. I awoke from this experience rather humbled.

The following night I went to bed with the full expectation of seeing him again, but instead, as I drifted between consciousness and sleep, I was whisked way to find myself in a great warehouse. I stood near the front of a line of innumerable young Filipino people waiting to be tattooed by an old Filipino woman whose arms were covered in traditional tattoos. The people in front of me were being tattooed with what looked like contemporary flowery designs. However, when I approached the old woman, she said that my tattoos would be traditional and she began to tap a tattoo into my skin with her hand.

Then the vision faded and I found myself again in my bed, wondering about the events of the past few days.

Over the course of the following months, I pondered my experiences. Although I had written them down, I felt that there was no way I could include them in my book, given that it was being written from a scholarly perspective. How could I even claim that I knew what these tattoo designs and symbols meant based on a few dreams I'd had? I felt that I would certainly be mocked for such a wild assertion!

But the old lákay's information would prove to be true.

Several months later, I came across documentation in a book about Filipino textiles, *Sinaunang Habi: Philippine Ancestral Weave,* by Marian Pastor-Roces, that confirmed nearly everything he had told me! Years later, in the Philippines, I even met the old woman who had tattooed me in my dream. Today I know her as Apó Whang-od; I was traditionally tattooed by her in real life. My book has led thousands of mostly younger Filipinos to understand the nearly lost knowledge of our tattoos given to me from the other side of the veil. As I have grown in my knowledge of my people's ancient spiritual traditions, I have recognized the depth of the symbolism of the tattoos that was offered up to me by my experiences with Apó Lákay.

Some of these symbolic meanings I will share here. Large trees in the Philippines were believed to house *anito* or ancestral spirits. Anciently, these ancestral spirits were believed to be active participants in the lives of their descendants. A giant fallen tree represented a break in culture and communication with the multitude of these ancestor spirits. Leaning up against a large fallen tree with my back against it symbolized a reestablishment of this connection, as the backbone itself is symbolic of the genealogical line of ancestor spirits extending through time. White clothing was traditionally reserved for the dead or those who are in mourning.

The white ba'ag represented Apó Lakay's condition of being disembodied and also his mourning for the lack of interaction with his descendants.

Seeing my face tattooed symbolized the achievement of a powerful relationship with the spirit world. In the past, tattooing of the face was an honor reserved for the bravest of warriors, with the understanding that their victories, success, and prosperity were achieved not on their own, but due to the collective influence of their anito family.

One would think that these experiences would be confirmation enough of my calling to serve my people, but apparently the Creator and the ancestors felt I needed additional confirmation. A few years ago I was invited by the Center for Babaylan Studies (a nonprofit organization dedicated to the preservation and teaching of Filipino indigenous knowledge, systems, and practices) to be one of their core directors. At the first retreat that I was invited to participate in, I was asked to perform a closing ceremony of my choice for the group. The retreat was held in Sonoma, California.

I had meditated on which ceremony I should perform, and I felt through Spirit that I should construct the *taltalabong* spirit raft used for making offerings to the anito and the sons of Kadaklan, some of our primary ancestor-gods. Although I knew that this was the offering that was requested, I still felt a tinge of anxiety as to whether or not it would be accepted or acknowledged so far away from the islands. I wondered, "Would it be accepted when performed by a mixed descendant who grew up in America?"

Nevertheless, I constructed the taltalabong and loaded it with offerings. At sunset at a lake in Sonoma, I chanted in our Native language to invite the ancestors, the sons of Kadaklan, and the spirits of the land in California to share in the offerings. I then launched the raft into the lake. Immediately, on the other side of the lake, several geese began honking and took to the air. A single white goose flew to the front of the black ones and formed a V formation.

I watched as they rounded the lake and flew from the left to the right, where we were all watching. They circled around and repeated the flight from left to right. In our culture, the flight of a bird from left to right is an omen indicating the approval of the spirits. Not only was the sign given by a flock of birds, it was also repeated! Finally the flock of geese flew off into the sunset, the traditional direction of the location of the abode of the ancestors. We stood in awe of these omens. I felt especially humbled that the Creator and the ancestors had allowed this traditional form of physical recognition to take place so far from the islands.

I had originally thought that the purpose of Apó Lákay's visits was to teach me about our tattoos. But I now know that it was to educate me about the reality of the realms that exist in close proximity to our own, the world in which he dwells, and the ways to access these planes. My change of paradigm has affected all aspects of my life. Since these revelations, I have been able to develop my spiritual abilities. This has brought my family and me guidance, knowledge, and comfort, especially when our loved ones have passed away. My shamanic receptiveness has enabled me to enjoy visits from my deceased brother and father. We are able to continue the relationship that we had in the mortal realm, although the lines of communication are different.

I am no longer fearful of being ridiculed for the information I gain through my experiences and I actively request the help of my ancestors in the writing of my books. Ancestors from both my Filipino and European lines play a greater role in my life now. They were particularly involved with the naming of my last two sons. I am encompassed by the love they feel for me, a descendant who listens for their voices in a world where so many of my generation have turned a blind eye and a deaf ear to the spiritual traditions of our inherited past. Fortunately, I have had many opportunities to teach others what I have learned, via my presenations at universities, museums, social clubs, and private forums.

Last, my ability to exercise healing energy has been awakened. This has been yet another blessing in a multitude of blessings that continue to unfold before me. Through these continuing experiences, my life is so much richer given that I have balanced my rational thought processes with open communication with the other realms of light. I now walk in grateful confidence before the worlds seen and unseen, ready to teach and to be taught.

Agyámanak ti adu kada kayó Apó Lákay kadagiti sirmatá nga imbingay yo kaniak.

(Thank you so much, Apó Lákay, for the vision you have shared with me.)

LANE WILCKEN is an independent researcher and scholar who has been studying the cultures of the Philippines and Pacific Islands for over twenty years. He is the author of *Filipino Tattoos: Ancient to Modern* and *The Forgotten Children of Maui: Filipino Myths, Tattoos and Rituals of a Demigod*. He serves as a *mambabatok,* a practitioner of Filipino ritual hand-tapped tattoos. Lane's grandmother Apo Catalina Lucas Coloma (Rivera) was a mangngilut and mangngagas (midwife and healer), and his grandfather Apo Roque Esmeralda Rivera was well versed in the oral traditions and practices of the past. Lane's great-great-grandmother Apo Honorata Eslabra Esmarelda was a mangnganito, or spirit medium. Lane graduated from Southern Utah University with a bachelor of science in sociology with a focus on symbolic interactionism. He resides in Las Vegas, Nevada.

22

The Non-Dualism
of Shamanic Psychotherapy

Joseph E. Doherty

*Normal consciousness is just one point on the spectrum of
reality, and there are many, many more.*

WILLIAM JAMES, M.D. (1842–1910),

HARVARD-TRAINED PHYSICIAN AND PSYCHOLOGIST

*In our dark times, a piece of us comes to an end. We must
find meaning in the darkness.*

THOMAS MOORE, *DARK NIGHTS OF THE SOUL*

At the age of forty-nine, as a traditionally trained psychotherapist with
more than twenty-seven years of experience in the field of mental health
and a plethora of personal experience as a psychotherapy client, I found
myself overwhelmed by what is most typically labeled "a dark night of
the soul."

I was at my wit's end and feeling stuck in the muck of the darkness.
In psychotherapy this is a condition that would be most likely diagnosed as depression. Earlier in my life, at other times such as this, I

had sought out the benefits of traditional insight-oriented, ego-based psychotherapy. This time I knew, at least on an intellectual level, that I was all talked out. I felt psychotherapy would only be a regurgitation of all I had previously learned; I knew I had gone as far as I could go with that paradigm of change.

Synchronicity played its cards before me at that very juncture. I was reading Thomas Moore's *Dark Nights of the Soul: A Guide to Finding Your Way through Life's Ordeals,* and trying to get a new perspective on moving through the morass, when a friend loaned me a book she was finding particularly illuminating. Because I could use any illumination I could lay my hands on, I accepted and began reading the book by Jamie Sams titled *Dancing the Dream: The Seven Sacred Paths of Human Transformation.*

Moore's book was providing me with a new and valuable understanding of my situation on an intellectual and egoic level, but as a Buddhist meditator of over twenty years it was clear to me that his advice of just "sitting through the darkness" wasn't going to offer me the assistance I was hungrily seeking. It was in Sams's book that I was encouraged to explore an entirely different paradigm for healing: the ancient discipline of shamanism.

Ever the left-brained skeptic, I was, of course, more than dubious. Yet I also was up against many dead ends with other widely recognized approaches. Already I was a yogi and a yoga instructor. I ate healthfully, and I took many natural supplements and Chinese formulas, along with acupuncture for brain health. Coupled with this, I worked out at the gym regularly.

However, the dark night still prevailed. And again, the universe was continuing to beckon me toward a different approach.

Out of desperation I placed a call to a woman who was both a psychotherapist and a shamanic healer. This choice was validated for me at a social event with my professional colleagues, when a new addition to our practice mentioned that before entering graduate school in the field of mental health, she had practiced as an assistant to a very powerful local shaman. Reluctantly, I scheduled a soul extraction and retrieval with Jan Engels-Smith,* and my journey of becoming a shamanic psychotherapist began shortly thereafter.

Seven years later, I am proud to formalize my studies and experience as a Ph.D. candidate in shamanic psychospiritual studies through Venus Rising Institute.† I feel honored to be a member of the first graduating class in the country for a program of this type affiliated with a major university, in this case the University of North Carolina at Asheville. I now practice as a shamanic psychotherapist.

Our Western culture, in which traditional psychotherapy was born and continues to exist, is one riddled with polarities: good/bad, right/wrong, black/white, self/other, either/or . . . to name a few. My Eastern philosophical training in Buddhism has allowed me to see these as dualities (both/and rather than either/or), as equals and mirror images of one another rather than opposites. However, my professional dilemma for the past five years has been the challenge of how to move beyond both of these models and form a practice that embraces psychotherapy and shamanic healing as a non-dualistic synergy and energy. To this end I present my model for shamanic psychotherapy.

Although the parallels in these two arenas have been recognized in some recent writings and research, such as that by Daniel Foor (by whom I was interviewed at the beginning of my own evolution as a shamanic psychotherapist),‡ I believe it is the non-dualistic approach in the integration of these two paradigms of healing that offers individuals a unique transcendent experience that exponentially increases the power of these modalities. Demonstrating, yet keeping separate, the healing power of these two approaches has proven, in my direct personal and professional experience, to have limited the benefits of each. But in the combining of the two, the benefit is clearly enhanced.

---

*For more on Jan Engels-Smith's work, please visit her website at www.janengelssmith.com.
†For information on Venus Rising Institute, visit www.shamanicbreathwork.org. Venus Rising is run by Linda Star Wolf, a shamanic healer (who is the author of the next chapter in this book).
‡See Daniel Foor's website, www.ancestralmedicine.org, for more on his work.

In psychotherapy we explore the self—both the conscious and unconscious aspects of the ego—to understand and then rid ourselves of unwanted and unhealthy thoughts, behaviors, feelings, and experiences. However, this exploration does not happen in a vacuum. A safe and trusting relationship with the therapist is the necessary foundation that allows the client to move forward and deeper into the psychotherapeutic process. According to relational therapy theory, the first cannot happen without the second.* In the West, we are a culture of thinkers, and therefore it is essential to provide many clients who are in therapy with the components of a cognitive framework before they can allow themselves to trust in a deeper energetic exploration. In my experience as a shamanic psychotherapist, this cognitive/relational experience lays the framework from which the journeyer can proceed to plunge into the depths of deeper shamanic healing. It is only then, through the support of this scaffolding, that the ego can relinquish its hypertonic grasping of the self, opening up a portal through which the journey to the soul can commence. And then, through a true and honest connection with the soul, we can have full and direct access to Spirit.

In traditional psychotherapy the id/ego/superego are viewed as manifestations of the self. In shamanic healing this tripartite self is only one aspect of the manifestation of our whole being, which is comprised of the trinity of Self/Soul/Spirit. Working at the level of the self, the therapist is, in essence, helping the client to uncover the combination to the "locked" ego. However, finding this valuable combination only places the tumblers in alignment, poised to spring open. Shamanic healing then proceeds to free open the lock, revealing the aspects of soul and spirit. It is only by working in the trifold realms of Self/Spirit/Soul that our deepest healing and transformation are invoked.

In *Soulcraft: Crossing into the Mysteries of Nature and Psyche*, Bill Plotkin, Ph.D, a depth psychologist and Earth-centered shaman, describes three realms of human development: ego growth, soul

---

*For more on relational therapy theory, see Judith V. Jordan's *Relational-Cultural Therapy* (Washington, D.C.: American Psychological Association, 2009).

embodiment, and spirit realization. He sees a healthy ego as "skilled in imagination, feeling, intuition, and sensing, in addition to thinking." He believes that "adequate ego growth is essential to personal well-being and cannot be bypassed through working in the other two realms" of soul and spirit.

Psychotherapy of the ego is comparable to shoring up the walls of a well as you dig deeper, seeking to tap into the source of water. We shore up the self so that it does not collapse in upon itself as we move deeper toward the untapped healing of the soul. I liken the experience of singularly exploring the healing of our wounds only through psychotherapy to that of riding in a glass-bottomed boat. From the safety of the boat we can see clearly the depths and riches of the vast sea below us, but it remains unexplored as we glide back and forth above it, only skimming the surface. Psychotherapy allows us to have a clear view of where we need to drop anchor and drop in! But if we cling to the security of our glass-bottomed boat of the ego, there will always be a barrier that prevents us from dropping deeper and moving toward a more complete healing via the soul.

Shamanism is like the scuba tank and the shamanic psychotherapist is the diving instructor. But it is the individuals themselves who must plumb the depths of their "soul self," which is often dark and frightening. The therapist provides the tools, but the individuals must learn to use them for their own highest good and well-being. In Shamanic Breathwork, a particular form of shamanic healing, the breath and the choreographed music relating to the chakras are the tools provided.* The breathwork facilitator is there to assist the journeyer, assuring that the needed "oxygen flow and diving tools" are consistently available to this brave individual as he or she moves beyond the ego and into the light and the dark of the depths of the soul. In other traditions of shamanic healing, drumming, rattling, energy extractions, soul retrievals, cord cuttings, sweat lodges, and plant medicines are among the tools that trained healers may offer.

---

*The primary resource for information on Shamanic Breathwork is Linda Star Wolf's *Shamanic Breathwork: Journeying beyond the Limits of the Self* (Rochester, Vt.: Bear and Company, 2009).

Working with a shamanic psychotherapist allows the individual to rely on the relational trust imbued through the process of ego exploration to then drop more safely into the work of the soul. Just as trust and safety, the first developmental stage of life according to Erik Erikson, are necessary to allow our infantile selves to begin to develop our fledgling ego in order to separate our self-identity from our caretakers, so too the trust and safety developed in the therapeutic relationship is beneficial in allowing that now developed ego to trust the shamanic psychotherapist and to feel safe enough to dive in to the depths of soul transformation.*

In Shamanic Breathwork the facilitator is trained to use his or her knowledge of the cycles of change to assess and assist the individual in moving forward along a spiral path, moving deeply from self (ego) to soul and into harmony with spirit. This is *not* a linear path, in the way that traditional psychotherapy is viewed. The shamanic facilitator is trained to see the family of origin as the point of stepping off the linear path and onto the spiral of change. Using the insight-oriented understanding of family issues and patterns gained in traditional therapy, we move beyond the linear path and begin our soul-based journey. As we are guided to move even more deeply into the woundedness of our ego through our soul work, we peel away the layers of our childhood pain. But unlike in traditional psychotherapy, we move beyond the limitations of the paradigm of words, and we are now working with the energy of the pain.

As we proceed around the spiral, time and time again, shedding the layers of our childhood pain, we begin to glimpse a view of our true and pure soul, the core of our being. This leads us to meeting our Inner Beloved, the next cycle of change. From here we are led toward our Sacred Marriage, through which our self and soul merge. We are then ready to drop fully onto the path of spirit. It is at this juncture that we uncover our truest and purest calling, our Sacred Purpose. It is here where Self/Soul/Spirit are so completely aligned that we will transform our wounded

---

*Erik Erikson's theories on developmental stages can be found in his seminal book, *Childhood and Society* (New York: W. W. Norton, 1993).

ego into our truest and fullest identity. Here we move from our self of a Human Doing into a Spirit Being.

We embrace fully at this time that we are in fact spirit beings having a human experience! It is through the guidance of a shamanic psychotherapist that we are brought to this place of stepping fully onto the path of our life, where we begin incorporating the lessons that we were brought into this lifetime to master.

In my practice of shamanic psychotherapy I also employ the elements of Nature to assist individuals in understanding and navigating their spiral paths and their cycles of change. These elements are incorporated into the teachings of the Venus Rising Institute, where my training has taken place.

Water/Earth/Fire/Air/Spirit are tools that indigenous shamans of all cultures share in common. In *The Healing Wisdom of Africa: Finding Life Purpose through Nature, Ritual, and Community,* Malidoma Patrice Somé describes in detail how shamans use these elements in ritual and ceremony. In shamanic psychotherapy I employ the elements as taught by Linda Star Wolf to assist clients in accepting and releasing the distress they experience on the Spiral Path of Transformation. These elements relate to the process of rebirth, which is necessary to transcend the limits of the ego and to move fully through the soul's transformation and fully embrace the path of spiritual wholeness. In the womb we gestate in the element water. As we prepare for birth we move into the element of earth. As we move into the birth canal we are propelled into the element of fire. As we are reborn we surrender into spirit. And as we transcend our ego fully we move into the lightness of air. As they come to understand the cycle of change and its corresponding element, the individuals I work with are then able to assist themselves in moving more fully into the experience, rather than resisting it.

Working with these elements of healing assists the individuals in viewing their experiences in a way that does not pathologize them, but rather aligns and attunes them with the most core healing elements of Nature itself.

Joseph E. Doherty (Jaguar Falcon Wolf), LCSW, MSW., Ph.D., is a licensed psychotherapist with over thirty-five years of experience in the mental health field. He is an Iyengar-trained yoga instructor. He is a certified Shamanic Breathwork facilitator and ordained minister of shamanic healing arts through Venus Rising Institute. His mind-body-spirit approach to healing with clients is a direct reflection of his own personal work of integration. He has taught at both the graduate and postgraduate levels on working with adults who experienced childhood trauma. You can visit his website at www.elementalhealing.org.

23

Baby, I Was Born This Way

Linda Star Wolf

I was born into a loving family and grew up with the good, hard-working, salt of the earth, Christian folks of rural western Kentucky. Although there was fundamentalism, there was also an innate closeness to the land and to family. I spent most of my early childhood outside with my grandmother Mammy Jones, in the garden and with the animals; I mostly preferred them to other children.

Mammy recognized my overly sensitive nature and my psychic gifts and treated my "strangeness" as something special to be proud of, teaching me that it was a part of God's gift to me. She helped to protect and cultivate my gifts and to connect the spiritual world to the beauty of the natural world and all of Creation. She helped me to see, hear, and interpret the world around me with shamanic eyes, to ground myself in the natural world, and to feel at home here on Earth. Mammy Jones infused me with her own special brand of faith, allowing me to trust that even though I was different, I was special, and I could do anything that my heart told me I could do.

Mammy also taught me to connect with the dreamworld and the art of dreaming. In the morning, as we ate breakfast, she always asked me about my dreams. We talked about what I saw and what that might mean. A few months before my twelfth birthday, I saw my

Mammy's death in a dream. It terrified me and I didn't want to tell anyone because I was afraid that if I spoke it, it would come true. The following morning at breakfast Mammy sensed that I was upset about something and eventually got me to talk about what was bothering me. I told her the whole dream and she reassured me that everything would be okay. A few weeks later she became quite ill and her health declined rapidly. She eventually agreed to go to the hospital but she never came home. My beloved Mammy passed away a few weeks after my twelfth birthday.

Not only was the loss of my grandmother a shock, but it created a huge psychic wound in me that lasted for many years. I secretly blamed myself for her death, believing that somehow I was responsible because I had seen the vision of it in my dreams. The pain of losing her was insurmountable and I was inconsolable. Although I knew my parents loved me, Mammy Jones was the one person in my life who really saw me for who I was.

As a teenager, I couldn't understand how to deal with my gifts without my Mammy to guide me so I wandered in the underworld for a long time. This was the turbulent '60s and '70s, and in my confusion, hurt, and grief, I ignored my sensitive nature and pushed my gifts underground as much as possible. I also developed several dysfunctional patterns for dealing with life, including addiction to substances and having a near-death experience with drugs before I was twenty years old.

The addictions turned out to be blessings in disguise and my early childhood and adolescent experiences eventually led me to a path of soulful sobriety. As I reclaimed my sanity and sobriety in my late twenties, I found that I was a natural wounded healer. I was working as a counselor in the addiction field at that time, and I sensed that there was more to be offered to those I worked with who were struggling as I had been. I could see myself in them; I understood that many of them were using substances to block out emotional pain and repress their sensitive spiritual souls. I became very determined to discover what that "something more" was—not only for me but for others who were seeking ways to live on this Earth that didn't involve being an addict and yet also didn't mean conforming to the mainstream status quo of what was considered acceptable and normal.

This yearning for something more led me to a path of radical transformation and reclaiming my lost soul parts through the healing power of breathwork. It led eventually to the shamanic path. I was doing a lot of breathwork journeying at that time and increasingly began to feel a call toward Native American, Mayan, and other indigenous teachings.

A Cherokee friend and teacher encouraged me to listen to a guided journey every day with the intention of finding a grandmother spirit who could help me heal my grandmother wound and give me the guidance to truly find myself and walk my path. During one of those journeys, a Native American grandmother whom I had never seen before came into my vision. She held my head in her lap and, stroking my hair, called me "gentle Star Wolf." I saw her face as clear as day and she felt incredibly real. When I came out of that journey, I was not sure if she was someone real that I needed to find in this realm or if she was a guide from the spirit realm.

It would be several years before I tracked her down in the physical world—or perhaps it was she who tracked me down. She told me shortly after we met that she had been dogging my tracks for years! One day I traveled to the Cattaraugus Indian Reservation in upstate New York. As I got out of my car, Seneca Wolf Clan Grandmother Twylah Nitsch opened the door to her back porch and walked toward me. Taking hold of my shoulders, she looked penetratingly into my eyes and said the words that would change my world forever: "What took you so long?"

I looked back at her in shock. Even though there were others close by, they ceased to exist in that moment and there were only the two of us, suspended beyond time and space. The whole world went into slow motion and eventually I found my voice, saying, "It would have helped if you had told me your name and where you lived."

"You were supposed to use your wolf nose, eyes, and ears to sniff me out," she replied with a wry smile. Then she added, "I gave you a name. What is it?"

I answered shyly, in a questioning manner, "Star Wolf?"

Her face lit up and she said very firmly, "Yes. That's right. Now come on inside and let's get to it."

There have been many shamanic moments of death, rebirth, and wisdom given to me during this life journey of almost sixty years. But my epic "no turning back" moment came that day on Grandmother Twylah's porch when time stood still and I looked into the eyes of the woman I had seen in my vision. Up until that point I had wavered back and forth between faith and doubt as regards my mystical experiences and psychic gifts. They seemed so big at times and I wondered if they were real. Sometimes I would believe and trust my deep inner knowing. Other times I would think, *Maybe it's just coincidence,* or *Why is this happening to me?*

When I met Twylah, the worlds collided and all doubt fell away. When worlds collide either you go psychotic or you evolve to the next level that's large enough to hold the truth that the multidimensional world is real. From that moment forth, I was able to stop alternating back and forth between rejecting and embracing my shamanic spirit. I began to accept that my gifts and my shamanic calling were real indeed.

Gram told me later that she frequently appeared to people in dreams and visions like she did with me because she was a dream walker. She told me that I was one, too.

We spent as much time together on the inner planes as we did on the outer ones—and she often confirmed what had happened during our inner connections when we would meet up again in person. She took me under her wing, called me her granddaughter, shared her teachings with me; she picked up where Mammy Jones had left off when I was twelve years old. I believed my own grandmother was in cahoots with Grandma Twylah to call out to me and guide me back onto my path. Gram confirmed that my Mammy Jones had sent me to her to help me heal the wounds of my past and to open to my shamanic gifts of the spirit.

Although I had been a counselor and teacher for many years, it was not until my reality shifted completely with the energetic exchanges between Grandmother Twylah and me that I found the inner strength to step fully into my true self and become who I was always meant to be. Gram helped me to complete the initiations that I needed in order to step forth into my sacred purpose as a shamanic Wolf Clan teacher and spiritual midwife for others. Grandma Twylah's message was clear: "Don't waste time. Be on your path and open up the path for others because that's what we are here to do. The Wolf finds the path and points the way but cannot make anyone get on the path."

Since that fateful time I found the courage to step out of the box of the mental health care system and the breathwork modality that I was teaching at that time and to birth a completely new form of breathwork: Shamanic Breathwork, which weaves together the best of everything I have learned. This includes my own direct experience with cutting-edge processes, from depth psychology and addiction recovery methods to ancient shamanic wisdom teachings that have been handed down to me. Through my nonprofit, Venus Rising Association for Transformation, I have ordained hundreds of shamanic ministers and taught thousands of people to awaken their own shaman within and walk in dignity with their sacred purpose. It is my great honor and pleasure in life to witness and support others in discovering and grounding their special gifts of Spirit into their beautiful shamanic path here on earth—as it is in heaven.

Mammy Jones passed from this realm in 1964. Grandmother Twylah passed over to the other side in August of 2007. My two grandmothers live on through me and in all those I've taught and counseled. Mammy Jones, Gram Twylah, and I all shared early December birthdays. Gram told me that we were all stubborn visionaries and Wolf women—pathfinders leading the way and clearing the path to help others from our own experiences as well as passing along the teachings that have been passed down to us. Whenever I find myself feeling in doubt in this turbulent world, I can still hear their peals of laughter breaking through the veils from the other side as my two special grandmothers remind me that they are still right here, walking with me every step of the way on the Wolf path.

LINDA STAR WOLF, PH.D., spiritual granddaughter of the late Seneca Wolf Clan elder Grandmother Twyla Nitsch, is a visionary teacher and shamanic guide to thousands. Her love for the Earth inspired her to write eight shamanic books and give birth to the Shamanic Breathwork process. Founder and director of the Venus Rising Association for Transformation and Venus Rising University, Star Wolf is a change agent dedicated to assisting others in releasing dysfunctional patterns and radically transforming their lives. She holds a doctorate of ministry and doctorate in spiritual psychology from the University of Integrative Learning and teaches people how to awaken to the bigger picture and step into a life of passionate purpose. Those who know her intimately see her as a powerful force of Nature and a catalyst for accelerated consciousness. Her website is www.shamanicbreathwork.org.

24

Shapeshifting
From Dying to Apprenticing

John Perkins

I lived with the Shuar, deep in the Amazon rain forest, a journey that began more than forty years ago. They were traditional hunters and gathers who had only minimal contact with the outside world and they spoke their own language.

At one point I became ill. I lost a great deal of weight in a very short period of time. It would have taken me several days of hiking through difficult terrain, heavy rain forest, and then a long ride in a rickety old bus to reach the nearest medical doctor. There was simply no way I could take that journey. I was, therefore, resigned to dying.

Late one afternoon the schoolteacher who spoke Spanish brought an old Shuar man to me. "This guy's a shaman," he said.

I had graduated from business school and had no idea what a shaman was. "You mean a witch doctor?" I asked, terrified by the prospects of such a person.

He gave me a condescending smile and added, "He can cure you."

Those words got my attention.

The old man looked me up and down. He stepped very close to me and, wagging his finger in my face, exclaimed, "You're dying!" Then he paused, watching me closely and added, "That's good." I later learned that the Shuar believe in reincarnation and the shaman felt that my life was about as bad as it could get; it was time for me to shapeshift into a jaguar, an ayahuasca vine, or something better than my current life.

I believe I started crying at that point. The shaman stared at me and spoke words that were translated as "Perhaps you're not ready to die. In that case, I could heal you tonight."

I decided to give it a try.

After dark, he took me on a classic shamanic journey. During the process I saw that I had been raised in a family that harkened back to pre-Revolutionary times in rural New Hampshire. We were very hygienic and ate rather bland diets: primarily meat and potatoes, with very few interesting foods such as garlic or onions. Now I was living with people who had very different habits. There was no soap; hygiene was basically unknown. The most common drink was a type of beer called *chicha* that is made by women chewing and spitting the manioc root and letting it ferment into an alcoholic beverage. People in the Amazon know better than to drink water from the rivers that are filled with organic matter. So they drink lots of chicha. Their foods were very exotic, including such things as squirming white grubs taken directly from a rotting tree.

I drank lots of chicha because hydration was necessary in the rain forest and there wasn't any Perrier. I ate lots of grubs and other exotic foods because there weren't any Clif Bars!

I discovered on the shamanic journey that night that every time I ate these foods or drank chicha I heard a voice, probably that of my mother, saying, "Watch out, it will kill you." I also saw that the Shuar were very healthy people. The men were all built like Rambo; they were hunters accustomed to carrying, on their shoulders, heavy wild boars and other animals they'd killed. The women were sexy and fertile. People lived to be very old, if they were not killed by a falling tree, a tipped-over dugout canoe, or some other accident that is not uncommon among hunters and gatherers.

That night I came to understand that it was not the food and drink that were killing me; it was my mind-set. I'd been preconditioned to believe that the hygienic practices and diets of these people were dangerous to my health. At that point I saw a new reality.

The next morning when I woke up I felt great—refreshed and healthy. My illness was gone.

A couple of days later the shaman came to me and, through his translator, proclaimed, "You're healed. You owe me."

I had no idea what to expect. But as it turned out what he wanted was for me to become his apprentice. It was the last thing in the world I desired at that point. I had graduated from business school and I had no aspiration to enter the shamanic realms, but this man had saved my life. I felt I had no choice.

That apprenticeship was very difficult. It required giving up a number of things, including certain foods that I had come to appreciate, and sexual relationships among people who were quite promiscuous! But I moved forward with it.

Thank goodness! It totally changed my life. The Shuar accepted me as an equal and I learned a great deal about them as well as about the importance of understanding relationships with the trees, the plants, the rivers, the spirits of the forest, and the world in general. It changed my life forever.

Following my time in the Amazon, I traveled to many parts of the planet and studied with shamans on every continent except Antarctica. Because of my training with the Shuar, I developed an appreciation for an aspect of human culture I'd never thought much about before. I also came to understand the power of shapeshifting and of our belief systems, and the importance of developing relationships with Mother Earth.

JOHN PERKINS is a former chief economist at a major international consulting firm, advising the World Bank, the United Nations, the IMF, the U.S. Treasury Department, Fortune 500 corporations, and countries in Africa, Asia, Latin America, and the Middle East. His *Confessions of an Economic Hit Man* (seventy weeks on the New York Times bestseller list) is a startling exposé of international corruption. Today John is a founder and board member of the nonprofits Dream Change and the Pachamama Alliance. He is the author of many books on indigenous cultures and transformation and has been featured on ABC, NBC, CNN, NPR, A&E, and the History Channel and in the periodicals *Time,* the *New York Times,* the *Washington Post, Cosmopolitan, Elle, Der Spiegel,* and other publications, as well as in numerous documentaries. His website is www.johnperkins.org.

25
A Doorway Called Africa

Misha Hoo

The icy gravel path crunched under my wheels as I cycled through the quiet park. There was hardly a soul about in the crisp February air and those who had ventured out hurried quickly into the cozy bars and restaurants that lined the fairy-lit canals. Amsterdam in winter was like a ghost town, with tourists taking off to the warmer climes of Spain and Portugal and many people making their yearly pilgrimage to Goa for a season of dance parties on warm beaches in southern India. I wasn't going anywhere in a hurry; in fact, I wasn't going anywhere unless it was in a long wooden box, I had recently vowed. Those were the dark days, when depression had intensified into deep despair and I had long given up on the idea that there was any solution or cure, anywhere.

I pulled my woolen hat further down over my ears and settled into the rhythm of pedaling my old Dutch bike across the expansive park. I was headed for a dockside building called "Africa" and what I hoped would be an awesome drum'n'bass party. The underground dance culture in Amsterdam was strong, with every kind of music on offer—from trance to techno, old school, dub step, and industrial. The dance floor was one of the few places where I felt okay, where the music was so loud that I couldn't hear the incessant negative rants that ran through my mind 24/7. On the dance floor, the familiar closeness of hundreds of happy sweaty bodies made me feel temporarily safe.

As I passed the lake I glanced up—its still surface was golden, reflecting the shining amber of the streetlights. I looked up at the row of tall lamps that lined the path and watched silently as the orange balls of light wobbled and grew bigger, and then each one doubled into two.

Oh, I thought, *the drugs are kicking in.* I put my attention back on the biking, reminding myself that I had a party to go to and I didn't want to take all night to get there.

A couple of days before I had confessed to a girlfriend that I hadn't tried magic mushrooms, even though they were readily available in "smart shops" scattered throughout the city center. That day was my birthday and she had proudly presented me with a big bag of dried Mexican mushrooms and gave me strict instructions on how to prepare them as a tea. I had followed her advice to the letter, holding my nose and downing a large cup of the strong brew before leaving the house. I could still taste the pungent earthy flavor of the mushrooms on my breath as I cycled brusquely through the chilly night.

Probably should have waited until I got to the party, I thought to myself. It wasn't uncommon for friends to get lost en route and never make it to a party at all, instead spending their entire night tripping out on the median strip in the middle of a busy intersection.

Classy, I thought, and then giggled as I imagined myself lost in the park all night.

Just a short year earlier I wouldn't have found that funny. In fact most of my life I had been anti-drug and, like most people, afraid of what they might do to me, afraid of losing control. Now all I wanted was something that would make me feel good at least for a while—a temporary respite from the overwhelming grief and sense of loss that clung to me like a huge heavy blanket.

I had spent the past year nursing my partner, who was suffering from an unknown terminal illness. He had some kind of autoimmune reaction wherein his immune system was attacking his own body and it was literally killing him. I sat by his bedside for months, willing him to live, trying not to focus on the row of hospital beds next to him that emptied with heartbreaking regularity as patients with terminal AIDS passed from this world. Thankfully he didn't follow them and slowly regained his health, but giving so much of myself to help him live had cost me vital life-force energy—soul energy, as I understand it now—and I had lost all connection to my own life as a result. My sense of who I was had all but disappeared and I became angry at how much I had sacrificed for him. My thinking turned morbid. I began to cry for hours at a time and, dazed and confused, I wandered through my daily routine on autopilot. Eventually I took a job overseas, hoping to start afresh, but clearly all my difficulties had tickets on the same flight as me.

Every day I would drag myself out of bed after arguing with those internal screaming voices for a couple of hours, my body weighted down like it was full of wet sand. I would compile a list of constructive things to do that day and shower and dress myself, fully intending to embark on a positive day of useful errands. Sometimes I even made it to the door before the wall of aching despair hit me. Then, with my hand clinging to the handle, I would lean against the door frame, head throbbing, tears streaming down my face, my voice begging for this madness to stop. As my vision darkened and my body slumped, my determination would slowly drain and eventually I would give up and allow myself to fall back down on the bed, fully clothed, to sleep for the rest of the day. Sometimes I didn't get out of bed for three or four days at a time.

Although looking back on it now it seems so obvious, at the time I had no idea that I was suffering from severe depression. My world had collapsed and from my perspective that's all there was. There was no solution; there was no other option; there was no other possibility. There was nothing outside of my own personal reality. My world had shrunk into a tiny ball of despair, and worse, in my opinion, it was all my fault.

In my youth I had watched as a close family member had literally been carried into a psychiatric hospital by two burly male nurses and there was no way that I was going to let the medical profession get anywhere near me. I was terrified of being considered insane and institutionalized. I was terrified of the ongoing rage and grief that alternately consumed my psyche, but most of all I was terrified that it was never going to end. My continual, persistent, and determined efforts to get through a normal day continued to fail until I simply couldn't try anymore. Suicide became the only option I had left.

So although I didn't believe in God or have any sense of spirituality, on my birthday I had made a pact with Him, with God, the Universe, or Whatever Else Was Out There. "If you don't show me something good," I had vowed, "if you don't show me something really good, something worth living for, then I am outta here."

The silent white walls of my room said nothing in reply.

I passed Central Station and headed east, leaning gracefully into the turn as I took a narrow underpass beneath the busy road and then followed the line of tall buildings along the waterfront. As I got closer, a steady thump of bass became audible through the noise of the traffic and I began to scan the buildings for names.

"Africa," I whispered as I searched through the dim light. "Where are you, Africa . . . ?" For some strange reason all the dockside buildings had been named after foreign lands—*perhaps a remnant of the days when the Dutch East India Company ruled the wharves,* I mused. I turned a corner and there it was—a huge brick building looming against the dark skyline. The empty block in front was full of bicycles, mostly lined up in rows, with some patches of scattered mayhem where someone had probably taken a tumble. *When one goes they all fall down like dominoes.* The thought was somehow comforting.

There was only one small door at the front of the building, and it was guarded by a couple of lanky security guys. As I approached I saw the name "AFRICA" stamped in bold white lettering above the door.

I clambered up the muddy slope to the entrance and greeted the door guys, who were mostly there to raise the alarm if the police showed up. As the heavy door swung open I was blasted by the fast percussive rhythm of hard drum'n'bass music and, squinting in the suddenly bright light, I made my way into the colorful, throbbing vibe. The huge warehouse was full of people. Brightly colored back-drops lined the walls with psychedelic art; people lounged in couches and on cushions, smoking joints and drinking spicy chai tea. The dance floor was a sea of thumping, writhing bodies all moving to the same groove.

Suddenly I felt like I was home. A warm tingling sensation ran up my spine and my eyes filled with tears. I looked down and took a deep breath, steadying myself against a wave of rising nausea. I looked up and saw a Native medicine man standing in the middle of the dance floor. He was dark-skinned with long black hair and clothed in some kind of white cotton dress. He was looking right at me. His face was so familiar and his gaze was so direct that I didn't question his presence there. In fact, I couldn't think at all. I stood completely still and stared back at him, and for the first time in years my mind was completely blank. I felt like I had known him all my life and yet I had been searching for him for lifetimes. As I stared at him I felt the music begin to move through my body and it took me into the mass of dancers.

Colors and light coursed through my vision as I surrendered myself to the dance. My feet were agile beneath me and I felt like everyone and everything around me was part of one great conscious-ness. My limbs extended and as I swept my arm across the horizon a curtain of bright sparkles showered us all in light. Everything was golden. Everything was connected. When I moved, the whole world moved with me.

Suddenly I became aware of the perfection, the intense beauty, the unquestionable divinity in everything around me. I had no idea that any of this had existed. I had no idea that anything could feel this right, this perfect. I had life bursting out of every cell in my body and then I realized that I was no longer afraid. My movements came to a halt and God was there—silent, present, waiting.

"Yeah, this is good enough," I said quietly, my hands clasped together in front of my chest, "this is good enough for me." Right then I made a decision to begin climbing out of whatever black hole

I had fallen into and to not give up until I experienced that kind of perfection every day of my life—until that state of spiritual awareness became my living reality.

In the years that followed I saw that same medicine man many more times. He continued to be my guide, leading me deeper and deeper into my inner world. Slowly I uncovered the traumas that had led to my state of depression and anxiety. I learned how to master my thoughts and balance my emotions. A lot of what I learned was taught from within, through realization and the necessity of healing myself. Every so often a shamanic teacher would come into my life and my understanding would take a giant leap forward as I assimilated techniques and gained context for what I had learned.

Through shamanic practices I discovered how to find my inner power and communicate with Nature, realizing that I could merge my consciousness with many layers of reality. Other guides have appeared over the years as I have explored Celtic, North and South American, Hawaiian, and African shamanism.

Once I made that commitment that night on that dance floor, in an old building called Africa, there was no looking back. It was like a whole new world opened up. My spiritual path had emerged and all I had to do was follow where the energy led me. The right book would turn up in my hands; the right teachers would appear just when I needed them. It wasn't easy and there were many more difficult times ahead of me as I journeyed through the psychic wilderness, developing my awareness and maturity, but the value of what I have gained by learning through my own direct experience is immeasurable.

Looking back, I realize that it was all part of my path. The depression, the despair, and the loss were elements of a truly classic shamanic initiation. Now that I have so many years of experience behind me I can see the signs and understand the symbolism; I can see how everything fits together so perfectly. When I look at my life, the big picture is indeed a divine masterpiece. It took me thirteen years of continual persistent and determined effort, but I succeeded. Nowadays I can see perfection in every moment and I can feel God within me in every breath.

Yeah, I reckon that's good enough for me.

MISHA HOO is a shamanic practitioner and teacher who has studied under spiritual mentors in Australia, Canada, the Netherlands, Hawaii, and Peru. She is an accredited Trance Dance facilitator and Reiki master and has developed her own system, Soul Weaving Energy Healing. She has also produced *Tarot in Black and White*. Misha currently lives in the World Heritage Daintree Rainforest in Far North Queensland, where she conducts a private practice in shamanic medicine and facilitates workshops and retreats. She has a bachelor's degree in world religion and English literature. Her website is mishahoo.com.

26

Sacred Journey of a Lifetime

✦

Holly Gray Schuck

In December of 2010, I led a trip to Chile with a group of women friends who had studied the Mystery Teachings of the Andes with me for several years. We were going to ride horseback in the high Andes to do ceremony with my mentor and friend, a shamana in the Mapuche tradition. We were an allyu, a like-minded community of women, who came together for teachings and ceremonies whenever we could, for we normally tended to our mates, children, and jobs in our small-town communities in the Midwest. We had grown to love and respect each other, despite and because of our differences, and we were all excited to be together on this trip of a lifetime. We had no idea how much we would learn and grow from our experiences and how they would come to shape our lives. We had no idea that one of our ceremonies would involve the mother plant, the sacred medicine plant ayahuasca.

Three days before we left for Chile, my mother passed away. I had been caring for her for eight months after she suffered a stroke that had made one side of her body unusable. Her spirit accompanied us in our journey. We arrived in Chile, and after loading and packing the horses, we traveled into the rugged Andes Mountains—a wonderful world with no electronics, a world full of natural forces and spirits that we came to honor and know in a more intimate way than we could in our daily lives. We were high on life, happy and laughing with each other as we climbed higher and higher into the mountains toward our base camp. The next week we participated in several sacred ceremonies high in the Andes, some of which were derived from other indigenous traditions as well as Andean rites of passage.

On New Year's Eve, we built a sweat lodge near a rushing stream, cleansing ourselves in its heat and then dipping into the cold mountain stream, preparing ourselves for the New Year. We feasted that night under a full moon that rose majestically over the Apus (mountain deities). We danced and drummed the New Year in—together with the cowboys who lived high in the mountains and who took care of our horses, prepared our meals, and tended the gardens that kept us eating fresh produce during our visit.

At a sacred waterfall the next day, we celebrated by standing under the waterfall, feeling the rush and gasping for breath as the shock of cold water poured over us. We basked in the high mountain sun, sitting contentedly naked by the singing stream, after giving our thanks and offerings to the waters of the Pachamama. The next day, on horseback, we crossed streams and waterfalls many times as we climbed high into the Andes, relying on our mounts to keep us safe. As the land receded below us, it seemed as though we were riding through the air into another dimension and time. We were so high up that there was no bottom; we could not see the valley floor below.

We climbed into the clouds and then left even them below us.

After resting for a day, we prepared for yet another ceremony—one that had come to us as a gift. We had been offered a powerful all-night ayahuasca ceremony and each one of us had to decide if we would participate in it. Known as the "Vine of the Soul" or "Vine of the Dead," this powerful plant, in combination with other sacred plants, is known for inducing powerful visions. Its helpers are the jaguar and serpent powers, who often are seen in ayahuasca visions; indeed, the name Vine of the Dead refers to the classic journey in which the participant dies to the mind-set and cultural paradigms that keep us trapped in a rational, mechanistic world as opposed to the imaginable and magical world of shamans and ancient peoples.

I asked for and set an intention for a vision—one that would carry me through the next years. I asked for a vision for my life—something to guide and inspire me as to how we as a people and the planet itself were to make it through the end of the Mayan calendar to a new Earth, a new way of being in the world.

We prepared for the ceremony with a special diet, prayers, fasting, and meditation. It was to take place at night with a master ayahuasqero. This master shaman had trained for many years, learning how to combine the medicine plants and in what quantities, and he had conducted many such ceremonies over the years. He was a young man with a wife and children and was well known for his skills and talents. His demeanor was soft and quiet, with a contained power that was palpable just under the surface—his energy was similar to that of a jungle cat. I had experienced a man with that energy before, a Lakota medicine man and tribal leader who had reminded me of a wild mustang.

My friend from Chile was also highly skilled and had partaken in numerous ceremonies with the sacred plant. Several of her friends joined us. Some were on their own journeys, and some came simply to serve us, especially those of us who were new to the powerful plant medicine.

That evening we assembled in a circle and began the ceremony at dusk, making our prayers and intentions for this powerful night. The evening was warm and the breezes were soft, with a humming vitality of the mountain air. We placed our sleeping mats and blankets, like spokes on a wheel, around the shaman's altar. He had a toy from his youngest son as part of his medicine bundle, or mesa. I sat across from him and my Chilean friend, and next to my partner on one side and my daughter on the other. Although I had participated in the sacred plant ceremony several times before, it had been many years ago when my children were young. At that time my son, who had been only thirteen years old, had participated in a men's ceremony in the jungle hut close to mine. But that is another story for another day.

This time my daughter, who was a young woman now, sat next to me and we squeezed each other's hand for reassurance. After the maestro prayed to the spirits and opened the sacred circle, we began to imbibe the distinctive brew. The taste was not as bad as I had remembered it, and I tossed it down quickly—sternly telling my stomach to settle down as it started to pitch and roll like an ocean ship. As I felt the distinctive sensations of the hallucinogenic plant take effect in my body, I calmed myself and my body by telling it how well I took care of it and that, tonight, it needed to take care of *me*. I continued to pray to my guides, monitoring myself and those around me. My partner was beginning to retch violently, repeatedly. My daughter inexplicably was singing songs in Spanish as if she had known them all her life. Even though she knew some Spanish, this was fluent dialect.

The maestro and my shaman friend were tending to my partner, so I turned my attention to the others. There were some quiet whispering sounds around the dimly lit circle, some quiet retching, and then silence. The candles guttered in the wind, and the air cooled. I pulled my blanket closer, or tried to, but noticed that I had lost the ability to command my limbs. I lay back, but as I did so, the effects of the brew came on full force and I was alarmed. I tried to communicate telepathically to my daughter and tell her I was sorry I had gotten her into this. Yet I could hear her continuing to sweetly sing the medicine songs as if she had grown up with them.

Chaotic visions followed and for a brief while I fought to stay on top of them and not fully succumb, but I was quickly being sucked under. Robotic, antlike creatures were scurrying around, up and down the passageways of my brain and body, too busy going about their business of cleaning to interact with me. I fought harder to gain some control, but my fear only increased when I was dragged to a machinelike thing—was it a locomotive? It had giant wheels and gears within gears—*Wait a minute!* I told myself. *My visions should be ones from Nature, not automated machines, wait, wait. . . .* Then I realized, *Oh yeah, this is the surrender part.*

At that point I thought to myself, *Give up, just go ahead and die, it's not so hard,* and I did. I gave up, and was sucked into a large machine.

Then I was dead. I didn't exist. But if I didn't exist, who was talking—or was it thinking out loud? Okay, I *was* alive, but where was I? I looked up and there was a hatch so I climbed up and went through it. And on the other side—was our circle! There was the altar, the other people, my friends, my partner, my daughter, and everything was framed in classic psychedelic, sacred geometric patterns. I was sitting up now, and we were clearly in a different dimension, a different reality.

As I watched, each of my friends sat up also. Although it was dark, except for the light from the candles, I could feel each one of them checking themselves out and adjusting to the altitude of this new and higher dimension. And then I realized that this was how it would be on this dimension after the shift, at the end of the Mayan calendar, the end of a 260,000-year cycle. We would all sit up and take our place, the place we have prepared for ourselves, the place that the Christos has prepared for us. It exists. We exist. And we are here.

The giant wheels I was ground up in were the Mayan calendar wheels; they were gears within gears. And I saw that as time ends, our world or reality would also end, and then simply begin again with the next heartbeat. The predominant theme of my vision was how we would all arrive safely, together, on the other side of the shift, how we would all sit up and take our place in the new world—a world of peace, harmony, and equity, and the beginning of a new cycle of time.

This vision has served me well when I have faltered or lost hope, and now that we are on the other side of the end of the Mayan calendar (12/21/12), I am so proud of my friends and family, our allyu, as we each sit up and take our place in this new world.

I have so many fabulous memories of that trip—the cave with pottery shards that we discovered on another day's ride high into the mountains; the cold rushing stream we bathed and drank from; and the power and presence of the mountain spirits, the water sprites, and the ancient ones. Throughout the trip we called to the condors that accompanied us, and gained greater trust in our horses. This trip of a lifetime to the Andes Mountains met all the desires of my intentions and more. It is *now* my intention to invite you all to come with me on a sacred journey. Let's explore together how ancient wisdom and practices can enrich our new world.

HOLLY GRAY SCHUCK, LICSW, MS, has over thirty years of experience in psychotherapy, working with individuals, couples, and families. She has studied with Alberto Villoldo, Americo Yabar, Juan Nunez Prado, Sun Bear, Serge King, Pat Burdy, Arna Lesham, and Luzclara. Her training also includes working with the healing methods of both North and South American teachers and healers. She currently has a private practice wherein she uses a blend of spiritual direction and traditional therapy. Holly has led trips to Peru, Ecuador, Mexico, Guatemala, and Chile, in Central and South America, and to Chaco Canyon and Canyon de Chelly to introduce others to the practices of the indigenous peoples. She is a level VII Frequencies of Brilliance practitioner and a fourth-level initiate of the Andean teachings of the Q'ero of Peru. Her website is www.sacredjourneys-wi.com.

27

A Pathway to Transformation

Raymond Nobriga

Reflecting back, my life has been a shamanic journey. My initiation began at the age of three and a half, when I fell out of my parents' car as it was traveling on a highway in northern California. An ambulance returning to a nearby hospital was right behind our car and, witnessing this event, picked me up and transported me to the hospital. There I was administered last rites. According to my parents' account of the attending physician's statement, my will to live was strong and I survived. They treated my concussion and the lacerations but could not repair the resulting partial facial paralysis.

Over the next three and a half years my parents took me to doctors at every major hospital in the San Francisco Bay Area. We were repeatedly told that no surgical procedure could correct my condition. I was very despondent and feeling sorry for myself due to the seeming hopelessness of correcting my disfiguration and "unique" appearance.

When I was seven, I was sponsored by a member of the Shriners organization, which allowed me to be examined by a physician at the Shriners Hospital for Crippled Children in San Francisco, a facility that specialized in the treatment of children suffering the effects of the polio that was rampant in the 1950s. Intrigued by my case, this physician designed a new surgical procedure that he believed would restore feeling to the right side of my face and provide some limited muscle control.

The surgery was performed and the results were successful. I was in recovery at Shriners Hospital for two and a half months, during which time I was not allowed physical contact with my family; all patients were quarantined due to the susceptibility of polio patients to viruses. The only way I could communicate with my family was by speaking with them through a window screen near my bed.

During the period of my hospitalization, the Shriners organization sponsored a college all-star football game as a fund-raiser for their hospital. We patients were each assigned a football player for whom we would make crafts or a piece of artwork, which would then be presented to the player during his visit to the hospital in advance of the game. The players brought each of us an autographed football and visited with us. My player was an All-American from Colorado, and during our visit he asked me if I would like to play catch with him. Of course I was thrilled by his offer, and as all of us patients were confined to the indoors, the two of us stood in the middle of the ward and played catch. It was then that I noticed the look of sadness in the eyes of the other boys who were confined to their beds and, due to their paralytic condition, could not participate. At that moment I realized how fortunate I was for my mobility.

This experience helped me to begin to shift my prior awkwardness of looking "different" to one wherein I could appreciate my "uniqueness." This moment still lives with me. Anytime that self-pity enters my consciousness, I reflect upon this experience and the feeling shifts to one of gratitude for this life lesson.

During my childhood, my grandmother cared for me while my parents worked. We often visited her mother, my great-grandmother, a healer for the Portuguese community in Oakland. She had an altar in the basement. It held statues of saints, healing oils, and candles, which she would use to help people. My great-grandmother was a devout Catholic who attended Mass daily, a fact that I could not understand given that

I struggled to sit through the one Sunday Mass that I was required to attend with her and my grandmother.

I often found my great-grandmother staring at me while she spoke in Portuguese with my grandmother. Of course, being sensitive to the disfigurement of my face, I assumed that they were talking about me. Looking back through the lens of today I believe she knew the spiritual purpose of my ordeal and was acknowledging this to my grandmother, which I am sure helped to relieve her of the sadness she felt.

These gifts and the experience of my great-grandmother registered somewhere deep within me as a touchstone, waiting for the time when I would call it up, make sense of it, and finally own it.

As I progressed through adolescence into adulthood, my interests became more focused on meeting cultural and family expectations. My desire to have a family and to achieve financial security were my primary focus and I had few shamanic experiences. Yet the shamanic foundation established through my Dreamtime and the connection with my great-grandmother served as a point of reference for my openness to further spiritual experiences.

I married, and this union allowed for the incarnation of three of the most beautiful and amazing souls I have had the honor of experiencing. At this time I also joined a new financial services company that was just starting up, and I dedicated myself to its success. As time progressed, these important aspects of my life were in balance and harmony. I was thoroughly enjoying all of the experiences of my children, and the company was doing extremely well.

And then something happened.

In 1991, while in Bandelier National Park in New Mexico with my business partner and a consultant discussing the future of our firm, we entered a kiva and I experienced being out of my body. The spirit world was calling. That evening I had a lucid dream about my father, who had passed over in 1986, and I recall feeling excitement and relief when I saw his beautiful, smiling face again.

In 1992 my adolescent son started sleeping on the floor of my bedroom on my side of the bed. After much prodding, he disclosed that there was an entity in his bedroom and that it made contact with him each evening as he was falling asleep. I offered to stay with him in his room and felt it pass through me. Although the entity was not malevolent, it was nonetheless quite disconcerting to him and to the rest of us. I reached out to anyone and everyone who I thought could help move this entity along.

Although these experiences reignited my connections to the unseen realms, I turned away from this aspect of myself as again I felt that a focus on family and career was of primary importance and there was no time to enter into and through the spiritual doorway I was being shown. I remember thinking, "I don't have time for this!"

It was a few years later that I started to experience a change in my personality: I went from feeling joyful and confident to being depressed and lost in the reality that I had created. I was now being consumed by the fear of losing the company that I had invested so much of myself in and of losing the loving relationships that I had established with my family and close friends. My personality began to turn dark and moody and I started noticing a strong inclination to become competitive with everyone. Not knowing what to do, I became obsessed with trying to control my environment, both at home and at work. My relationships, all of which are incredibly important to me—relationships that I had nourished in a healthy way—started to become filled with tension. I was hurting people with inappropriate comments, and I had become impatient with everyone, including my family members, who were becoming increasingly fearful of me. All of this was a beautiful mirror for the fear and hoplessness that I was experiencing internally, yet I still didn't understand what was happening to me.

Each time I would attempt to go deeper into the feelings of despair, I would judge myself for not appreciating all of the beauty and successes in my life. My thoughts would be along the lines of *Take a look around at others, what do you have to be depressed about?* However, words and thoughts that had supported me in the past now only served to deepen my sense of despair.

A friend who was witnessing these changes in me suggested that I go see his father-in-law, who was a shaman. When I met with him and shared all that was happening with me, he listened intently, and after a few more sessions, he remarked that "I wasn't ready" for the Work. Feeling a tremendous sense of rejection and hopelessness, I wondered, *Now what?* I knew that I was on the path of leaving this earthly realm much sooner than I wanted if I didn't take steps to prevent that, yet even a shaman couldn't help me. I thought, *How much further into darkness must I go?*

Not long after this I received an answer to my question.

A few months after meeting the shaman, there was a major exodus of employees from my firm. This exodus included my business partner. The fear that I was losing all that I had worked for was becoming a reality—or at least a strong possibility. What was most painful for me was that both my professional life and my personal life were eroding and apparently my anger and verbal outbursts had much to do with that in both scenarios. In any event, my old world was becoming annihilated, along with my sense of who I was.

At this time I was told by the same friend who had put me in touch with the shaman initially to contact him again, so I set up an appointment and he and I met. This time he said, "You are now ready?" I recall the tremendous sense of relief I felt upon hearing these words, for he was right. I was now ready to surrender to whatever process he had in mind.

In my first session with him, I experienced a tremendous sense of freedom from all thoughts of fear, and my need to be in control dissipated. I felt a sense of serenity, a feeling that I hadn't recalled experiencing in years. During the session I had a vision of myself standing on a dock at the edge of San Francisco Bay, and in the slip was a huge ship with the initials of my firm written on the hull. As I stood there watching this image, the ship exited the slip, turned, and sailed out to sea, passing under the Golden Gate Bridge. I knew then that I was being asked to leave the firm in order to follow my spiritual path. Ten months later, without soliciting offers, I received an offer to sell the company, which I did. This experience instilled in me an ability to trust the guidance and support available in following my path and, as importantly, to surrender to the calling.

During another journey I received an image of a wooden paddle. On one side of it was written the word "hurt" and on the other side the word "heal." Seeing these two words, I immediately chose the word "heal." I recall my choice being made without deliberation or hesitation.

I continued to work with the shaman, doing personal healing work for another year and a half, during which time my connections with the unseen world, experienced as both ancestral connections and spirit guides, continued to strengthen as they became more available to me. The shaman then began to apprentice me in his tradition.

After his passing, I wondered, *What's next?* Some time later a friend told me about a workshop that was being offered by a Peruvian shaman. Although I was not familiar with this tradition, I was intrigued to learn more about it. I attended the workshop and instantly developed a deep connection with don Oscar Miro-Quesada, a *kamasqa* curandero. At the same time, I developed a curiosity about the mesa, an altarlike arrangement of Spirit-infused artifacts that is part of the Peruvian tradition. When the opportunity came in 2001, I accompanied don Oscar on a pilgrimage to Peru, where I experienced the ceremonial traditions of both the north coast and Andean regions, which resonated with me deeply. I also immediately felt the power of these sacred Earth-honoring ceremonies.

During this first of many journeys to Peru, I participated in a mesada ceremony in the north coast city of Tucume. I was seated near the curandero (shaman) who was the ceremonial leader and I was viewing his mesa (an altar he was working with). I noticed that among many stones, shells, and other sacred items were photos of Catholic saints. An image of my great-grandmother's altar flashed before me as I was struck with new understanding: through my great-grandmother's daily attendance at Mass, she was strengthening her relationship with the saints who supported her during her healing ceremonies, similar to the way this curandero was invoking the assistance of Jesus Christ and the Christian saints to assist him in this particular ceremony.

Not only did this insight provide me with clarity regarding my great-grandmother's daily pilgrimage to Mass, it also shifted my understanding of the importance for maintaining a "right" relationship with the spirit realms. It is only through honoring and maintaining alignment with the realms of spirit and Nature that guidance and support may be received.

On that same journey in Peru, I experienced the ceremonial practices of the Andean paqos (shamans) at sacred sites. Offerings there were made to the spirits of Nature as a form of sacred reciprocity for the abundance and gifts received. As a result, an important foundation of my practice is ceremony, as it is a way of maintaining a reciprocal relationship that allows for the intervention of the spirit realms.

In 2002 I was guided to pick up my life and move to Mt. Shasta for the next step in my spiritual evolution. I now reside in Mt. Shasta and have developed a retreat center to support opportunities to share wisdom teachings, healings, and ceremonies.

It has been my experience that the calling of one's soul must be acknowledged, for any attempts to ignore it will result in suffering. It is also important to recognize that once we respond to this calling, we need to trust that guidance and support will be available to assist us in making the required changes in our life so as to allow us to follow the path that has been laid out before us.

Surrendering to and walking this path has given me great compassion for those experiencing their own struggles, and a heartfelt connection with everything in the visible universe and all the forces that lie behind it, which represent the greater reality of life.

I continue to call upon the experiences and wisdom learned during this journey, which have provided invaluable tools to me as I walk this sacred path of life.

I remain grateful for it all.

RAYMOND NOBRIGA underwent an extensive apprenticeship with master shaman don Oscar Miro-Quesada, supplemented by his numerous journeys to Peru to study with the indigenous healers and ceremonialists of the highland regions. He offers to others the wisdom teachings he has received and the rich and varied experiences gained through his service to the natural and spirit worlds. Ray has experienced the extraordinarily transformative power of this tradition and has committed himself to serving others in their process of transformation. Ray maintains a healing, teaching, and ceremonial practice incorporating his many years of training and experience. Ray is the founder of the Sanctuary at Mt. Shasta, a retreat and healing center in Mt. Shasta, California (www.thesanctuaryatmtshasta.com). Ray is a sanctioned teacher of the Pachakuti Mesa Tradition: Cross-Cultural Shamanic Arts for Personal and Planetary Renewal workshop series and an ordained minister. Ray formerly hosted a weekly radio program titled *Self, Soul, and Consciousness* on the VoiceAmerica Internet radio station.

28

Shamanic Awakening

Nadiya Nottingham

In my native Irish tradition we have shamanic stories about the silkie, which is a creature, often female, who removes her skin to reveal a human body underneath. Typically, she takes a man as a husband and lives as a good wife on land, usually in the northern windswept fishing villages of County Donegal.

On my own shamanic journey I taught myself to meditate by the ocean in the old seaside town of Sandycove, south of County Dublin, where James Joyce lived. My siblings and I grew up playing around the Martello tower where he lived and worked. I have very early memories of the cry of the gulls around that delightfully tiny harbor serving as a call of the wild for me; it seemed to speak to my very soul. The gulls were *our* silkies; they sat on the rocks and piers, and they were comfortable enough with human proximity to let us see their enormous bodies, their startling yellow eyes, and their marvelous webbed feet.

Their great colonies were side by side with us sunbathing humans; they were our neighbors and we theirs. We both lived in this ocean place together, lending to a sense that this must have been how our ancestors lived: side by side with the creatures and being aware of their own "creatureness."

By the time I was fifteen or sixteen I was disillusioned with organized religion and I began to ask the sea for help. Near our home was a lovely old tree by the ocean and I would sit under it and call out my prayer to the ocean spirit. A seagull would always sit somewhere nearby, and with the stiff salty breeze reddening my cheeks, the gull's cries seemed to echo my heart's call.

Through the difficult moments of a convent schooling, I would look out the window and find solace in the wheeling of those birds on the other side of the thin pane of glass that separated us. "Dear Gull," I would beam out, "take me away from here, let me know what it is to fly with you." That wish did come true, but not before I had gotten seriously sidetracked.

Many of my friends had started drinking and smoking cigarettes and pot. There was heroin too, but thankfully that was a step too far for me.

I had my first cigarette when I was about twelve. When my grandmother found out I was smoking she was delighted to have a smoking companion. Becoming a confidant of Grandmother Lily's was one of the first defining moments of my adolescence and we soon drew closer together. I felt so grown-up being trusted by her. She was no fan of the nuns and seemed all too happy to be in cahoots with me behind their backs. Convent girls were ripe for temptation—at least this little dreamer was.

Fast-forward three decades to New York City. Through a process of dying and rebirth, I have become a successful shamanic practitioner. After having been exposed to the hazy blue smoke-filled bars of the '80s and '90s, my first "death" came in the form of my left lung collapsing. Years of sex, drugs, and rock 'n' roll had taken their toll and I became a ninety-eight-pound waif, down from a weight of one hundred and twenty-five. I hung by a thread and you could have knocked me down with a feather.

New York had first beckoned me in 1982, when Dublin was beginning to feel oppressive. My mother, whom I'd always been very close to, was drifting away from us by way of alcoholism. My family's many attempts to have her stop drinking were futile. In addition, I'd split up with my musician boyfriend of three years. I was a skin care buyer in an apothecary, a sweet but unexciting job for a twenty-year-old with longings for a walk on the wild side.

As another rainy summer came to an end by the Dublin coast, a few friends got together for drinks. My friend Sharon had just returned from a long visit to the United States and she was tan from the great weather and infused with a kind of sparkle I'd not seen in her before. She was full of enthusiasm about America, but most especially New York. "Nadiya," she told me, "the moment you set foot in New York an electric charge goes through your whole being."

I'd never heard a place described in those kind of terms before. Furthermore, I had some kind of sense of what that charge was. I wasn't sure why, but I felt that what Sharon was referring to was something I would recognize.

In the years preceding my lung collapse, I had spent many summers on Fire Island, a beautiful, fragile sandbar off Long Island Sound. One could usually be seen there with a cigarette dangling from one's lips while a flute of champagne was close at hand and the cocaine was abundant.

One day an old man I knew invited me to dinner at his oceanfront house, which was a shack really, with broken chairs and an old woven rug, fishing rods hung from the ceiling, and a photo of Marilyn Monroe over the woodstove. Compared with the high-end houses nearby, his house had an authentic charm, and this man, George, was a genuinely kind and good-hearted being.

George wanted company and I needed new friends who didn't stay up till every bottle in the house was empty. He invited me to be his summer guest, carte blanche, and I gladly accepted. George had another friend who graced us with a daily visit: a large, white-breasted seagull that stood on the deck and waited for the scraps of fish that were usually forthcoming.

Through the course of my friendship with the gull, I reignited my shamanic root spirit, which was a welcome and sustaining substitute for my previous bad habits. I immersed myself deeply in yoga studies in the United States, and after traveling to India, I became a qigong teacher and had a daily meditation practice. I felt like I was doing all the "right" things; the life I now led was a very healthy one. Underneath it all, however, I knew I was missing something. My real fear was that I was missing being "bad"—but I was wrong. What was missing was something so much more fundamental.

The next leg of my journey would take me to that missing link.

In the mid-2000s I met and fell in love with a man who had traveled to the Amazon. He introduced me to ayahuasca. The "teaching vine" of the jungle would teach me more in one night than anything I could have imagined. This goddess plant looked into my soul and reminded me of who I really was.

One of the profound joys of my childhood had been listening to my mother's exquisite voice. She loved the little songbirds that came to our window, and she sang like one herself. After her death, it felt as if a song had left my heart. The circumstance of her passing, at the age of fifty-two, was tragic and premature.

I couldn't bring myself to sing after she died, but the songbirds took on new meaning. Every time I was in audible range of a peep, peep, peep, my whole being would not only tingle, but a vibration that seemed mountain-deep would echo though me.

On daily walks with my Jack Russell terrier in Central Park and Riverside Park, I began to have encounters with red-tailed hawks. I started having dreams and visions of these raptors, and soon it seemed that they were allowing me to come physically closer to them than they had in the past. One such hawk sighting for me was at extraordinarily close range; a female was sitting on a six-foot-high tree stump on the edge of a path in Riverside Park.

I froze in my tracks as I came across her; she took a look me and did not move, but continued to devour a squirrel. Her gaze seemed to say, *I know you're not a threat; you're a "bird person."* As winter turned to spring, she and her mate showed themselves to me almost every day.

My excitement intensified when Hawk showed up as a power animal alongside an old friend, Wolf. Hawk and Wolf seemed to work well together. Wolf had been showing me my gifts for building community; now Hawk appeared to bestow and strengthen the gift of inner vision. My intuition, which has always been very strong, strengthened considerably. I could sense when friends, clients, and family needed help or even just a phone call. It was mind-boggling, a gift I rarely talk about, as it defies description and is unpredictable and deeply personal.

It came to be that the opportunity to go to Brazil on an ayahuasca retreat presented itself. It meant ten days in the forest with an ayahuasqero shaman and his partner, who was an incredible dancer—a woman who became like a sister to me.

This occurred at the beginning of summer when my friend George had become quite ill. Now in his mid-eighties, he suffered from a variety of ailments, including heart trouble. He was thin and frail when I spent a June weekend with him before my Brazil trip. Though he was weak and slept a lot, he still found time and energy to perform his trash-collecting duties in a golf cart that whizzed up the boardwalks of Fire Island. George was a man of his word and someone who could be depended on to "chop wood, carry water," as the Buddhist saying goes. He detested having any sand in the house, and we would laugh about the fact that a man fanatical about having sand in the house should be living on a sand dune on Fire Island.

So after my visit to George, off to Brazil I went. Upon arrival, my companions and I drove two hours into the countryside, crossed a river by boat, and frog-leaped over rocks and stones to find our hiking trail. We then, a ribbon of trekkers, snaked through a sandy path in a forest in northern Brazil. Our bags were on the backs of some overworked donkeys trailing behind us.

We arrived at a most beautiful stone structure, high on the hillside of a river valley. In it we found good food and comfortable beds—nothing fancy, just sheer beauty illuminated by candlelight.

On our second day in this paradise, a misunderstanding transpired between me and a woman I knew from New York. She wrongly accused me of something I didn't do, and although I tried to explain my side of the story, she was not open to listening. To come all this way, to be in this Garden of Eden, for this? How could it be?

If this was to set the tone for the retreat, what would I do? Suddenly the remoteness of the place felt like a trap and all I wanted to do was run away.

After our evening meal everyone planned to go down to a river for a gathering. Some members of a local indigenous tribe were coming to sing and dance with us. I lagged behind in the dining area, slumped in a hammock. I had no desire to join in. I was depressed and I felt alone and misunderstood, and I certainly didn't feel like dancing or singing.

Just then the retreat manager came by. "Nadiya," she said, "the Funio tribe is here and they need someone to guide them down to the river. Do you have your flashlight?"

"Yes," was the only word that came to me. As I pulled myself out the hammock I turned to see four amazingly beautiful human beings— strong, stocky, bare-chested men—who wore feather headdresses over their jet black hair. I spoke no Portuguese and they spoke no English, so they smiled and waited for me to guide them down to the river.

The first few steps were lit by candlelight, but as we left the candlelit area we were plunged into total darkness until I turned on my flashlight. I remembered to point out to them a small tree stump that was right in the middle of the path, and they laughed at this, then I laughed too. In the next minute they started singing, and my heart broke open. Here I was, in the forest, leading some tribal men on a path to the river. They were singing and I was crying and laughing at the same time. Their song was so simple it sounded like "Yah hey, yah hey, yah hey, yah hey." I could sing that too, so I sang along with them. I looked up and the sky was brilliant with stars, which seemed to twinkle back at me the message: "Yes, just sing and laugh."

When we got to the river everyone was there by a huge fire. Each person looked so pure. The river shone behind us in the night and the rest of the world disappeared. I forgot who I thought I was, and I forgot I had been depressed. I only remembered that I was one with everything. At that moment I was river, fire, song, and community. We sang and danced around the fire for hours.

"Yah hey, yah hey, yah hey, yah hey!"

Over the next ten days of drinking indigenous medicines, partaking in a sweat lodge, hiking, dancing, singing, participating in fire ceremonies, river swimming, body painting, and storytelling, we each transformed and, like the snake, we shed old skins. Like Lizard, we grew new tails, and as humans we walked on new legs, with big blazing hearts.

On our last night the Funio tribe built another fire on the riverbank, and after we'd sung a few songs the chief asked us to dance an animal that had healed us, to call out its name to the stars.

For a moment I was sure that I would call out Hawk, because this had been my most recent spirit helper in New York City. However, when I opened my mouth, Gull came out, as if by magic. There had been no trace of Gull in my thoughts up to that point. But as soon as I said the word it made sense, so I danced a Gull dance and made laughing Gull sounds to Fire and River, along with my fellow travelers Bear, Jaguar, Eagle, Whale, Nightingale, Turtle, Snake, and Condor.

Three days later, thanks to the amazing magic of airplanes, I was back in New York City. The phone rang. It was Andy, my friend George's grandson, calling to tell me that George had passed over while I was in Brazil.

I asked him which day Geoge had died and it turned out that it had been July 19 at night, the exact time that I was dancing Gull in the forest.

At that moment I understood very clearly the true meaning of a spirit animal, or power animal, as they are known. In the fiftieth year of my life, it was revealed to me that for all these decades this animal spirit has flown between worlds as a helper, a protector weaver of soul friends, in this case my beloved George. I couldn't be with him at the end, but we both had Gull as our power animal and we felt like the full power of the ocean spirit was tying us together in the great mystery of life.

NADIYA NOTTINGHAM is a native of Ireland. A Celtic Priestess of Bridget and shamanic healing practitioner, she combines her training in medical qigong with the sacred flow of water. She was trained by Master Sat Hon and Masters Liu Dong and Liu He in qigong and by the Foundation for Shamanic Studies. She frequently travels to South America and her native Ireland to teach and study. She lives in Dutchess County, New York, where she has a private practice, and she is a senior teacher and workshop leader at New York City's Integral Yoga Wellness Spa, where she began her yoga and breathing studies in 1992. Her website is www.nadiyanottingham.net.

29

A Luminous Re-Membering

don Oscar Manuel Miro-Quesada

When we surrender the need to figure it all out and cultivate the ability to let it all in, then our Earth-walk becomes a sacred dance of healing service on the planet. More than the world needing saving, it needs loving.

DON OSCAR MANUEL MIRO-QUESADA

Editor's note: The following is adapted from *Lessons in Courage: Peruvian Shamanic Wisdom for Everyday Life,* by Bonnie Glass-Coffin and don Oscar Miro-Quesada (Rainbow Ridge Books, 2013). Reprinted with permission.

I am Oscar Manuel Miro-Quesada and this is my story. It is a story told within the immediacy of the present moment, even as it recalls the past. It is a story about how I came to serve the Earth by returning to the origins of a once-forgotten tradition. It is a story about how honoring these ancient wisdoms can awaken us all to the spiritual dimensions of life.

I was born in Lima, Peru, on August 21, 1951. I was youngest of five half-siblings, a result of my mother's third and father's second marriages. My coming back into wholeness as a soul on this good Earth began at first breath. This divine ally of both Earth and Heaven filled me with so much more than oxygen in that first awakening. Spirit itself filled my lungs as life took hold.

Yet what began so easily became a struggle for survival as I grew. As ever increasing episodes of severe asthmatic hypoxia set in, my breath was simply not available. I felt distant from Spirit, distant from life itself. I was a young soul encased within a dangerously frail physical body. As a seed that had not yet sprouted, my soul remained dormant, deep underground. Rather than expansion and growth, my soul sought contraction in order to survive. Rather than movement, it welcomed stillness. Rather than the radiant sunlight of day, it came to anticipate the darkness of my childhood room as an artificial harbor.

In addition, during my first nine years of life, I learned many ways to appear sane as my family descended into deep dysfunction where violence and danger had become the norm. Within all the chaos, my breathing became more and more constricted and the asthma attacks more frequent. I missed day after day of school as I struggled just to breathe. Meanwhile, I found refuge in small spaces, under tables, in corners. I crawled around in the classroom as perplexed children pointed fingers, laughing and mocking me. I was like a scared animal. Hiding.

Viewed from the perspective of a heartfelt shamanic initiation—a veritable rite of passage—I now understand the true miracle of love that was at the root of my illness. The severe asthma and family dysfunction that was part of my life for so long had been the very path to my redemption. It pointed the way for my return to wholeness. It paved the road from the dark night of my aching soul to the luminous realms of my shamanic ancestors.

I was ten years old, and the finest physicians in Lima had concurred that my very survival depended on my leaving this coastal city with its smog, humidity, and pollution, to relocate to the dry central highlands. Even then I felt a stirring as we rode up the winding roads away from sea-level Lima into the central Andes. As we traveled, we followed the river Rimac, called such by Quechua-speaking peoples of the highlands because it is the river of the "one-who-speaks." My destiny was calling out to me and I could feel the murmuring voices of my ancestors tumble down the mountainsides into its flow.

Our destination was the town of Chosica, halfway between the coast and the highest peaks of the Andes, where mountain lords are named and honored with ritual offerings to this day. There, high above the village, giant stones and enigmatic citadels are venerated just as they were during ancestral times. The entire region is known as a place of visitation, of sightings, and actual contact with star-beings. It was there where I found breath through an encounter with the beyond.

It was a December night in 1961. The air was cold and the sky was full of stars. My mother had put me to bed and then returned to the kitchen to clean up after dinner. From deepest slumber, I awoke with a start. My eyes were wide and round in surprise and growing desperation. My mouth was just a slit, and I felt my chest disappearing. My body was completely numb: there was no breath at all. Panic cannot even describe the sensation. I tried desperately to call for help, yet I could not move or speak. The world began closing in on me as darkness pressed down against my chest. The Earth opened to swallow me, and I felt myself pulled down through the mattress of my bed, deeper and deeper into this abyss. My body felt cold. The pounding in my ears that was my heart became faint, then fainter still; then all was silent. I relaxed and fell into total drowning.

I was dead.

From far away, I began hearing someone call my name. It wasn't my birth name at all, but a nickname my father had given me years before because of my curiosity and my countenance. "Eager Beaver," he had called me, or Beaver for short. It felt good to have an animal name. I identified with it. Faintly, I began hearing it in my right ear, then in my left, "Beaver, Beaver, come back. We need you. Beaver, come back, Beeeeaver . . ." Suddenly, with a gasp of air, I was pulled from the abyss that had swallowed me. I found myself sitting upright in my bed in total darkness.

With open eyes, I gazed around the room. Slowly, as I regained consciousness, more fully I began to feel the presence of extraordinary compassion and indescribable love, healing, and grace. As I gazed

deeper into the darkness, there appeared a quivering field of luminosity that gradually settled into three humanlike forms. Standing seven
feet tall, their heads were almost touching the low ceiling of my room.
As they became increasingly more detailed and separate, their appearance became discernible. All three had long white beards and luminous
blue eyes. They were ancient yet ageless; wizened, yet completely unen-
cumbered. They wore white robes, and their long hair grew into wispy
trails of luminous spiraling light. They were three angelic beings, three
Shining Ones. I now know them to be three expressions of the Divine
that have been described in tales and legends since the dawn of time:
luminous beings, perfect, harmonious, whole. They were beyond all
dichotomy and division. They were Absolute Love.

These three beings communicated in unison a thought that mirrored
exactly what I felt. A resounding gift of awakening to my true place of
origin reverberated deep within me. The thought-feeling coursed from my
head throughout the entire length of my body as they stood before me. It
felt pleasant, like the vibrational lingering of sacred words once spoken. In
that moment, my entire experience of being in a physical body shifted. I
recognized my own essence in the same light that they embodied.

That awareness alone would have been enough for me to embrace the
experience of death that had come upon me. In that instant, I could have
just let go, returning with a peaceful heart into the hands of our Maker.
Yet somehow I knew it was not my time.

No sooner did I know it than the Shining One to my left bent his tall
frame toward me and placed his transparent lips to my chest. He began
to breathe the asthma out from my lungs into himself. For what seemed
an eternity, he sucked in through his lips, extracting from my frail body
all residue of the illness that had so far accompanied the evolution of my
soul in this lifetime. Afterward, he raised his head and offered that den-
sity in breath up to the heavens. I saw the crack between the worlds in
that moment. All my suffering, fear, doubt, and insecurities were taken
skyward as he blew forth to the heavens. When he finished, the portal
between worlds vanished as quickly as it had appeared.

Next, the Shining One to my right placed his right hand, with a luminous open-fingered palm, upon my sternum. He then placed his left palm on top of the right one. As he closed his deep blue eyes, I felt a concentrated willing: a bestowal of his essence into my heart. My entire being was lit from within as I lay motionless on the bed.

Meanwhile, the Shining One who stood between the other two opened his eyes wide, looking straight ahead. His Buddha-like hands danced with flowing light. He touched his luminous fingertips together in various gestures. Once the hand gestures were complete, this Shining One rested his arms by his side and gazed toward me with his infinitely compassionate eyes. It was then that the communication between us began.

I entered a realm between dream and waking where images floated seamlessly along. The first image I was gifted by that luminous being was of returning to Lima. I saw the great turmoil that would ensue as my father and mother separated, yet I saw myself being free of asthma forever more. The telepathic transmission of the events of my life was extensive: the jobs I would hold, the relationships I would treasure, the children who would be born and those who would be lost to me in the dance of eros that accompanies the search for self. I saw the teachers I would meet, and I saw the artistry of what I was born to do as my service to the great web of life.

As the movie of my life began to fade from view, the last message reverberating through the depths of my soul was this: "Remember the rituals. Remember the rituals. Remember the rituals."

For the next several years, my recollection of that transformational moment was clouded. All that changed when in August of 1969 I met the famed maestro *huachumero* don Celso Rojas Palomino from Salas, Chiclayo, during what was to be the first of many night *sanpedrito* ceremonies.

During that first night, after the tobacco offering was given and after his patients had been cleansed with the sacred objects on his altar, out of the center of his *banco* a light started to circulate. I blinked my eyes in amazement. The light continued to rise from the mesa. As it emerged, it coalesced into a large oval pulsing field. As I continued to watch, the same three wizened Shining Ones that had visited me and healed me of asthma eight years earlier appeared before us now. As they began to come closer, I stared in open-mouthed wonder. No one else seemed to see them, not even don Celso's assistants who were sitting just to his left. Was I dreaming? Was this really happening?

At first I didn't notice don Celso's sideways glance. Then he elbowed me firmly, jarring me from my reverie. "Do you remember them?" he asked me.

"Yes, I do," I stuttered. At that moment, my entire reality shifted. I felt transported back in time to a moment I had all but forgotten. In less than a nanosecond everything that had been shown to me at age ten during that near-death experience came back into my awareness. And I remembered it all. In this second visitation by the three Shining Ones, I tapped into the noosphere—the ineffable yet universal field of information that some call the Akashic Record.

In that moment, all contrasts, all polarities, all separation, all interpretation, all need to have a nice comforting orderly world was annihilated. It was all destroyed. And I found myself floating up in space and dissolving as a separate entity, as an individual, as an ego-mind, as a personality. In that moment, the one known to this world by the name Oscar just disappeared. I was *absorbed* within the All. I remembered my purpose for being born, and this time it stayed firmly imprinted in my psyche. All that I had witnessed and forgotten at age ten came cascading back, free of censorship and dimensional filters. I realized how incomplete our sensory experiences are as I peeked behind the veil of the eternal *now*.

As soon as the ritual ended, I asked don Celso if I might apprentice with him, and he agreed.

After that, as I began practicing the rituals of my ancestors, the memory of that moment was released in me again. It was then, when I began to quiet myself, communing with the Mystery from a place of deepest surrender to wholeness, that I came to realize this truth more fully: Illness equals action without alignment. It is estrangement from the sacred as we project the causes and consequences of our suffering onto others. It comes from looking outward rather than inward for acceptance, approval, and love.

In all sanctioned lineages of shamanism the world over, the symptoms of illness are symbols of the state of your being. While you may be ill, you may be in pain, you may have experienced deep tragedy or longing, you are not just suffering passively. Instead, you begin to see this particular illness as a call to enter into conversation with powers that beckon you to assume new responsibilities of being human.

Each of us has catalyzing moments that open us to an awareness of Source within ourselves. Like many who recognize the power of the spiritual in their lives, it was the depth of my suffering that primed the pump of my awakening. As I opened to my reality of being born "of spirit" as much as "of matter," I gained an expanded view of myself. I allowed *love* to be who *I am*. In this awakening, I connected deeply with the Ultimate Ground of my Being. And in so doing, I entered into a true sacred alliance and path of healing service in honor of All Our Relations.

This Great Work is not so much about changing the world as it is about changing oneself in the process. As we commit to this quest, and the graceful honoring of all life that will naturally flow from our actions, unhindered evolutionary transformation is effortlessly unleashed upon the world—in paraphrasing Joseph Campbell, we have learned to "follow our bliss!"

DON OSCAR MANUEL MIRO-QUESADA is a respected kamasqa curandero and altomisayoq adept from Peru, visionary founder of the Heart of the Healer (THOTH), originator of the Pachakuti Mesa Tradition cross-cultural shamanism, and coauthor of *Lessons in Courage: Peruvian Shamanic Wisdom for Everyday Life.* An internationally acclaimed shamanic teacher, healer, and Earth-honoring ritualist, don Oscar is also an OAS fellow in ethnopsychology, an invited observer to the UN Permanent Forum on Indigenous Issues, and a member of the Birth 2012 Welcoming Committee and the Evolutionary Leaders Circle convened, respectively, by Barbara Marx Hubbard and Deepak Chopra. His work and shamanic training programs have been featured on CNN, Univision, A&E, the Discovery Channel, and the History Channel's *Ancient Aliens.* For more information please visit www.heartofthehealer.org or follow him on Facebook.

30

My Shamanic Initiation
The Fire of Transformation

Mona Rain (Smith)

I had come for my first shamanic healing not really knowing what to expect, but knowing I'd been led here by a greater consciousness that I was still struggling to understand. Miracles happened that day, awakening in my spirit, in my mind, and in my body. I was asked to lie down, to relax, to close my eyes and envision my transformation and call my helping spirits to be with me . . .

I surrendered to the process, fully willing, still not knowing how this would or could happen. I only knew I was led to this man by a strange, strong consciousness within that was guiding me. The rattling began. I sank deeper into my awareness as I heard the prayers being spoken, as the rattle transfixed my soul, awakening an energy from deep inside. Suddenly, I was engulfed in a spray of hot fire, over and over again. Fire below me—Shungo! Fire over the entire front of my body—Shungo! Again and again—Shungo! Shungo! Around me—Shungo! Intense heat penetrated me, filling my senses as I surrendered without fear, without trepidation, to the energies, to the sacred fire and its ability for complete transformation. I immersed deeper and deeper into another state of consciousness. *This is it,* I thought. *This is what I have yearned for my entire life . . . I am finally home!*

As a term of my employment in an outpatient physical therapy center I was required to have the hepatitis B vaccine. However, after the second injection in a series of three, I began to experience flu-like symptoms, asthma, loss of memory, irrational thinking, and weakness throughout my entire physical body. At the age of forty-one, my menstrual periods stopped immediately, never to return. Additionally, I couldn't walk fifty feet without stopping to rest, totally out of breath.

As I sought out medical diagnosis from doctors and specialists, I learned that my entire immune and endocrine systems had been affected. Tests and more tests, IVs, and various medications helped only moderately. For over two years I searched for answers and healing. I tried alternative health care modalities; nothing helped for any length of time.

Throughout all of this, I was a practitioner of craniosacral therapy through the Upledger Institute. I was adept at accessing alternate states of consciousness through my training and personal experiences. In an advanced continuing education workshop on the immune system, I received some startling news when I was in alternate states of consciousness. Bone cancer was settling/developing in my energy body, my thymus was destroyed, and my immune system had no idea how to function anymore. This was it, I realized. I needed to come to peace with my life that was deteriorating at a rapid pace.

As my spiritual awareness surfaced in my search for the meaning of life and I was pondering my mortality at the age of forty-three, I was led to a lecture given at a local spiritual center by author/shaman John Perkins. I had seen John and his books years earlier at an Omega conference in Weston, Florida. At that earlier time, I found his presence intriguing and his books fascinating, but I had no idea what shamanic realms were and was not ready to receive such information that was so strange to me. Now, several years later, I was anxiously anticipating this meeting!

I attended, and I scheduled a personal follow-up healing with him immediately. That lecture and subsequent shamanic healing have forever changed the course of my life . . . my personal life, my health, my professional life, and my passion for the gifts and abundant possibilities that exist by utilizing the shamanic realms in our everyday life.

I attended his weeklong intensive, Arutum, which focused on accessing one's own personal power and connecting with the four sacred elements, one's shamanic guides, shapeshifting, alternate states of consciousness, and journeying, journeying, journeying all day—every day. Shamans, curanderos, and curanderas from Brazil, Peru, Ecuador, and the United States assisted us.

It was during this weeklong intensive that I experienced my first shapeshift. I shapeshifted into the great energy of the transformative snake—*amaru*—and went into a "time of no time." I existed in another realm but walked in my physical body, unable to ascertain what was happening to me.

When the journeying had been concluded, I followed the group to the lunch break, but I had no interest in eating. Instead I was totally fixated on the stones in the garden and the pillar of cement holding up the walls. I rubbed up against them, feeling their coolness, and desiring only to be curled up next to them. John and several others were called over to "call me back." I remember nothing of that twenty minutes in my conscious waking mind. It was here I accessed another realm of healing—I was able with the others to call my spirit back and heal my physical body and my energy matrix.

In the weeks after that intensive workshop my energy levels increased exponentially each week. I was able to begin walking for exercise and then I was able to power walk, work without extreme fatigue, and sleep uninterrupted. I began to recover my mental capabilities, and my health. Then came the time to travel.

Of course I was drawn to South America, and I knew I had to experience the fire cleansings for myself. Again, taking an enormous leap of faith, I traveled alone to a foreign land. I did not speak any Spanish, and I had only met my American guide briefly in an empowering journey with the *yachaks* of the high Andes in Ecuador, from whom I learned the fire cleansing for myself. The incredible fire cleansings shapeshifted me and because of them I was able to regain my health and my life. I returned to Ecuador six months later and was initiated into my "path of light."

As I returned home to the United States, I pondered what I could do to assist the global consciousness in a more Earth-honoring way. I realized my soul desired to shapeshift those around me as I myself had shapeshifted. I wanted to bring this awareness to my loved ones, my friends, the people I worked with, the community, and even the strangers I interacted with in my daily life.

Thus, I began a monthly full moon circle, which included a fire cleansing ceremony; I also offered complimentary mini cleansings to those in attendance. This circle continues to this day, each month, although the ceremony itself has transformed and moved locations to adapt to the needs of the community it serves. In addition, I began to offer classes on basic shamanic journeying and Earth-honoring practices, as well as leading small groups to South America.

Today, I am healthy and strong again. I travel, walk, and hike in the mountains without tiring. I now work full-time and am physically comfortable once again. I have not been on medication of any kind for over twelve years, and my immune system is functioning normally. I rarely get sick.

My healing practice has grown in that I have more shamanic clients. It has evolved into an ecoconscious practice where I treat Earth-honoring CEOs, presidents of corporations, corporate executives, and doctors and healers practicing alternative healing modalities who are in need of balancing, renewal, and spiritual connection in their lives to better assist their businesses and practices. I love thinking of it as the trickle-down effect: as I assist them, they assist so many others in turn!

I have discarded the medical massage component of my practice, and long ago I also gave up my outpatient physical therapy practice. I did, however, retain the powerful craniosacral techniques and now blend those with the shamanic healing techniques to satisfy the needs of each client. As well, I regularly pray on the lands here in North America with indigenous elders and others. I have also traveled to Peru, seeking out sacred sites and sacred plant medicines to explore and to offer prayers with. My life, in every moment, is a shamanic one. I observe and

I am grateful for the synchronicities and for the shamanic resonance in my world around me. I explore other experiences of many varied shamanic traditions to pray with, to learn from, and to share with.

Each time I travel, each time I experience another sacred site, each time I pray, each time I work with a client, each time I experience another soul, I remember. I remember the ancient voices, the ancient prayers, the ancient energies, the star brothers and sisters, and the galaxies. I remember my beginnings, my endings, my lifetimes upon lifetimes. I follow the guidance of the spirits of the vibrating essence of Pachamama. These experiences have given me tremendous gifts and insight. I believe in sharing this with others, for others have come to share with me. As we awaken, we awaken those around us; we are all part of the universal whole.

I am tremendously grateful for all of my experiences, to all the spirits in this realm and in the alternate realities, and all the possibilities of existence in the shamanic realms.

Thank you, Itzhak Beery, Shaman Portal, John Perkins, and the sacred fire cleansing tradition of the Tamayos of Otavalo, Ecuador.

Shungo!

MONA RAIN (SMITH), LMT, has been a *chacaruna* and healer for the past twenty-five years. She is gifted in bridging ancient shamanic traditions and holistic healing practices. Mona studied craniosacral therapy and acupressure at the Upledger Institute, taking advanced course trainings, including therapeutic imagery and biofeedback. As well, Mona studied transpersonal psychology at the Synthesis Institute in Miami. In 1998 she was initiated into her path of light and the fire tradition in the high Andean mountains. Mona is a Pachakuti Mesa Tradition carrier in cross-cultural shamanic arts. She maintains a private healing practice at the Shaman Spirits Cave in Boynton Beach, Florida, and at the Center for Human Development in Hollywood, Florida. She also offers workshops, mentoring, exploration of the divine feminine, drumming circles, ceremonies, Ecuadorian fire cleansings, and spiritual vision quests to Peru. A licensed massage therapist (LMT) and craniosacral therapist since 1990, she lives in Florida. Her website is chacarunahealing.com.

31

The Power Animal Experience

Debra Fentress

For years I had been in an empty, unhappy marriage. I stayed in it because I felt it was better for my daughter to have a dad around, although I had to be a buffer in that relationship. I simply felt I alone couldn't give her what she might need.

I knew that I had somehow lost my own personal power. Over the years, I tried therapy, journaling, and a host of other methods . . . all of which helped, but I still felt like I didn't have it in me to make it on my own, particularly with a child.

One weekend, I attended a workshop held by noted author and shaman Hank Wesselman. I had read his book *Spiritwalker* and was excited at the opportunity to learn from him and discover what he and the workshop had to offer. I come from a pagan lineage, whose many rites and journeys are similar to shamanic work; I was eager to experience those similarities for myself. Additionally, I knew that shamanism placed an emphasis on personal power, which was just what I needed.

The workshop took place on the side of a hill overlooking an ancient Indian burial site. Our view was beautiful and you could feel the energy of the ancient ones. And Hank was a great teacher. There was an energy about him that was powerful yet gentle. He was also very tuned in to each person and who they were. Over the course of the two-day workshop, he led us through various exercises, which all led up to the retrieval of our power animal.

When it was time to discover our power animal, Hank paired us off. As we spread out and took our places, I was nervous. I had come to the workshop knowing only the hostess. My partner was a man who seemed to have kind, healing energy but he was probably as nervous as I was. Neither one of us was quite sure whether we could pull off what we were supposed to do.

I think Hank sensed the nervousness of the group, for he began to walk around, speaking encouragingly and beating a drum softly. I lay down on the mat because I was to be the recipient first; with the help of my partner, I would find my power animal. As I lay quietly, I could feel myself relaxing, my mind slowing and then drifting. Finally I experienced only a sense of peace. In what seemed like minutes, my partner was gently helping me to sit up, blowing the power animal into my crown and heart chakras and then relaying what he had experienced in his part of the journey.

My power animal was not at all what I'd expected. In fact, it didn't even exist in this world. And I didn't like that creature! I had to move on because it was my turn to journey next on behalf of my partner. I felt a little strange as well as nervous, but everything went well. I brought back his power animal and the exercise was over.

We finished the workshop, said our goodbyes, and went home.

That night I had a dream in which my power animal came to me and I turned away from it. He kept trying to get me to accept him and let him in. I was adamant that he could not be with me. Suddenly, we were physically fighting. Given that he was so much larger and stronger than me, I didn't stand a chance, but I fought as hard as I could to get him off me. At that he fought harder, even scratching my arms and hands until I woke up by falling off the bed.

I was panting and out of breath. I felt like I had been fighting. Then I noticed my arms—there were red welts running down to my hands; they looked like scratches. And I was so physically tired.

I finally got back to sleep, telling myself that what I'd just experienced was just a dream. Before long, however, another dream started.

The power animal was back. I was scared this time and begged him to leave me alone . . . to not hurt me. He began to explain that he wasn't there to hurt me but to *protect* me. Whenever I needed help or strength, all I had to do was call on him and he would be there. As he spoke, my feelings toward him softened and everything began to make sense.

From that night on, I began to feel a sense of power. Within three months, I got certified in neurolinguistic programming, filed for divorce, started a coaching program, and moved my daughter and myself to a new city. And I haven't looked back.

I fully believe that if I hadn't taken that workshop with Hank and received my power animal I might still be in that dark place. I now teach my own workshops on shamanic practices, and through my coaching program, I coach others who want to find their own power and light.

As a lifelong student of personal growth, DEBRA FENTRESS studied with Hank Wesselman and Helen Bangs and was a lead trainer for Advanced Neuro Dynamics, an international training company. Debra has a background in psychology and is a published author, master trainer of neurolinguistic programming (NLP), master practitioner of Time Line Therapy, certified hypnotherapist, certified spiritual counselor, and creator of Neural Pathway Restructuring—Changing Your Past to Create Your Future. Debra is dedicated to assisting people create lives of love, joy, and happiness on a moment-to-moment basis. She has coached CEOs, government agencies, corporations, and individuals to improve their lives, both professionally and personally. Her website is www.SpiritsMuse.com.

32

Pandora's Box

Wendy Whiteman

I have been a shamanic practitioner and a shamanic guide for others for fifteen years. I have had numerous experiences with Nature and its impact on the human condition. We must always remember that as a member of the human kingdom, we are made from the attributes of the three lower kingdoms . . . mineral, plant, and animal. It is no wonder that our reflection can be found in all of Nature and with our eyes wide open we can find our healing. I have seen some of the most wonderful healings take place with people who suffer from depression, addiction, fear, and poor self-esteem. If we approach Mother Nature and our own healing with the reverence they deserve, we will find healing.

I have had teachers who have been shamans, whether they called themselves that or not. The most influential was a Navajo (Diné) medicine man, a hand trembler,* and singer from the Gallup area of New Mexico. He was very traditional in his medicine ways and served his reservation as a medicine man for many years. Since I am a Caucasian woman, his approach with me was more shamanic than traditional Diné. His understanding of natural law and the mind-body connection was fascinating, considering that he was "uneducated" by Western

---

*Hand tremblers are diagnosticians who use the altar and divination skills to find out what is wrong with a patient.

193

society. What this shaman taught me is the important and necessary connection between ceremony and practice. One without the other is a dis-connect from the laws of the universe. The practices bring the grounding and centering. The ceremony brings a reverence for the possibility of divine intervention.

The case that brought the most shamanic impact to both myself and my client came to me a few years ago when a group of people came to see me. They had come from the United Kingdom to New Mexico for a four-day retreat, which included medicine walks in the high desert of Taos, shamanic practices, and ceremony. Each person came with a particular issue that needed clarity.

A young lady, Sue, is the client I will focus on. She was in her twenties with a high-pressure modeling job. She spent too much time away from home, which made her feel rootless. Her other issues were her weight and issues having to do with eating. And she had a propensity for smoking pot. The young lady was ready for a change but found it very difficult to effect any kind of change in her life. We decided to start with the pot smoking, as she and I both agreed it was masking all of her other issues. Rather than having me choose the location for the medicine walk, I asked Sue to journey with the help of an ally to find a physical place where we would then go to perform her medicine walk. She was also to determine whether or not the ally would help her find some clarity on her issue.

When she returned from her journey, she described the place as being very rocky. A river was also a feature that she had seen. Her ally was a large raven who took her to this place. Sue said that she rode on his back and viewed the area from above. She felt confident that this was her medicine place and the raven was her guide.

The next day I took her to the Rio Grande Gorge, which is home to the Rio Grande. The gorge was filled with giant ancient volcanic rocks and the river was below. We put down a small altar and gave offerings to the spirits of the land. I always use an altar as an anchor for my client and myself. We start here and we end here.

Sue was smudged and then she was to leave the altar and me and start her medicine walk. She had as much time as she needed to walk and observe and listen to the voice within. She had made a prayer at the altar, asking that she find some understanding for her pot addiction and how to quit. She felt a sense of urgency that she had never felt before . . . like this was a make-or-break opportunity.

Sue walked down the mesa path through the large sage bushes, "scanning" as I had taught her to do. Scanning is a method of taking in as much of your environment as possible, through heightening your sense. This is a safety procedure, as well as an information-gathering technique. She was very nervous, as she was not an outdoorsy girl and this terrain was very foreign to her, even treacherous in many ways. She started to cry and said she felt hopeless. Sue remembered the raven in her journey and called out to her ally, asking for help.

Within minutes she saw a lone raven circling above her. She said she couldn't believe it, even though ravens are common in New Mexico. As she walked down the path, Raven continued to circle above her. Sue then decided that she wanted to follow the raven instead of having the raven follow her, so she sat down on the path. Raven circled and then veered off to the right, heading for an area filled with giant volcanic rocks and a view of the river. He landed on one of the rocks. Sue followed him down the slope, then climbed the giant rock. Raven was above, watching her.

Sue found an area that she felt drawn to and sat down to view the river and watch Raven. She said she no longer felt alone and was hopeful that some answers would come to her. She lay down on the rock to journey, but as she did so, something caught her eye. It was a little metal tin can that was lodged between two large rocks. It was out of her reach, though, so she decided to resume her attempts to journey. She lay on her back and looked up to the big blue New Mexico sky and her ally. Raven squawked at her, fiercely flapping his wings like a parent reprimanding a child.

She closed her eyes and tried to journey again but that seemed to make Raven even more distraught. So Sue sat up and said, "Okay, Raven! Maybe the answer is right here before my very eyes." She then had a chill go though her and she knew it was associated with the tin can. She knew that she had to get it and open it up. So for an hour she tried everything she could think of to get that tin can. "My need became stronger and stronger," she said. "Like my desire for pot . . . when I really need it I will go anywhere and do anything to get some." Sue added that she was even performing some dangerous moves in order to obtain the tin.

With the help of a stick she was able to knock the tin out of the crevice and it fell a few feet farther down the rock pile. She straddled two rocks and finally got the tin between her fingertips. Slowly she was able to get herself back to an upright position. Her first thought was how obsessed she was over this little tin can, which was very old and quite rusted. "It was an old mint container like the ones you can buy at the grocery store checkout stand. I did all this for a silly can?" Sue said. She looked up to see if Raven was still there. She had been so obsessed with the retrieval of her tin that she had forgotten about Raven. He was gone!

She started to doubt herself and felt that she had wasted all her time with the silly mint can, which she couldn't even open because it was so rusted. The old pattern of doubting herself came back, as did her fear of failure. This was the moment in the pattern when Sue wished she had some pot, so she could escape her emotions. She decided to quit the medicine walk and return to me.

Sue climbed back out of the rocky area onto the mesa and found her path to the altar. When Sue arrived she sat down with me by the altar and said, "This was a waste of time, mine and yours . . . this great Raven came to me and I followed him to this rocky area, just like in my journey yesterday, but then I got all caught up in trying to get this stupid tin can out from some rocks I was sitting on."

Sue pulled the tin out from her pocket and handed it to me. I said, "Sue, did you open it?"

"No . . . it won't open," she replied. "It's rusted shut." She continued to berate herself as she told me what had transpired on her medicine walk. I could no longer hold a straight face and began to laugh . . .

because I had seen this before with other clients. I asked her, "Why do you think that the medicine walk is over?"

At my question she looked really stunned. "Because I got nothing!" she finally replied.

I looked down at the tin, which was sitting on the altar. I said, "Really? This tin is nothing? You risked injury to get it and you still doubt your intuition and the process of the journey? Are you ready to open Pandora's box? Everything you experienced today was part of your answer, but the clarity lies inside this tin. I think you will know it when you see it. I don't know what is in this tin, maybe nothing, but then, *that* would be the answer you seek."

I got out my knife and gave it to Sue. "Open . . . says me!"

Sue pried open the top of the can and then gasped, dropping the tin.

What rolled out was what changed my view of shamanic practices forever. Old marijuana buds . . . yes, pot!! Neither of us could speak, as this was beyond bizarre and bordered on being impossible and improbable. The chances of this happening were one in a million, but given that shamanic practice and guidance were involved, the odds drastically switched.

We discussed the unbelievable find of marijuana, the very symbol of her whole trip to America from the United Kingdom, and all of its meanings for her.

That night we did a sweat lodge for Sue. In the lodge, her emotions poured out of her. As a model, she was no longer living her authentic self. The job was killing her, literally. She told us about her professional life and the vices and pressures it included: little sleep, diet pills, uppers, downers, alcohol, sex with agents or no job, travel twenty-hours and hit the runway one hour later . . . It was not glamorous, it was hell. We discussed the invisible energy cords that ran from her to her addiction. They were so strong that she could travel thousands of miles from one continent to another, sit on a rock in the desert, and still attract marijuana to her.

Sue saw that she no longer had control of her own life. She had given it over to so many other people and substances to maintain a life that was killing her. She was able to trace her lack of self-esteem and hopelessness to choices she had made in the past and understood that it was time to make choices again, albeit ones that were more appropriate for where she was now. The concept of "I am the victim here" had to go. She was able to see that the victim role was keeping her stuck and that she had to be the hero and the director of her own life. Her life had been a choice, not a lifelong sentence.

Sue spent the following day at the altar giving offerings to Raven and the rocks and developing a healthier and more productive reverence for pot. She did some more journeying and then we did a final release ceremony at the river with the tin of marijuana. She had opened Pandora's box and in it had seen all the evils and illnesses of life she had succumbed to. But just as in the story of Pandora's box, she found hope. Sue found her authentic self emerging and the strength to heal herself.

I stayed in touch with Sue for a couple of years. She went back to London and within those two years she broke ties with her old boyfriend, got married to another, moved to South Africa, had a baby, and left modeling. She was happy and had become the heroine of her own life.

Sue's experience reinforced for me, a shamanic practitioner and guide, that there truly are no accidents. Receiving guidance from the ordinary and non-ordinary world requires working with the laws of the universe. This is not hocus-pocus. Although my Navajo teacher would not refer to the law of cause and effect, because he had not heard it put that way, he was a believer that we are responsible for everything that happens in our life. Every moment is a choice and we are capable of righting the wrongs and creating a balance in our life once again.

WENDY WHITEMAN has lived on the high mesa in Taos, New Mexico, for the last seventeen years. She is the author of *Sacred Sage: How It Heals* and *Sacred Sage Spirit Medicine*. Her journey with Native and shamanic studies began with Michael Harner and Grandmother Twylah Nitsch. Her most significant teacher was Elton Thompson of the Diné People. Wendy has been in business for twenty years dealing with Native art and ceremonial herbs. She has a bachelor's degree in psychology, is a certified aromatherapist, artisan distiller, and author, and has participated in many years of ceremony and shamanic practice with teachers from the United States, Peru, and Mexico. Her website is www.wolfwalkercollection.com.

33

Sacred Place

Peter Brown

I was walking on a logging road that wound its way up the side of a volcano in the Sierra Mountains of California and was struck by the fact that I was being pulled or asked to follow this particular path. It was the continuation of a path that I had been fortunate to embark on with the guidance of a *marakame* in the Huichol tradition of Mexico and a *granicero* in the Nahua tradition of that same country. It was a path leading to a sacred place, a place to which one pilgrimages to gain gifts for oneself, one's community, and the beings in all of the realms.

As I proceeded down this shamanic path, the presence of this volcano, this mountain, was making itself better known to me. On this particular trip, I placed an offering of chocolate and a candle in thanks, asking nothing of the mountain in return.

As the year progressed, however, I thought more and more of about the mountain. I studied its geology and the history of human development on it as regards the original people who had lived there. An urgency to start working with the mountain was beginning to develop within me, and thus the following summer, after the snows had receded, I returned to place another offering of respect. As I was approaching the mountain, the most magnificent buck that I had ever seen, almost a caricature, appeared from the north and walked in front of me to the south, and then stood very still on the side of the trail.

The deer is a central figure in Huichol culture and because of this I deemed my sighting of it to be confirmation that I was indeed to start working with the volcano. The problem was, I didn't know where to begin. I presented my offering of thanks and went home.

The next time that I had a chance to sit and talk with my attending shaman, I told him of my experiences and my belief about the mountain. I was looking to him for counsel. He told me that it was very dangerous to begin a relationship with a Kakayari—a deity that has taken land form such as a mountain, lake, or river—unless you have a person helping you along this path. I was told that if you just start making offerings, not knowing the customs and rituals or even the being of the Kakayari, then you are opening yourself up to problems. It is not enough to just hear the Kakayari calling.

Several years passed as I awaited the instructions from my elder. I was getting antsy to start the work. I set a deadline in my mind, telling myself that if I did not get instructions/assistance/guidance, I was going to just do it. I was going to approach this god, this Kakayari, give the offerings that I thought best, and ask to work with the Kakayari. I figured that this was taking too long. The Kakayari had called me, hadn't it?

With the coming summer, I planned to take my leap and make an offering and ask for gifts and blessings from the mountain. But as I was formulating this, an elder shaman called me and said that he was coming to help me work with this mountain. He arrived in the spring to take a look at All That Is and Was. *Finally,* I thought, *I'm going to get my answers and start all this work.* Protocols, instructions—everything I needed I would receive. Finally, I was on the road after all these years.

Well, it was not quite so simple. A few weeks later, I was in southern Mexico at the annual welcoming of the rains ceremonies, and I was given a feat that I had to accomplish. *Then* I would be given the instructions on how to work with this Kakayari. I would be taught the proper offerings to make, the location to place them, the correct time of year to go, and the prayers to sing. My particular trial is not of import. I was to meet with my elder again in November, and I would perform my task. If I accomplished it, then the rituals and the ancestral names of the Kakayaris would be presented to me.

I was disappointed by yet another delay, but I understood that I was not ready to fully step into the mission before me. Thus I worked to prepare through the summer and fall. Come November, I was called upon to demonstrate my mastery of the ability to be fully present so that my words would be heard and my offerings accepted by the Kakayari. My first attempt failed. I was given a chance to try again, and this time, I arrived. I had completed the task in a manner that my elder felt meant I could now be heard by the Kakayari. When I finally received the instructions in the winter, I eagerly devoured them. I learned that I could not, in any event, have started my work with the mountain until spring; the additional months of waiting proved to be just another test.

Upon reading the rituals, a *nierika*—a doorway to an ancestral tradition that has lived for millennium—opened. A tradition and connection to a sacred place and way of life that had been let go, that had been lost for hundreds of years, was starting to emerge. Through the simple act of learning the rituals and the ancestral names of these places, I felt I had established a new connection to the energies of the mountain. I was being enveloped.

I learned that I was to work at this time with two Kakayaris—two different mountain gods. The Kakayari that had called me required that I also place offerings and prayers with this other god. I was awestruck. I sat in dis-belief. I was being given the duty, the gift, and the task of working with these Kakayaris. The gravity of this work for the community was starting to sink in. I had been guided to a sacred place and an ancestral tradition. I was to assist in its revival and the continuance of the human role in this relationship. I was working in this land so that an ancestral way could be preserved and maintained.

The Council of Elders and the lake that they surround oversee a geographical area much larger than its own physical domain. All the elders had roles to play overseeing this and other realms. The lake is where all existence in this realm comes from and returns to. I had learned their stories and was to work with them in a manner that allowed for the renewal of a tradition and a compact that would benefit the beings in all of the realms.

After much preparation, I undertook my first task of working with them. I was to build an altar on each of the two mountains I had been instructed to work with. I was to consecrate them and "bond" with them over a three-day period. One mountain was to be worked with in the spring, the other in the fall.

I climbed the first mountain looking for the appropriate place between two peaks to build the altar. This location would be a portal where offerings would be placed to be recognized by the spirit of the mountains. The offerings are presented so that one can work with the mountain for the benefit of the community at large.

I spent a lot of time in the early afternoon of that day making sure that I was in the proper location. My confirmation of this was found in the clear blue Sierra sky, where there was one cloud, and it was over me.

After building the altar, I started to write some notes to myself, but my pen immediately stopped writing . . . was it out of ink? The next morning at sunrise, I began my fast for the ritual that I had been given so that I might work with this deity that had taken the form of the mountain. As I reread the instructions, one section leaped out at me. It said that by reading this sacred information, the "sacred talk," I had liability now.

When I read those words, I definitely felt a greater connection to what I was doing, and again I felt enveloped by the ancestral ways of the region. The liability was a responsibility and an expected exchange that is required in any relationship. The difference, though, is that the gods are a bit more exacting than most humans.

My first day on the mountain passed pleasantly; I started to fall into a rhythm with the animals, the insects, the sun, the wind, and the birds. During the second day, I was standing looking over the land when a large "head" came rushing down the mountain toward me. The immediate presence of this almost translucent being who appeared from the mountaintop stopped about fifteen or so feet away from me, floating ten feet off the ground. He had a forceful, strong, deep voice. I was fully conscious as he spoke to me. I had not been sleeping or visioning. I was standing looking up toward the volcano through the doorway of its protectors when the being arrived to speak. He was approximately eight or so feet across and ten feet high. I stood in his presence. Not having the ability to write down what was transmitted to me, I only have the recollection of the feelings and words that were presented to me.

The human role had been unfulfilled in this relationship for many years and the deity was not so much angry as disappointed that people had ignored him and the Council for so many years. He felt this negligence was harmful. He left me with the impression that he did not think much of my presence there, nor of my ability to carry my mission through. He was willing to wait and see, but he was not holding his breath.

I completed my time on the mountain and closed the ceremony. I walked back into the world knowing that I had successfully accomplished the proper ritual and that I had been recognized by the mountain, even if it was with skepticism.

The second part of my calling dictated that I go to another mountain in the fall. A few days before heading out, I was riding my bicycle near the ocean when a coyote walked up the trail I was riding on. I stopped, because the coyote chose to stay in the middle of the trail. I acknowledged it and then thanked it for being there, at which point it sat down and looked at me. After a while I thought that this had gone on long enough. I believe that I had heard all that coyote had to say. I started to walk down the trail toward the coyote, because I had to get back.

Well, the coyote stood up and started to show its teeth, basically telling me to stop. I did. He then sat down facing me, and we exchanged some more information about my upcoming trip, about my need for awareness, and about how gifts can appear as horrific events. After this exchange had taken place, after I had allowed the message from the coyote to be heard by me, he stood up and wandered down the gully and I continued my ride home.

My work with the second Kakayari in the fall began much like my encounter with the first in the spring. In preparation for undertaking a ritual to open a nierika, I had begun the requisite hike. It was a very cold night the first night out, given that I was almost nine thousand feet up in the Sierras. I went into my bivy sack very early because there was a strong wind, and clouds covered the sun.

I woke to an overcast sky as dawn was approaching. I ate and drank one last time before the start of my three-day fast, and then I got out of bed to perform the bonding ritual that would allow the nierika, the doorway, to open. Afterward I got back into my bivy to wait for the sun to reach higher in the sky and warm up my camping spot. I fell back asleep, to be awakened by pattering on my bivy. I pulled it back to see a red sky with winds blowing and snow falling. My immediate reaction was alarm, but after a bit I realized what a blessing it was to have snow fall on the altar at this time, for I had learned that snow is the anticipation of the blessing of water. It is a sign of a blessing to come.

As the sun worked its magic and the day warmed up, everything started moving very slowly. Not only was I in a slightly altered state due to my fast, the cold, and the altitude, but this place was very still, very dense, and very quiet. The denseness of the place held a palpable gratitude, a deep silent thanks.

Everything about the day had a whiteness to it—a glow. I lay in my bivy and everything seemed good. Everything seemed possible. These words, though, do not properly describe what I was feeling. I suppose you could call it bliss . . . appreciation . . . reciprocity . . . and gratitude.

I felt thanks in my body. I understood, even *was,* thanks. Thanks to everyone and everything. It was a state of being. I *was* this state of being. It was this mountain—it had permeated my being. The doorway had opened, and this mountain god had spoken to me. This god had imbued me with its being. I prayed that I would be able to retain this sense of its spirit after I had left the mountain, that it would be always present within me.

As the day progressed, the mountain god began to speak to me in a new manner. My thoughts and feelings shifted from being in that wonderful, magical state of thanks to being obsessed with a personal relationship of mine that was out of balance. I could not get it out of my mind and was thinking of the history and pain of my relationship with my parents. Then I started to think of ways to get back at them.

This mood of mine went on well into the night. No matter how long and how hard I tried to think good thoughts, such as the love and appreciation I had felt earlier in the day, I felt the opposite; I felt psychotic. All had gone cold. My life was one with no connection; it was a life with no thanks, no gratitude, and no exchange.

Then it dawned on me. This experience was being presented to me viscerally because I really needed to deal with this incredible emotional block that was holding me back. This blackness, this coldness, was the opposite of gratitude. It was the opposite of the warmth that we feel within our being when we are open and giving and connected to one another and the living world. My emotions were limiting my ability, making me incapable of offering exchange, grace, and thanks. That night, my dreams initially were ones of destruction, but by the end of the night, they were about construction. This god had brought me full circle over my three-day sojourn on the mountain.

I closed the ritual at sunrise. The mountain god had given me knowledge of a life that acknowledged the importance of gratitude and a life that did not. After one makes a request (in the spring), one needs to express gratitude (in the fall) for the gifts received in the intervening time. For relationships to be full and to fulfill the human role in the world's existence, we need to openly express our gratitude for what we have been given.

The world is grand. The spiritual realms are accessible to us when we work with the rituals and offerings that the gods have given us, and which we recognize in turn. Here I am, a human who has lived amongst these great beings for decades and sensed that there was something amazing just in front of me. But the gods did not make their presence known until I had performed the rituals that they had offered up to make themselves accessible. It is through the enactment of these rituals that humanity performs its role, contributing to the ongoing reciprocity that exists between mankind and the other realms, in order that both are sustained.

PETER BROWN lives in Olympia, Washington, under the guidance of Mt. Rainier and has an active healing practice. His spiritual path began when lightning struck a fir tree, shooting down its sixty-foot length and traveling through the ground into a young Peter. Decades later Peter understood this to be a calling as he entered the *consultorio* of the eighty-year-old Nahua weather worker, Don Lucio Campos. Peter continues his work in Mexico at the feet of his elders as well as through sacred sites in the United States. Peter is a Huichol marakame, a Nahua weather worker, an initiated Firekeeper, a lay spiritual healer inducted by the Plant Spirit Medicine Association, and a certified flower essence practitioner. He holds a bachelor's degree in sociology and a master's in community media. His website is www.peterbrownhealing.com.

34

The Awakening
of a Medicine Woman

Katherine Gomez

As I was growing up, even at a young age, I knew I was different from everyone else. I couldn't explain it, nor did I understand it. I didn't have many friends and people thought I was a little strange; I could sense their uneasiness around me. My mother had the "gift of knowing" and the "gift of healing." These gifts were something that no one in our family ever talked about. It was as though they were invisible, although I would hear my mother say over and over again, "I knew that was going to happen," or "Last night I dreamed . . . is going to happen," and sure enough, it did. I'm not entirely certain that my mother understood that these were gifts since she never talked about them as such. And because these occurrences were part of our everyday life, I considered them to be normal.

She had given birth to me when she was thirty-four, which was, in those days, considered late to have a baby. I had a very close relationship with her because I was the youngest of four; my three siblings had married before I reached my teens. Therefore, I felt like an only child. I loved listening to my mother speak about the *remedios* (remedies) she had learned from her mother and how and why they were used in our culture. I would pay attention and memorize everything she said and did as it pertained to these remedies. I was intrigued and fascinated when she spoke of old wives' tales and told stories of people who would go to curanderas (healers) for cleansing and for the healing of folk diseases such as *mal puesto* (curses), *mal ojo* (the evil eye), *envidia* (envy), *mala suerte* (bad luck), *susto* (soul loss), and *espanto* (fright), to name just a few.

After I married, I continued to share much of my time with my mother, in addition to being a mother myself as well as a busy wife who also held down a full-time job as a hospital medical transcriptionist. While I worked, my mother babysat our daughter, from the age of eighteen months until she was seven. When I was twenty-seven, my mother passed. This left a huge void in my heart, and I felt very lost in life, as though I had no identity of my own, no purpose here in this world. I set out to discover my true identity and purpose by delving into everything esoteric that I could get my hands on . . . tarot cards, crystals, numerology, astrology, and runes were some of the tools I used, hoping to find my niche.

This went on for a few years, and while everything I delved into was quite interesting, nothing seemed to jump out and grab me. One thing I began to notice during this time of trial and error was that as I transcribed patient medical reports, specifically those for cancer patients, I was beginning to determine and/or "know" what treatment plans would or wouldn't work regardless of what the doctors' orders were. I also found that I could determine approximately when the patient would die. I would routinely check back with patient records to find that I was right. I found this not only frightening, but profound. Later down the road I realized that my intuition was kicking in as preparation for moving forward into the next steps of my spiritual journey.

Then our family lost a nephew at age twenty-nine to alcoholism, which was overwhelmingly devastating to all of us. In order for my brother-in-law Joseph Winterhawk—the boy's father—to heal, he returned to his roots, to his Ute ancestry, for traditional healing. He participated in the sacred sweat lodge ceremony, and over time, he was trained to conduct them. He would invite me to participate, but being claustrophobic, I always declined. I couldn't bear the thought of being all closed up in that small structure in the dark.

After six months of persuasion, and to appease my brother-in-law, and with the promise that I could get out of the lodge at any time if need be, I finally agreed to take part. On the day of the ceremony, I was feeling a little nervous and wanting to back out so I wouldn't freak out and make a fool of myself. However, something impelled me to follow through with it.

Other people were there, some I knew, and some I didn't. We all followed my brother-in-law's guidance on what to do, how to do it, and when to do it. As I entered the sacred lodge and took my place, the doorway's flap was still open and everything was fine. Then the flap was closed and the ceremony began to unfold, and something magical and mystical began to happen. I began to feel a loving, healing presence, an energy that embraced me with a love I'd never felt before. It was *amazing*! Instead of feeling all closed in, I felt like the universe was opening up to me, as if it were welcoming me home. The prayers and songs felt incredibly sacred, and the cleansing steam felt overwhelmingly purifying. The smell of the Earth was like nothing I had ever experienced before.

Throughout the ceremony, I grew to know that this loving presence and energy that embraced all of us was our ancestors sharing their wisdom, love, and healing, which each and every one of us so desperately needed. "This is it! This is it!" my inner voice shouted. "This is what I've been searching for; this will begin my Earth-walk!" The ancestors informed that they had connected me to my true self and that I needed to research my ancestry in order to move forward to fulfill my destiny.

I am forever grateful that I was persuaded to become part of this most sacred ceremony that enlightened me, that awakened my "memories" to who I truly am and to what my true Earth-walk is.

In researching my ancestry, I discovered that I was born into the Huache tribe of Mexico and that I come from a long bloodline of healers. My inheritance of curanderismo (an ancient healing art originating with the indigenous tribes of Mexico) has always been embedded deep within my heart and my soul through this ancestral bloodline.

Since participating in the sweat lodge, I have studied, trained, and apprenticed with many elders who have taught and trained me well. I am grateful for their love, guidance, and assistance on this most sacred journey. Today, I am a ceremonialist, shaman, and teacher, accomplished in the Native American, Incan, and Mayan traditions of our ancestors. I work with my gifts of knowing and healing to serve and teach others. This is a sacred path that I will always walk with the guidance of the Creator and our ancestors.

Aho!!

KATHERINE GOMEZ, ND, was born into the Huache tribe of Mexico. She began her true spiritual journey as a healer in 1991, becoming a Reiki master and teacher. In 1994 she became a massage therapist and she has organized and taught women's healing circles since 1996. Her path has been inspired by her teacher Elder Joseph Winterhawk of the Southern Ute Tribe of Colorado, who gave her the name Walking Medicine Woman. Katherine became a naturopathic doctor, iridologist, and herbalist in 1996, which awakened an abundance of ancient memories of knowledge and wisdom. She is a graduate of the Four Winds Society. As a ceremonialist, shaman, and teacher accomplished in the Native American, Incan, and Mayan traditions, her heart's calling is the vital development of the well-being of the physical, mental, emotional, and spiritual elements for each individual.

35

Warrior Wisdom

Colleen Deatsman

Like many shamans and shamanic practitioners, I never intended or wanted to be a healer, a shamanic practitioner, a teacher, or even an author. I wanted to be a biologist of one flavor or another. I wanted to be outdoors, immersed in Nature, exploring and helping to save the precious and beautiful gifts of Mother Earth, which so many people take for granted. Mostly, I wanted to preserve the forests, explore the oceans as a steward of Jacques Cousteau's *Calypso,* and save the whales. I joined the environmental stewardship organization Greenpeace at an early age, honed my aptitude for endurance swimming, and worked hard to prepare myself for a life of hanging off whaling ships in cold, rough seas posting huge banners with "Save the Whales!" painted across them in bold red letters. Apparently, however, Spirit, and my soul, had a different plan for whom I would serve and how I would do it.

I grew up in a small rural town in Michigan where I spent nearly every waking moment outdoors, sometimes with family or friends, sometimes alone. I learned how to play, swim, climb trees, camp, fish, hunt, ski, wander the fields and forests, talk with the animals, and know Nature as a cherished friend. When foul weather, parental guidance, and other circumstances forced me indoors, I was often found avidly devouring books about the lives and spirituality of Native Americans, mountain men, and indigenous peoples of diverse ethnicities. Visions filled my thoughts and dreams. I longed to live as they did and many still do: enveloped by the land and sky, honoring the waters, in balance with the elements, reading the omens, and talking with the spirits.

Desiring to put my Nature connection to productive use, I entered college at eighteen with exuberance and big dreams of becoming the kind of physically fit, Nature-loving, activist-biologist that Greenpeace couldn't resist. All was going according to plan until I landed in class with a calculus professor from hell. No matter what I did, how hard I tried, and how many times I went in for special assistance, there was no way I was going to pass this class with her at the helm. Having taken algebra, geometry, and advanced math, I was well prepared for college math, but calculus, well, that was an animal of a different color. I didn't "get it," she couldn't/wouldn't help, she was the only professor that taught this course, and it was a requirement for a biology degree.

I was clearly at a crossroads.

That uncomfortable challenge changed the course of my education and my life, as crossroads often do.

I earned a bachelor's degree in parks and recreation administration with an emphasis in therapeutic recreation with special populations, and after working for several years, getting married, and becoming a parent, I went on to earn my master's in rehabilitation counseling and secured my licensed professional counselor accreditation.

As an adult, wife, mother of three, and weekend warrior athlete with a full-time counseling career, the endeavors and stresses of my life began to take a caustic toll on my health and well-being. My focus, time, and energies were caught up in daily living and excelling in all that I did. This created an imbalance in my soul, energy field, body, and connection with Spirit. I would not recognize or understand this imbalance until years later when a major physical breakdown demanded my attention.

For nearly ten years I fought the unidentifiable degenerative culprits that were later diagnosed as chronic fatigue immune dysfunction syndrome (CFIDS), fibromyalgia, and environmental sensitivities, the symptoms of which were a chronic sore throat, swollen lymph glands, sleeplessness, extreme fatigue, low-grade fever, a below-normal body temperature causing a frozen-to-the-core feeling, headaches, heart problems, mental confusion, muscle weakness and pain, neurological disorders, urinary tract irritation, and depression, to name just a few.

These conditions tend to cluster together in a syndrome that moves throughout the body, constantly shapeshifting in appearance and form, thereby defying diagnosis and treatment. This mysterious syndrome destroys life as it renders its host's weakened immune system susceptible to every cold and flu virus, bacteria, allergen, and environmental toxin/chemical that floats by. Every single symptom of this illness is chronic, painful, and excruciatingly debilitating. Combined collectively, this created the crippling loss of my life as I had known it. I could no longer do all of the things that I had wanted and needed to do. My active life diminished to mere survival and many days I was unable to get out of bed or function at all. I am sad to acknowledge how many days I probably wasn't very present with my clients and family, and how many other days I could only crawl downstairs like a crab to the phone to reschedule appointments.

Disheartening as that was, it was amplified by the fact that these symptoms were completely foreign to me. In my youth, prior to the illness, I had been full of energy and enthusiasm for life. I had a fulfilling counseling career, ran marathons (26.2 miles), and bicycled many centuries (100 miles). I did intensive speed-work training runs and competed in 5K running races, often winning awards in my age group. I was an involved and engaged mother of three children, all very active in sports and extracurricular activities. There were very few weeknights or weekends that weren't spent at an event of theirs.

When this monster illness began sucking away my active life, I thought at first that it was just the flu or a cold, something that would go away. But it didn't. Instead, the symptoms lingered and worsened with each passing year. My spirit and passion for life began to evaporate as I struggled. Sadly, I lost more and more of myself and my energy to live, to the point of contemplating, and nearly attempting, suicide.

Back in the late 1980s the medical community didn't have a diagnosis, understanding, or clue about what was happening to people presenting with these symptoms. Without a diagnosis or understanding, there was no sound treatment or potential cure available, and there were no prospects on the horizon. Chronic pain plus chronic fatigue plus chronic flu-like symptoms plus no help equals deep frustration.

Finally, in the mid-1990s when my blood tests came back positive for Epstein-Barr and cytomegalo viruses, I was finally also given the diagnoses of CFIDS, fibromyalgia, and environmental sensitivities. This was good news and bad news, as my empathetic Dr. Chebli explained: "We have a diagnosis, but we have no known effective medical treatments for these viruses." I was advised to go home and rest.

I went nuts inside! Was he crazy?! I refused to live my life as a victim of these illnesses. I decided to live.

Another crossroads.

As the warrior in me came alive, I began looking for witch doctors and healing alternatives. I tried every practitioner, herb, supplement, and technique I could find that claimed to boost the immune system. This included echinacea, blue-green algae, pycnogenols, massage, acupuncture, chiropractic, and energy bodywork, to name a few. All of these helped me to function, but they didn't cure the beastly illness.

Something was missing—something deeper.

As if on cue, once this realization occurred, it happened. By a twist of fate, a door opened—a door I had to walk through. Former coworkers of mine put the word out that they were hosting a basic shamanism weekend workshop taught by Myron Eshowsky through the Foundation for Shamanic Studies. This workshop was described as being an experiential introduction to shamanism, shamanic drumming, and the shamanic journey.

My mouth fell open as I read the flyer. Shamanism—the spirituality of the many peoples I had read so much about for many years—was being offered right here, just twenty minutes from my home!

A powerful urge to attend welled up from within, yet logic brought the whole thing into question. I wasn't sure what to do. At the time, making the commitment to attend meant that the money could quite possibly be misspent if the syndrome flared and prevented my attendance. In the end, however, I couldn't shake the inner knowing that attending the workshop might be the way to connect with the healing and spiritual life I had so desperately craved. I signed up, and four weeks later, with sore throat, swollen glands, fatigue, and chills, I forced myself out the door.

Another road crossed.

Though I had never experienced anything like this workshop before, it felt oddly familiar to be sitting on the floor in a circle with a room full of strangers. The facilitator was humble and gracious, and I couldn't help but sense that I was in the right place. I didn't know why; I just knew it was okay, perhaps important, to be there.

I was excited and nervous; would I be able to journey? The answer came as soon as the drumming began. I didn't go anywhere. I lay there for quite some time on my fleece blanket, on that hard floor, enthralled with the drumming. That drumming. Wow! It was nothing short of amazing. The beat entered me and I began to move my feet to its rhythm.

The next thing I knew I was dancing around a fire wearing wings. I flew into a nearby swamp and slid down an algae slide. Sliding down further, and further, and further, I let go of the fear and tried to enjoy the ride. I slid down into the Earth and felt her protection and nurturance blanket me in warmth.

Moments later I emerged at the surface of a clear mountain lake; the wings were gone. I swam out and sat quietly at the lake's edge, relaxing in the sun. The nearby willows rustled, and out stepped a huge, powerful moose that spoke to me telepathically. What had begun as a comforting, warm reception from Moose unexpectedly shifted into an important lesson. He described in detail specific ways and situations in which I was wandering from my soul passion and participating in activities that were distracting me from more important endeavors. He shared that the causes of my physical challenges were separation from Spirit, my soul-self, and energy mismanagement. The syndrome and its cluster of symptoms was a physical manifestation of power loss. It was my wake-up call to heal myself with Spirit energy, and then step forward to help others do the same. In other words, I was being called to task in a compassionate way to get back on track with the vision of my soul.

I was amazed, yet I knew all of this to be true. I felt humbled and grateful—and empowered to make changes. I expressed my regrets and my desire to connect with Spirit and my soul work. He nodded and suggested that I make shifts from being too busy "doing" to taking more time for "being"—walking in Nature, drumming and journeying daily, and honing my sense of perception, awareness, and connectedness in everyday life. Then we just "were" together, quietly sharing an essence of vibrantly colored, wavy-fine mist that floated back and forth between us.

The eerie call of a loon, followed by various screeches, hoots, squawks, and tweets, floated in and out, causing the colored waves to flow and undulate. Hundreds of spirit shamans dressed in regalia from all around the world entered the room, drumming their healing and sharing the power of the spirit worlds. The whole room vibrated so loudly and so strongly that it seemed as if the roof would blow off at any moment! The penetrating vibrations pounded my body, heart, and soul until I could no longer stand it. I silently screamed out and at the same time felt myself crack open down the middle, letting out the pain I had been holding, allowing the vibrantly colored waves to flow in and soothe me. My heart ached from expanding so much. I reached up and rubbed that area on my physical body. I was all at once aware that my previously frozen body was warm from the inside out and that each of its wounded cells felt nurtured and loved. I was full of a powerful energy that was exquisite beyond words.

When the drumming changed, I was unable to return to consensus reality when the callback signal came. I had connected with my power animal, an incredible source of energy and personal power that had been missing since my childhood. I was very still and patient in my journey, something I had not been at that time in ordinary reality. I felt at home and connected, which was also something I did not feel in ordinary reality in those days. For the first time in many years, I was in a place where I belonged. I was so full of life and energy that I was shaking uncontrollably on the floor in the workshop room. Gradually, ordinary consciousness seeped in and I felt a deep quiet. I heard soft crying and realized it was coming from me. I had found my home. I had found my healing power. I had found my soul. I had found my connection to the All.

I gathered myself together and crawled back to my space in the circle, noticing several others doing the same. I blinked my eyes over and over again trying to focus; the world looked very different somehow, even though nothing had physically changed in the workshop room.

And then it hit me—the lightbulb lit up. An understanding seeped into my consciousness that my body was changing right then and there. I was healing. Wow, I was healing! What a miracle that was!

My head was swirling as it all came rushing in. Realization after realization that Spirit had just gifted me with the tools and energy to heal, to be whole once again, and the methods to help others do the same flooded in. *Wow!* I screamed inside with joy and amazement. *I am alive with soul purpose!* A big smile ran across my face as this really sunk in. This was big—very big!

That evening, upon returning home, I was not ill or fatigued. I was super-energized. I enthusiastically shared the learnings, my insights, and excitement with my husband, and then I went out for an exhilarating five-mile run. "I have been given the gift of a second life!" I joyfully squealed as I ran through the woods on that cold day in March over fifteen years ago.

And this has been the case since connecting with the power sources of the spirit worlds. The illnesses are gone. The pain is gone. The fatigue is extinct. The depression has lifted. My immune system is strong and vital. My life is full and rich with dynamic health, physical fitness, and the blessing of the call to assist others on their journey to healing and wholeness. My heart is full of gratitude.

Thank you, helping spirits!

Today a new sun rises for me; everything lives, everything is animated, everything seems to speak to me of my passion, everything invites me to cherish it.

NINON DE L'ENCLOS (1620–1705)

COLLEEN DEATSMAN is the author of *The Hollow Bone: A Field Guide to Shamanism, Seeing in the Dark: Claim Your Own Shamanic Power Now and in the Coming Age, Energy for Life: Connect with the Source, Inner Power: Six Techniques for Increased Energy and Self-Healing, Journey to Wholeness: Personal Healing through Spirit and Soul-Self Connection,* and numerous online and magazine articles. She holds a master's degree in rehabilitation counseling and is a licensed professional counselor, certified hypnotherapist, shamanic practitioner, energy movement healer, Reiki master, and certified alternative healing consultant. Colleen is also an expert by personal experience, having healed herself with spirit connection and energy movement from chronic fatigue immune dysfunction syndrome (CFIDS), fibromyalgia, and environmental sensitivities. Her website is www.colleendeatsman.com.

36

Spirit Chases Me

Randall Sexton

My first ayahuasca ceremony was winding down when a small black bug-eyed troll jumped into my body. I wasn't afraid, just curious; I was noticing what was happening. At first I thought the troll had come from the Ethiopian guy one mat over, and that he had jumped into me to escape the shamans who were working on him.

After noticing I had a visitor in my body, I also realized I was paralyzed. Completely paralyzed. I was lying on my right side and whenever someone would come near I would try to wiggle my eyebrows to get them to notice my predicament. I lay in this state for what seemed like an hour when I remembered that the shaman had told us, prior to the ceremony, that we could blow spirits out of ourselves. Gathering a large breath, I blew, and sure enough the troll disappeared and I could move again!

I spent a few weeks processing this experience and finally realized that none of my demons came from outside of me, but that I was the source of all my demons.

I never planned on lying in a hut in the Amazon, and especially purging at both ends!

My health care career had begun relatively normally. I had gradually worked my way up from a nurse's aide to a registered nurse. However, my life was to start changing in ways I didn't understand. And it all started on a Sunday afternoon, not in the jungle, but in a modern emergency room.

I barely caught a glimpse of a blue-and-white polka dot dress and a white hat as the medics entered the triage room in the emergency department. Things were busy for a Sunday afternoon and thankfully the lady on the stretcher didn't seem to be in critical shape.

Walking quickly into the room, I glanced down at the bed to see an elderly African American female wearing her Sunday finery and clutching her purse to her chest. When I asked her what was wrong, she listed multiple somatic complaints and then added that her pastor had "tossed the bones and put a spell on me."

In that instant, I "heard" what I should do. I told her that I could help her by putting a barrier around her that would protect her from the pastor's spell. The blood-pressure cuff had already been placed on her left arm, so I pumped it up until I saw her wince and then quickly dropped the pressure. I did the same to all extremities, told her she was now safe, and left as a physician entered the room.

That occurred almost forty years ago and was the first inkling of what my path was to be, although I had no idea what I'd just done. Years later, it became clearer when a massage therapist friend gave me a book titled *So You Want to Be a Shaman*. I never really paid much attention to the book, perhaps because my friend had told me about spirit guides that appeared whenever she was working with a client. My mind just couldn't quite wrap itself around her stories; however, the book never seemed to leave me alone.

I gradually began to realize that something was missing in my nursing practice and in the health care field in general. Earning a master's degree in psychiatric nursing did little to ease my dissatisfaction, so I enrolled in a school of Oriental medicine.

It turns out that Chinese medicine is a very complex and theoretical form of medicine that views the body not as a machine, but as a garden to be cultivated. At this same time I was also learning a form of Asian body therapy, Zen shiatsu, which I began to use in my practice. Many clients came to me to give it a try, after having failed to get results from other types of treatment. I had great success using this modality with them and quickly fell in love with this healing protocol.

Another event was to make me question the rigid scientific viewpoint that I held. I received a phone call from my brother telling me that our father had suffered a cardiac arrest in his physician's office. Because I was six hours away, I phoned the physician to learn that my dad had been telling jokes with the physician before having his pulse taken by the good doctor. It was twenty-eight beats per minute. "I started running around trying to get an external pacemaker set up when your dad arrested," the doctor told me had told my brother. "We got him back and across the street to the hospital where he arrested again. Once more we revived him and he's on his way to a medical center by helicopter."

After a week in CCU, my dad went home with a pacemaker. I happened to remark that he was lucky he'd had a doctor's appointment that day, or he probably would not have survived. He informed me that he'd had no intention of visiting his doctor that day, but he was on the way to the grocery store when three guys got into his pickup truck and forced him to go to the doctor's office.

"Who were they?" I asked.

"I don't know," he replied. "I couldn't make out their faces."

He was correct; he didn't have a doctor's appointment that day.

A few more years went by and while in a bookstore in Hawaii I noticed a book called *Shaman, Healer, Sage* by the medical anthropologist and psychologist Alberto Villoldo. I couldn't resist any longer—I took the plunge and enrolled in Alberto's Four Winds Society, the renowned energy medicine school.

At Alberto's school, there were quite a few physicians, as well as psychologists and nurses. They were all searching for what Western medicine was lacking . . . a soul. One physician, who also held a doctorate in cellular biology, told me that he was frustrated with the lack of progress in his patients. Well, we saw some dramatic progress during our training! One psychologist exclaimed, "Talk therapy will be so boring now!"

Part of our core training in shamanism involved training in each of the four directions, and before I left for Utah, for the session involving the West, a psychic client of mine in India told me that she could see me partway up a mountain, in a hut on stilts. She added that I would get a "message from the West." When I arrived in Utah, I discovered that the condo (hut) where I was to stay was indeed partway up the side of a mountain and the pilings under me in the parking garage certainly resembled stilts.

I thought I had received the intended message after a pretty intense session near the end of the West session. However, the next day at noon, after class was over, I went shopping in downtown Park City. I walked into a shop and the lady behind the counter said she was expecting me. Turns out she was a shaman from Peru!

We talked for a short time and she performed some energy work on me and told me things not only about me, but also about my son and wife. She gave me a meteorite from Machu Picchu, which now lives in my mesa (prayer bundle/altar). She finished by teaching me a healing exercise and clearing up a lot of "trash" that I had been hanging on to.

I currently work as a psychiatric nurse practitioner at Fort Riley, Kansas, treating soldiers of the First Infantry Division. In my position, I struggle to combine Western psychiatric medicine with what I've learned and experienced of shamanism. This can be difficult at times, especially because there are official guidelines I must follow.

However, my last ayahuasca ceremony helped me develop my practice. During the ceremony the side of a jaguar appeared directly in front of my face. I went inside him, but I was afraid and came back out. He appeared again and I stepped inside him again. My body boundaries completely dissolved and for a brief moment I was afraid. Then I saw through the eyes of the jaguar that I was one with everything . . . the trees, water, sky, plants, and Earth. There was no *me,* separate from Nature. I also realized that in order to help others heal, I had to step inside of their experiences.

Stepping inside of others is what I do, no matter how much time I have per session with them. I quickly track what is happening and ask my guides for an appropriate intervention. I also try to "modify" an intervention so that it might appear more appropriate for this modern world. I am grateful for what I have learned from the spirit world. I'm also grateful to all my shamanic buddies (whether they are health care professionals or not), who have taught me to experience outside of the scientific box I was trapped in. It is now my hope that I can have some impact with the military by making them understand that soldiers do not have to continue to suffer, and that "evidence-based medicine" has a challenger, who would be me.

RANDALL (RANDY) SEXTON is a psychiatric nurse practitioner serving active-duty soldiers at Fort Riley, Kansas. He is a graduate of the Four Winds Society and is inspired by the soldiers he treats. Randy has participated in ceremonies by the Q'ero in the mountains of Peru and with the Shipibo medicine people in the Amazon jungle. Randy has studied Chinese medicine philosophy and the Japanese art of Zen Shiatsu. He holds black belts in the martial arts of hapkido and tae kwon do and is a t'ai chi practitioner who teaches t'ai chi to soldiers for psychological health. Randy holds master's degrees in psychiatric nursing and business administration as well as a post-master's certificate as a psychiatric nurse practitioner. He is comfortable walking in both the scientific and spirit world.

37

Shamanic Impact

Niramisa Weiss

I got sick, really sick, around twelve years ago, the same time I started to practice yoga regularly. Normal life became impossible and the future, if I had one, was uncertain. However, the fear of annihilation propelled me into survival mode. I was going to save myself, no matter what. I found myself regularly on my knees, in private, praying for help to whatever god might be listening.

And help came.

Fortuitously, I found myself in a quiet space for a long period where I was unaffected by the moods of others and I started to dream. In dreaming, all manner of spirit beings visited me. I wrestled with an angel and overcame it. On waking each morning, I felt unseen hands stroke my hair and a strong sense of unconditional love and care for me permeated my soul. I began to feel invulnerable. God really loved me and He would never let me down.

I had fasted and detoxed repeatedly and the sickness was subsiding, but I remained unwell. Then, from the shadows of the past, came the sickening realization that there had been a period of my life that had been really, *really* bad. I tried to remember what had happened, but I only ever got so far before I came up against nothing. I knew that going beyond was the key to everything. I pronounced my intention to the Universe that I was finally ready to heal.

And then the *lwa* came—ancestral archetypal spirits hailing from a tradition legions away from my own. From the depths of Great Spirit they brought me gifts, tangible material objects that appeared randomly in odd places, and through them the lwa introduced themselves. The darkest, most fearful of the Haitian gods walked alongside me through my healing journey and I knew that nothing, *nothing,* could hurt me with these giants of Spirit guiding me.

I knew so much about the lwa that I hadn't been told. And I remembered having had knowledge about them when I was a child too. I knew each one's special day and special color and what energies each of them represented. Everything about them made sense, as if I had known it forever.

The lwa held my hand through ayahuasca ceremonies in Peru, shamanic healing rituals in Glastonbury, and Buddhist meditations in Spain. Eventually they led me to a group who were practicing Gabonese Bwiti ceremonies with iboga bark in southern France. During the iboga ceremony I remembered. While the drums roared and the harps twanged, picking at my soul parts, the people danced frenetically and I returned to the point in my memories where there had always been a blank. Instead I saw an eerie gray mist around the scene. The lwa led me along the path I had walked long ago and I saw what an innocent sixteen-year-old girl, who thought she was much older, had been subjected to—a horror so intense that the only sensible thing to have done at the time was to bury it. I saw her unconscious awareness that nobody who loved her could help her, and even if they could, they would choose to abandon her instead; they were also incapable of withstanding such a journey. If she was going to survive, she had to forget.

All this I remembered.

And the lwa stayed with me, stroked my hair, told me I was safe, and terrified those with dark intentions and those too stupid to understand the power of the magic.

And I did my healing.

I only see light and love coming from the lwa and the Vodou practice. The fear around this Haitian religion and those similar to it comes from faulty human judgment. The practice, the lwa, the ceremonies, the beliefs—they are all founded on the Light, there is no doubt in my heart about that.

Later the lwa reminded me I had known them in a previous life as well and that I had served them well. Over two centuries ago, during one of the most shameful acts of inhumanity, I was kidnapped and taken from Dahomey, West Africa. There, I had been the daughter of a king and knew the respect and love of my people. The iron ring around my neck I wore on the boat burns me to this day. What else to do but cry for help from the spirits of our motherland? In Haiti, in captivity, we served the lwa as best we could and with only Spirit as ammunition we brothers and sisters sharing no common tongue overcame the French with their warships, guns, and cannons. Even so, our freedom came at great cost and the repercussions persist to this day.

It has been many years since the Bwiti ceremony in southern France where I uncovered hidden sickening memories. Remembering what had happened to me when I was sixteen failed to bring me the instant relief I had been expecting. I went to the police and gave a statement. I would stand up in court if necessary, except the memory is getting foggy again.

After remembering a great fury burned inside me, a rage so intense I pushed it into addictive behaviors and depression. I found myself regularly on my knees again. And then Elder Brother came, quietly and with no magic or fearful histories. He leads me along my path through life now. And he has taught me how to forgive, how to bless, and how to see that the only reasonable response to any of these experiences is an indescribable gratitude to Great Spirit. He is teaching me how to love. And this goes on.

Elder Brother tells me to remain with my shamanic brethren, to connect with them often, and to practice the way of respect for all living things. He teaches me the true yoga and introduced me to Patanjali. He shows me the heaven in Hinduism and Judaism and the interconnectedness of all our spiritual belief systems. He gave me

Nandi as a pal. And the Shekinah, Holy Mother Mary, speaks to me constantly.

Whenever the regular world threatens to take hold again, I'm reminded to remember who I really am. And this I will *never* forget.

NIRAMISA WEISS is currently writing books at Elder Brother's request. She has written two nonfiction books that explain one of the cornerstones of his teachings, *The Liar* and *Forgiving the Unforgivable*. She is also writing fiction under the pseudonym Margaret Murphy. Her novel *Life without the Liar* is a many-lives romance based on her own healing journey. Her second novel, *Antichrist: The Exorcism to End All Exorcisms,* will be available summer 2015. The lwa feature heavily in her novels. Niramisa has a doctorate in computer science. She is a qualified yoga teacher but prefers jnana and bhakti to asana. She has recently started playing the piano again, something she never had the confidence for in the past. The journey continues. Her website is www.niramisaweiss.com.

38

Pine Spirit Medicine

Rita Baruss

"Hi, Rita!" a bright child's voice called out. I released the thought-bubble I was in and glanced around, momentarily disoriented. It had been years since a small child had called out to me. Indeed, as I looked around I didn't *see* any small children, and the reality of where I was, in a new neighborhood where nobody knew me by name, came into focus. However, directly in my line of vision, as if illuminated by a spotlight and standing out from their surroundings, were several pine trees grinning and waving their branches at me.

Seeing them, I realized that it was Pine Spirit that had spoken in my mind in the clear voice of a small child.

I had been communicating consciously with spirit worlds for a number of years, through shamanic practices taught to me during two brief seminars I attended that were presented by teachers organized by the Foundation for Shamanic Studies at different locations all over North America, to introduce Michael Harner's core shamanism practices to as many people as were interested. In so doing, I had met many animal, human, and angelic guides. However, there had been nothing in any of my training and experiences that had ever suggested engagement with plant consciousness.

While I had been doing occasional journeying with local groups that met for this purpose, my Earth-walk marriage had gone through a divorce, as a result of which my children remained willingly living in their familiar home with their father, who could support them in the lifestyle they were used to. I moved out to live on my own, which left me with time on my hands. I quickly realized that the place in which I felt the most comfortable was my gardens, and the people I felt most comfortable with were those who were interested in plants. Thus it was that I came to be engaged with the Herbalist Association of Nova Scotia, which hosts an annual herb fair. One of the herbalists, who knew of my involvement with spirit worlds, asked me to do a presentation on Plant Spirit Medicine at the next herb fair. It was as a result of this request that I did the shamanic journey that would change my perception of reality and, subsequently, the course of my Earth-walk life.

Having had no previous contact with plant spirits, I underwent a shamanic journey to my familiar guides to ask them to connect me with a plant spirit.

They introduced me to Pine Spirit. Pine Spirit came into my mind as an illuminated pine branch and into my perception as a delightful, gracious, loving energy. When I asked how I was to start to learn about Plant Spirit Medicine, Pine told me to go out and introduce myself to all of the real pine trees in my neighbourhood.

Thus it was that, after my journey, I put on my windbreaker and my walking shoes and, feeling only slightly ridiculous, I rehearsed the following greeting in my mind: *Hello Pine, my name is Rita, how are you?* I had no idea what to expect to hear back. Indeed, I didn't really expect anything except for a good walk—it all seemed harmless enough.

Well, it turned out to be an eye-opening and hilariously entertaining walk. First of all, I had never noticed how many pines were in my neighborhood. "Hello Pine, my name is Rita, you are beautiful," I said to a vibrant young tree that I passed. I then became aware of a strange, sultry voice, speaking in a Southern drawl. It made some sassy comment in my mind, something I never would have thought of on my own, and it was so funny that I burst out laughing.

Before me, as I continued my walk, there was another pine to greet, and then another. After each greeting, there was a comment in some sort of unusual voice that was not a part of my normal thinking processes at all. Yet I recognized the voices as something I would have heard in a movie or a restaurant while traveling; they were vaguely familiar to me from experiences long past. In other words, they were part of my memory bank, but not part of my current daily thinking.

In this way, Pine made sure that I was not confusing its speech with my own mind, so I would have no doubts that it was indeed Pine Spirit communicating with me. When I commented on this, Pine said, *Well, if I spoke Greek to you, you would not understand a word of what I said, so I can only use what is in your own mind already. Aren't you glad now that you have done so much reading? It has given me such a rich memory bank to draw on.*

After that walk, I became very conscious of pines and I saw them everywhere, as if illuminated by spotlights and standing out from their surroundings. I continued to greet them. Moreover, if I was lost in my own thoughts walking by them, they would call out to me.

Meanwhile, I was learning to recognize the presence and voice of Pine Spirit. Whenever I was ready for listening and learning, all I had to do was to picture the illuminated pine branch in my mind and ask for a lesson. Often I did this while I was outside walking.

For the first two weeks or so, Pine not only informed me in words but also showed in pictures, like brief little film clips, how it is that plants make oxygen for us to breathe. Pine showed me lush rain forests and told me how, in the wintertime when our plants are dormant in Canada, we still have a rich supply of oxygen. This is because air currents from the rain forests distribute the oxygen from the rain forest around the planet. This oxygen not only works on the physical body by animating and energizing our cells, but emotionally it is calming and relaxing, mentally it is stimulating, and spiritually it is the carrier of consciousness.

It took me about two weeks to fully absorb and integrate this information. I had been a yoga instructor for over twenty years, teaching people how to breathe consciously and how to use the breath to release tension and energize the body. I had been reciting the benefits of conscious breathing, telling people that it enhances immune cell counts, lowers cholesterol levels, balances hormonal functioning, soothes the nervous system, lowers anxiety levels, and so on without ever wondering or questioning how this was so. I would point out all of the breath-based therapies that were thriving everywhere and detail how basic meditation practice involves watching the breath and becoming aware of the breathing process. I myself used the connection to breath as a focusing technique for activating my psychic awareness.

Well, Pine allowed me to take my own sweet time in realizing that this is Plant Spirit Medicine at its most basic because all anyone has to do to benefit from this medicine is to breathe consciously.

When I finally had my aha! moment, putting two and two together, being awed at the amazing beauty and gift of it all, there in the street, in front of my feet, was a good-sized pine branch.

I instinctively recognized it for what it was and bent down to collect my good-job award even as my practical brain started to look for reasons that this pine branch was on the road. I do a lot of walking, and I am generally quite aware of where I am stepping, given that doggie doo and broken glass are not uncommon city street findings. However, I couldn't remember ever being aware of a substantial pine branch at my feet in the streets of this well-maintained town.

Seeking to find a rational explanation for the branch, I looked around for the pine tree that it must have blown off of in the prior night's wind, but there were no pine trees in any of the surrounding yards. Finally I spotted some pine branches just barely reaching over the roof of a house about two blocks up the road, but even that was a stretch. Thus, I had to accept that it was Pine Spirit who had organized that branch to manifest at exactly that place at exactly the time I got the lesson it was presenting to me.

My conversations with Pine Spirit continued. The next thing that Pine showed me was how plant spirits choose their people. In a visual presentation, Pine showed me pictures of my life, starting from early childhood. Plant spirits were present and actively engaged with my consciousness and energy fields. I was shown how I had been drawn to places where plants abounded, how I felt balanced and energized and re-instated in universal love, comforted, awed, and brought to my favorite sense of myself by the plant beings.

I was awed and amazed and I asked why the plant beings helped people as much as they did. Pine told me that the plant spirits were try-ing to cultivate friendships with humans because they need our under-standing and engagement in order to be able to evolve and realize *their* highest potential, just as we need them for our mere survival, never mind our highest potential.

Thus it was that I came to the realization that doing one of my favorite things, which is hanging out with plants, is a valid, nay, even necessary activity for the survival of the human race.

Over the following months, my conversations with Pine contin-ued. We talked about many things of mutual interest to us. Pine was a truly gracious, accessible, and outgoing spirit, a teacher and a wonderful introduction to Plant Spirit Medicine.

It has been a number of years now since the journey where I was intro-duced to Pine Spirit. During these years, plant spirits of many different plant species have become my most frequent shamanic guides. I have moved out into the country to live with a wonderful plant medicine man whom I met as a result of that first seminar I presented. I have found a job as a gardener with a small company doing restorative land-scaping; it is appropriately named Helping Nature Heal. And I am pas-sionately engaged with the caretaking of the soil and plants of the land I live on while trying to perceive and understand plant consciousness so that I may be able to communicate some of the ineffable marvel of it to my fellow human beings.

Rita Baruss was born in Leeds, England, to Latvian parents who had been driven out of the country of their birth by WWII. Rita emigrated along with her parents and siblings to Canada. Rita grew up in Toronto, Ontario, and after completing a year of studies at Trent University in Peterborough, Ontario, Rita traveled in Canada, the United States, and Mexico. Rita has worked as a seamstress, security guard, child care provider, writer, artist, baker, cook, gardener, yoga instructor, energy healer, and shamanic practitioner. She is the author of two published children's stories, a poetry book, and many self-published short stories. Rita is currently living in Laurilay, Nova Scotia, with a wonderful plant medicine man, working part time as a gardener, instructing yoga classes, and engaging with the people and circumstances that her life is presenting to her with as much spirit presence as possible.

39

Communal Song and the Art of Healing

Elizabeth Cosmos

Alberto Costas Aguas was born a brilliant healer. This was his gift and his mission in life, during which time he met the Guaraní, a people indigenous to the Amazon. Through knowledge passed down from their oral tradition, they knew he was coming. They entrusted to him sacred wisdom for healing with love and beseeched him to share their sacred teachings with the world. The teaching that they shared with him he called Ama-Deus, which is Latin for "to love God."

I met Alberto and learned the Ama-Deus healing method when he was ailing. I did this in order to carry on his mission after his death—to teach, preserve, and spread the message of Ama-Deus to the world. In my personal practice and my teaching, many times the beauty and power of this healing method were demonstrated. However, when I was unexpectedly visiting a Guaraní village, I directly experienced the profound force of love in the same way that Alberto did. A definite shift occurred in my heart-center, expanding my consciousness to what I understand to be heart intelligence.

I had planned to return to Brazil to further my investigation into Alberto's personal background and to make a third visit with the

Guaraní in order to purchase some of their crafts. In anticipation of returning to the village, throughout the year clothing had been collected, which would be distributed among the village's children. Upon returning to the village, the clothes and gifts for the *cacique* Tata Ti were dispersed through several hours of pleasantries, which produced a constant influx of people from the village.

When the formal etiquette and gift-giving were complete, Tata Ti had a large smile on his face and he repeated the word *aguyje,* which means "thank you" in Guaraní. In response, I told him, "Tere guahe porâite," meaning, "You are welcome."

I searched the small crowd for the women who made and sold the crafts. They were normally out near the informal gathering, waiting for their turn to interact. I looked to my good friend and interpreter, Teodoro, with a question on my face.

"Teo! Where are the women with their crafts?" Teodoro gestured for me to go further into the village. "Are you coming with me?" I asked.

"They say it is okay for you to go to them. I will be there in a moment," he replied. With apprehension, I moved into the interior of the village in search of the women with their crafts. The prospect of moving deeper into the village unescorted was new and I felt a little unsettled, but soon I felt lightness and an ease of acceptance as I walked further into the group of thatched houses. Stepping up a small hill and spotting the women with their shawls spread out on the ground, I wondered how they had known that I was coming to this specific spot. I hadn't seen anyone run ahead to announce my arrival.

They smiled and gestured for me to come closer to look at their work. I sat on the ground with the women, and they talked with me and presented their crafts. The women with their infants wrapped on their bodies returned to nursing or playing with their babies as my eyes and hands sifted through and selected from all the wonderful, colorful handiwork of carved wooden animals, woven baskets, beautiful feathered earrings, and intricate beaded necklaces and bracelets. Teodoro eventually joined me to help me choose from the many items and translate the transaction.

Darkness descended quickly and we fumbled around in the semi-twilight, paying the women and helping them to pack up their things. The women quietly slipped away in the darkness. As Teodoro and I turned from the now empty space, I had no idea how to find our way back. Teodoro extended his hand and we carefully began to navigate our way through the thatched houses. A young man approached and exchanged words with Teodoro, who then turned and shrugged his shoulders, saying, "He wants us to follow him."

I was grateful that someone had appeared to guide us. We descended the slope carefully in the dark, and I realized that we were passing near a large thatched dwelling. As we rounded the corner of the structure, the young man gestured for us to enter it. I held my breath as we passed through a small door and entered a large room that I knew instantly to be the Opy, the house of prayer. Neither Teodoro nor I spoke; we only looked at each other in amazement. I had no idea of the reason for this occurrence or what was going to happen next.

I was very touched to be there, to be included and accepted into this gathering.

The Guaraní hold the Opy to be sacred and usually outsiders are not allowed inside. My heart was pounding as I quickly scanned the dimly lit space. My eyes adjusted to the candlelight, and Teodoro and I followed the gesture from our escort to sit. The interior room had simple, low wooden benches along two sides and an altar opposite the entrance. It was about five feet high and composed of a narrow board set on two posts. On the altar were candles, rattles, and other musical instruments—including ones I had witnessed earlier, which had been played during our welcoming visit.

We moved silently to the far corner near the altar and sat on the low bench. I quietly set my bundle of crafts at my feet. A young boy who seemed to be around ten was smoking a pipe and praying while he circled the circumference of the room and passed in front of the altar and each person sitting on the benches. We both fixed our eyes on him so as to understand the meaning of his intentions.

As this was happening, the Opy was filling up with children and adults who positioned themselves on the small benches on either side. One man picked an instrument from the altar and sat opposite us. He began singing softly while playing.

The young boy made several full circles around the inside while chanting and smoking the pipe, passing close by all who were seated. Each time he passed the altar, he directed a forceful stream of air on each item on the altar and also on the larger musical instruments, the *takuá* (which looked and sounded like rain barrels) that lay propped below the altar. This boy was performing a preparatory cleansing ceremony. Soon after, everyone gathered and the door was locked from the inside.

The chanting youth then commenced the ceremony, beginning at the opposite side from where we sat. He inhaled from his pipe, then directed a forced breath directly on the top of each person's head at the fontanel spot of the cranium. The benches were low, which allowed the young boy to easily perform his cleansing movement on everyone—even on my friend who was of taller height.

Many of the gathered children were lined up facing the altar. The boys standing closest to it began to sing; some used rattles, the *mbaraká*. The girls lined up behind the boys and used the takuá by rhythmically pounding them on the ground in sync with the singing. The girls answered loudly to what the boys sang out, and both boys and girls moved their feet in specific ways and differently to different songs.

Cacique Tata Ti placed a jar of water with tobacco leaves on the altar and then returned to the end of our bench and began smoking a pipe near the door with another elder. As the children sang he smoked and prayed.

At one point during the singing, a young boy not more than five years old entered and looked for a place to sit. The only available space was a very small opening between me and another adolescent. This young child did not hesitate to squeeze himself in next to me. I expected him to feel a sense of repulsion when our skin touched, much like experiences with children at home when they had no choice but to sit by an unknown adult, but this child exuded no feeling of strangeness. This experience was so endearing. The feeling in my heart grew large and warm.

This heart feeling was a combination of being allowed to participate in this ceremony, the comfort of the child sitting next to me, and the accepting nature of all the people inside the room.

At this point, I ceased being an observer. Closing my eyes and listening to the children sing, feeling the pounding takuás and the shaking rattles, unified my senses.

The sound of the rattles was explosive in the house of prayer and the accompanying loud singing began to quiet my mind. The takuás were pounding out a reverberation that not only was projected onto my physical body, but also was coursing through my legs via my bare feet on the dirt floor. As I was first registering these physical experiences, it was as if the collective sounds swayed my body in a rhythm with the music. I let go and felt myself surrender into this swaying, feeling a release of tension in my body as I did so.

Recognizing familiar words such as "Ñande Ru" in the song, I joined in, chanting in a loud voice with the girls. Very quickly I felt in harmony with the group. Our collective intention of appealing to a higher power was all too evident and we easily slipped into a strong feeling of praise and gratitude for life.

At some point during this devotional singing, which lasted for more than an hour, I became aware of a pulsating, loving presence expanding my heart-center. There seemed to be no separation, and the feeling of oneness permeated the Opy. The group called out to God—Ñande Ru—with great yearning, asking Him to hear our prayers, and, blissfully intoxicated, I felt myself floating beyond the boundaries of my body.

After this expansive feeling I was brought back to my physical body as Teodoro moved from his spot. Without breaking from the singing I quickly scanned the room, locating him with the cacique at the end of the bench by the door.

Cacique Tata Ti was praying over Teodoro's head, holding a jar of water and tobacco leaves. He dipped the tobacco leaves into the water and touched specific areas of Teodoro's body, particularly around the head and the back of the neck. He repeated touching these places while he prayed. Feeling peace and happiness for my friend, my heavy eyes closed easily, and I slipped effortlessly back into the rhythmic singing.

In a moment, however, the singing abruptly stopped, and Teodoro returned to his spot. Resting in silence, we watched as the instruments were placed on the altar and everyone silently cleared out of the Opy. The last to leave, we stepped out in a daze and found ourselves alone, amazed, and entranced. We stood in the light of a full moon in a cloudless sky.

The canopy of trees in moonlight silhouetted my friend as I looked around and spoke in quiet reverence, my first words since entering the Opy. "I feel overwhelmed with joy. I have no words, I just feel so wonderful. My heart feels like it will burst, and I'm so humbled with the sharing of these loving people."

Dreamily, Teodoro responded, "Hmm, yes, it was so wonderful."

Looking around, I saw there was no one in sight. "Where did everyone go?" I wondered aloud.

"I don't know, but we now have the moon to help us out of the village!"

"What just happened in there, Teo?"

"I received my Guaraní name, Karai Tupã."

I caught my breath, saying, "Really! What an honor! What does Karai Tupã mean?"

"It means 'God helper.' You know I have *you* to thank for this. I did not know my baptism would happen now."

I replied in a burst, "Oh no, it is I who need to thank you!"

"Please listen, I need to say thank you, and I will explain why." Standing in the moonlight surrounded by thatched huts and the stillness of the forest, Teo proceeded to explain. "The cacique said to me the reason the baptism took place tonight was because you were singing. The cacique summoned me when he saw you become immersed in song, and this action allowed my baptism."

I was speechless as I recalled my mentor Alberto's explanation of how the people felt that song brought them closer to God and how they came together unconditionally every evening to sing. As soon as a certain feeling, or what Alberto explained as a specific vibration, was reached with the singing, then and only then would the ceremonies for healing take place.

I felt the unity Alberto described in surrendering to the pounding of the takuás, the shaking of the rattles, the smoke, and most of all, the singing.

In that moment, I understood that I would never fully comprehend the depth of all that had taken place. However, the expansion of joy and exuberance in my heart-center was genuine. For me, this encounter was a spiritual gift, an authenticated experience of Alberto's story about how people came together each night to sing songs of praise until a sense of harmonious connection was achieved, before proceeding with the ritual. Communally, the participants tapped into a stream of consciousness that was love.

My humbling experience in the Opy was a direct knowing of the power of their song, but more so, of the communal power of love and reciprocity. And this lives on in my heart. Alberto had begun every class by saying in his rich and passionate voice, "They are always giving, always sharing."

Teo and I walked away in awe of this beautiful evening spent with these gentle, giving people. We drove home in silent wonder.

This experience and the expansion of my heart-center opened me to better see the world through a prism of unconditional love.

The experience of love invokes the desire to know the Source as a continual living experience. The need to connect with others, to love and be loved during our earthly experience, is the force that directs us back to Source. I still hear Alberto's words ringing in my ears, "You cannot heal until you first love. Love is in all healing no matter what technique you use. Without the love, it is impossible to heal."

This simple, unexpected opportunity gave me a direct experience of heart intelligence. The importance of this intelligence of the heart is unfolding globally and is crucial to mankind's evolutionary path. I believe we are all created with a soul purpose: to love and be loved. In thinking love, my thoughts take me to the highest source of existence, what is understood to be the Source of All.

Then love becomes Love.

ELIZABETH COSMOS, author, teacher, and practitioner, has been involved in spiritual healing for more than thirty years. She was responsible for the founding and development of a comprehensive, hospital-based integrated medicine program for alternative therapies at Saint Mary's Hospital in Grand Rapids, Michigan, where she lives. She is also the founder of the International Association of Ama-Deus, LLC. Her work has been featured in such international publications as *National Geographic*. Beth is an ordained minister in the Science of Mind Church for Spiritual Healing and earned her doctorate in energy medicine at Holos University Graduate Seminary. She is the author of *Ama-Deus: Healing with the Sacred Energies of the Universe*. Beth travels globally, teaching and sharing the Ama-Deus healing method. Her website is www.ama-deus-international.com.

40
Temples of the Earth

Zacciah Blackburn

I was an all-around American kid. God and country, Eagle Boy Scout, football player . . . recruited to the U.S. Naval Academy to play football. I had just made the starting lineup on the academy's very competitive team and I was on campus in advance of the school year practicing for what would no doubt be a grueling season ahead. One August morning in 1969, I woke up in my dorm room, alone. The banner headline of that morning's *Washington Post* screamed out: "400,000 Jam Rock Festival in Catskills." The headline was accompanied by a giant photo of throngs and throngs of people in a mud hole, clamoring together for three days of love and music.

For the first time, I "got it." I understood what the love-ins, long-hairs, and peaceniks were all about. Having been bred in conservative Texas (just think "George Bush" if you don't understand what I mean . . .), I had no previous concept of how or why the countercultural revolution was taking place. But in that instant, when I read the news-paper, it became very clear to me that this was a moment of irrevocable change. Somehow the image and words about what was then happening in Woodstock, New York, cracked open an egg of perception somewhere within my psyche and in a flash I suddenly understood why people of my generation were rising up against the status quo.

As I read the article, someone standing a few feet behind me spoke over my left shoulder. "This is where you belong," the voice said, in distinct yet almost whispered tone. I turned to see who was speaking; I had not heard anyone come into the room.

And no one was there.

It's God or someone speaking to me, I heard my baffled mind say. This was a voice unlike any other, with a clarity, a purity, a conviction, and integrity about those few words. I listened and let my heart flutter through the possibilities of my making the trek to upstate New York to attend the festival. *I have no civilian clothes, no money,* my thoughts raced. *If I leave these walls I'll be committing desertion. By the time I get there, the festival will be over. It'll all be for naught . . . and my family will disown me.* (This had already happened to every brother of mine who had sought to define his own path.) I struggled with the ramifications of going to Woodstock, and reasons not to go clouded my brain. Yet this pure strong tone, this voice from another world, one that I did not know or understand, had spoken. And I trusted it completely. I knew it was authentic.

But in the end, I cowered from the outward ramifications of what I imagined would happen should I take action and go.

Two years later, I had a very important decision to make. My future had come down to one defining moment: I had to set down in writing whether or not I would commit to six more years of life at the Academy and in active service in the Navy. I was struggling once more, and as I did so, military officers hovered over me, waiting for me to make my decision.

Again I heard the same voice from the other side, saying with earnest comfort and warmth, *But you don't really want to be here.*

Yes, yes, that is true, I thought. *I don't know what it is I do want, but I know this is not it.*

Many more ramifications came with that decision, but I was prepared now to face them. I knew that my family would be disappointed that I would not choose the military as my career and I would have to face their dashed expectations. But I couldn't focus on that. I had to (survive) make a choice, and it was apparent to me by now that there were greater choices to be made.

Thank you, my body quivered, although I did not utter a word.

During the next two years, the choices I made led to visions and experiences beyond my comprehension. They took me on a unique path of exploring world cultures, spiritual beliefs, and especially music. It was now the early '70s, and a friend had bequeathed me a bamboo flute. At this time, they were barely known in the United States. As I learned to play it, I was invited to Kirtan sessions, African drumming parties, and many other events that led me to study with masters of many traditions. I made flutes for a living until, while raising my two children alone, I began to turn back to those early voices, visions, and the destiny that would help me unfold. Through the years of study and music, I turned more and more to the instinctual voices guiding me to prayer and service, in ways I often did not understand. I found exquisite teachers in this world who guided me in preparatory stages for all that was to come.

I began to spend every spare moment I had in Nature. I loved its beauty and instinctually could hear its explicit song. I would sing prayers of gratitude with my flutes and, eventually, with simple drums and voice, chant deep intonations that came from the ethers. I often did not know their meaning, but I felt one day that some linguistic specialist was going to hear them and say, yes, that is an ancient language of the peoples from long-ago _____ (you and I can fill in the blank). I knew that these chants had meaning; sometimes I heard the words in English as I spoke or sang them.

I was living in the state of Vermont and one day I set off on a hike to climb a mountain, stopping en route to visit a friend who made power objects. He was of the Wampanoag people and two elders happened to be visiting him. I courteously and respectfully engaged them in conversation as long as I was able, then rose to excuse myself to find my mountain to climb. One of the elders turned to me and asked, "My son, where are you going?"

I turned to her and responded, "Grandmother, I am going to climb a mountain!"

She turned back to me, staring into my soul, guiding me. "My son, you don't need to climb a mountain. You need to go to the canyon!"

She went on to tell me of a sacred place, a gorge, not too far away, that held ancient ways of knowing and was some form of interdimensional space. I did not fully understand her. She told me how to find a doorway of stone, then said it was important to use it, and told me how to do that.

It took me a year to find that doorway, although I found the canyon that day.

It became my sacred temple. I went every day I could get away from work and the responsibilities of being a parent. It spoke volumes of ancient wisdom to me, in many ways. I would sit upon the great stones in the river canyon, staring at the great forms of the ancestors and medicine allies around me. The stones took many forms. I would "feel" into those forms, and sound sacred tones from deep within me, of what I was experiencing through them. The stones would awaken and I would experience profound shards of light extend from within their cavities and explode into my field like lightning bolts of luminous wisdom. These extending shards of light would often take on unknown geometric forms.

I was not aware of all that was happening, but more and more, I heard the Ancient Ones speaking in this temple complex. I returned again and again.

One day I was standing on two rocks, with part of the river rushing through them between my legs. I suddenly let go of a deep grief that was holding me, binding me. I gave it all away. Tearing it from my shoulders, I released it into the waters, thanking the Ancient Ones for taking it and cleansing it for me. This was a long process, but when it was over, I felt a tangible force turn me physically around and face me upriver toward the most spectacular part of the canyon and its great waterfalls. I heard a voice state, *Now turn, and receive the joy and blessings that are coming into your life!*

I did this, and in so doing, I felt the wonder of everything—the beauty of Nature and all of the unseen forces of life itself cascading into my being, much like the great waters cascading over the falls before me in the canyon.

When complete, I was filled with gratitude, I was overflowing with joy.

I turned and thanked every creature and being, seen and unseen, on this Earth, the heavens above, and the worlds below. I turned and turned, giving thanks in all directions, over and over, as I climbed from the canyon. At one point I had to stretch way up and pull myself over a giant boulder in my path. I turned to thank all beings again, and then continued on my way. As I did so, a great voice from behind me bellowed out: *He just doesn't get it, does he?!*

I turned over my shoulder to see a great stone face in the canyon wall become animate. It was one of the stone beings, coming alive, saying now with kindness to me, *It is* we *who thank you!*

That was a moment beyond all memory, for in it I truly began to understand what was waking upon this Earth. I understood that by honoring all within our Mother Earth and within Cosmos, we would create the catalyst that would birth a new world, as foretold by the mysteries and prophecies of these times.

There were guiding principles I learned in that sacred canyon, as well as at other ancient sites I visited. I learned about right relations and how to appropriately approach the living beings guarding and protecting these ancient sites so as to access the wisdom therein. These guidelines are very specific techniques that have worked time and again at simple sites in the backlands of Vermont, at the great stone temples of Great Britain, Egypt, and Peru, and elsewhere on this planet. By respecting and honoring the living wisdomkeepers and guardians of each place, profound wisdom has been revealed to me.

Perhaps one of the most astounding experiences of this kind took place in a small stone chamber in rural Vermont. There are nineteen such chambers in the state, and dozens of them in the Northeast, all built by ancient peoples. Most archaeologists dismiss them as nothing more than colonial root cellars. However, farmers of the region do not agree with the archaeologists' assessment and the very old gold coins, writings, and other evidence of distant cultures that have been found on these sites lend fuel to the debate as to the true origins of the chambers.

I took two friends to see one of these stone temples. It is known as a calendar site, given that numerous archaeoastrological alignments have been discovered within its complex of stones, which covers several acres. This site also features five stone chambers within a radius of a few miles.

We performed our practice for entering sacred sites, asking for permission to do so from the guardians and wisdomkeepers there. We entered the chamber and sat down to hold ceremony. The elders of the site (from unseen worlds) came forward and asked me to "hold my consciousness in a particular way, and sing these sacred tones." They gave me voices I didn't imagine I could duplicate. I felt embarrassed to even try, although I have been known to make some pretty odd sounds when the time is appropriate in order to enter an altered state of being.

I initially resisted, but then the better part of me took control and I immersed myself, and my voice, into the states of awareness the elders were defining for me and the sounds that were being emitted. We had an exquisite journey and experience.

We came back feeling greatly enhanced and clarified; we were doing pretty well.

After this we enjoyed other aspects of this sacred site, and then we rested, watching the sun set across the horizon, across the back of sacred Mount Ascutney, the "Grandfather" mountain of this region. We had a deep conversation about our experiences. Soon, however, it started to grow dark, and we knew we had to wind our way back to the car to be sure we safely made it past several dry spring holes and foundation holes close to the path.

The path back led past the door to the sacred chamber, and as I passed by, I felt an unseen force come out and turn me back toward the doorway. This was disturbing to me as I was intent on returning to the car before darkness fell completely. At this point, the force came out again and pulled me harder, turning me back, drawing me into the doorway. Part of me freaked out, which was not a normal reaction for me in the face of unseen mysteries. I pulled myself together, basically telling myself that there was nothing to be afraid of in the chamber. And to prove it, I entered it.

By this time my friends had realized that something was up. Catching up with me, they entered the chamber with me. We simultaneously let out a gasp, saying almost in unison, "Oh my God! Do you see that?! How is it possible?"

In the small chamber, the walls of which were comprised of rough-hewn, stacked stones, and the ceiling of which was made up of great, smooth, multi-ton stones, we saw, not these rocks, but a great Gothic-style cathedral made of crystalline panes of glass and upheld by metal latticework. We could see the stars above us, penetrating us with their light, just as if we were standing outside looking up at the stars in that very moment in time.

We all saw the same thing whether our eyes were open or closed, and we were full of wonder and astonishment. At some point, I came to my senses, realizing we were experiencing a very sacred act. I intentionally reentered a very reverent state of mind, and almost immediately I made contact with the living beings of this place.

They said to me, "Zacciah, what you have done, through coupling these particular states of consciousness with these particular sacred sounds, is to open the key to the gateway to the Library of Knowledge that we stored here when we built this temple eons ago."

I understood their words, and I walked through the temple library with them. I would never be the same again.

These mysteries have continued to unfold for me time and again, in ancient temples, in powerful, natural Earth sites, and in practices utilizing sacred sounds coupled with sacred states of consciousness, worldwide. But perhaps what truly amplified this experience came just two months later, when one of nine living wisdomkeepers of the five million Olmec Otomi Toltec Teotihuacan peoples of Central Mexico came to my house and stayed with me for most of a week, as we prepared for a workshop we were teaching together the following weekend. This wisdomkeeper handed me a clay statuary of a head. It was obviously one of the Olmec Otomi peoples. He said, "Here, I want you to get acquainted with this, so you are not scared when you meet him."

He continued, "We do not have a written language. We never needed one, for we stored our ancient knowledge in the 'invisible books' in our temple libraries. Olmec is our ancient mother language. It comes from Lemuria. Our ancestors came from both Lemuria and Atlantis. We access this ancient knowledge in the 'invisible books' by coupling particular states of consciousness with specific cosmic sounds from our mother language. I want you to be familiar with this guardian face, for you will see him when I take you there. Here, I want to take you there now."

With almost the exact language of what the temple elders had spoken just two months before in a little-known ancient stone chamber in central Vermont, a living wisdomkeeper of an ancient people was standing in my living room, telling me exactly the same thing.

He then took me there.

✧ ✧ ✧ ✧

ZACCIAH BLACKBURN, PH.D., is a gifted intuitive, teacher, and sound healer, trained in classical healing and shamanic traditions and sacred sound cultures. He has been involved in the field of healing music, sound, and shamanic practices for over thirty-five years. He teaches internationally, his work focusing on therapeutic sound, spiritual development, and indigenous Earth mysteries. Zacciah utilizes sound coupled with sacred intention as a therapeutic tool, in mystical settings, for personal healing and transformation, in private therapies and workshop programs, providing illumined expertise in esoteric practices. He conducts tours worldwide of sacred sites, utilizing and sharing his skills for Earth-healing rituals with participants, incorporating sacred sound. Zacciah is director of the Center of Light Institute of Sound Healing and Shamanic Studies in Ascutney, Vermont. His website is thecenteroflight.net.

41

Direct Dialogue
with Mother Earth

Michele Gieselman

I had never heard the term "shaman" or "shamanism," until one day when an awareness of it became very strong. For no explicable reason, I felt an energy of excitement and longing connected to this new consciousness, this new word. What did it mean? I had to find out.

Then, it happened, as it does when you are being led. I was invited to lunch and during the course of the lunch, my friend shared with me that she had attended a course in shamanism and was excited to tell me that a course similar to the one she had taken was going to be presented in the valley where we lived.

Was I interested? she wanted to know.

"Yes!" I told her. At the end of our visit, I didn't have a strong understanding about shamanism, but I knew I had to find out more. The excitement and longing were building.

The first moment I realized I was to be a part of these teachings happened when I walked into the initial session to join the circle. I felt I had come home; everything about the program seemed as if I had experienced it before. Little did I know the amount of gifts and affirmations I would receive during this journey.

As a child out in Nature, I always felt complete. I would swim in the river from late spring until late fall and welcome the autumn, with its rich earth smell and glorious colors. The first snowfall was enchanting; it was a white sparking blanket beckoning me to play. It was wondrous! There were times when I wanted to crawl inside the Earth to know how it would feel. That first weekend of the shamanic training I did find out.

It was January, and a typically cold and blustery Canadian winter. We held our seminar in a retreat center that was set out in the country and nestled right beside a beautiful lake. Before we arrived, we needed to find three stones that represented one of the four directions. At this seminar, we were focusing on the South direction. These stones needed to be retrieved from different areas of the land, depending on the direction we would be working on. In this case, I needed to select my stones from a body of water. Selecting my stones, my Khuyas, was a labour of love and a sweet connection to Mother Earth, our beautiful Pachamama. I was to bury these stones somewhere on the grounds of the center and visit them throughout the weekend. I chose to put my three stones down by the lake, around the roots of a tree.

Each time I went down to check on my stones, it was as if I was entering into another reality. The wind blew, the snow swirled around me, and I loved it. I knew that my Khuyas were absorbing the energies of the lake, the trees, the wind, the snow, and the cold. All of this magic would accompany me and my Khuyas when I brought them back to be part of my mesa (medicine bag). Creating this bundle awakened a memory that I had done this before.

The sacredness surrounding the creation of my medicine bundle was amazing. As I created it, I realized that Mother Nature would always be a part of me, and I would always be a part of Mother Nature. That was an aha moment for me. Through this experience, I felt a strong and permanent connection with the Earth and this has given me an invincible foundation.

My initial shamanic training took place over a period of two years. During that time, I participated in different ceremonies, rituals, and healing modalities. One of the ceremonies was the fire ceremony, which initially I didn't understand the significance of. I seemed to be spending a long time in the cold—rattling, singing, and doing my best to ignore my chilly feet. It took me a while to realize that coming to the fire was equivalent to being at the altar, communicating with Spirit or God.

At the ceremony, I asked the fire to take my heavy energy, *hucha,* and give it all to the flames and to Mother Earth. Every person receives this energy when they are living on Earth. It is not always negative, but it is a heavy energy that prevents one from functioning optimally. Hucha empowers Pachamama. To her it is food, not waste, and in return for her energetic meal, she offers Sami, refined energy, to the person doing the cleansing. In Joan Parisi Wilcox's *Keepers of the Ancient Knowledge,* priest Juan Nunez del Prado says, "When we give hucha to the Pachamama, we are giving her food. . . . When we are working with heavy energy, we are working with real, living energy, and this real, living energy empowers Mother Earth. She needs living energy, and if you release hucha to her you are empowering her. Also you are empowering yourself."*

Sweeping the heaviness into the flames and then receiving fresh new energy into my body filled me with gratitude. I was grateful for the fact that I could come to the altar and be cleansed in this sweet and powerful way. My heavy energy was pulled into the flames through my breath, and using a pushing action with my hands, I was able to pull it from my three centers: my stomach, chest, and head. In return, I received energy that was pure and light.

This was another aha moment for me, and today, each time I approach the fire with my mesa, I feel love and a huge acceptance of who I am and what I have to offer.

Another one of the rituals I participated in was that of creating a *despacho.* This is another method that embraces the Pachamama and also

---

*See Joan Parisi Wilcox's *Keepers of the Ancient Knowledge: The Mystical World of the Q'ero Indians of Peru* (London: Vega, 2002).

engages the person involved. As I prepared a gift of love for the Earth, I was giving a piece of myself as well. In return, I received the Sami, the pure energy from Mother Earth. I gathered gifts and wrapped them in white and presented them to the Earth. In this, I included candy and chocolate and Native objects from where I live, which is important. What an extraordinary way to honour Pachamama!

In my healing practice I use the modalities that have been taught to me. The mesa, my medicine bundle, is paramount in all that I do. The use of my mesa, the breath, and the calling of the archetypes from the four directions is a gentle and very successful way to deal with a blockage or other issues a client may be experiencing. The shamanic journey has been a path of awakening for me and I know now that I am in touch with Spirit at all times.

The most influential instruction I received in my shamanic training was from Peruvian Jose Luis Herrera, who lives in the Sacred Valley in Peru and whose shamanic expertise is derived from a combination of much experience and detailed research. After many weekends spent enjoying the teachings of Jose, in 2008 I was very fortunate to take a trip to Peru with him. I was welcomed into his country with such graciousness and was invited to experience the magnificence of the mystical system of the Q'ero Indians of Peru. This experience for me was a journey to the Source, from whence the knowledge of Jose's shamanic teachings had come.

One of the rituals I was privileged to be a part of was creating a despacho in honor of Ausangate, which is the spirit of the mountain, otherwise known as the Apus or Lord of the Mountain. We hiked up the mountain and camped there for three days. We were honored to be in the presence of an *alto mesayoq*, a mover of the living energy of the universe, and a *pampa mesayoq*, a steward of the land. The alto mesayoq talk directly to the mountain spirits, the Apus; they are the keepers of ancient knowledge.

The despacho was as big as a dining room table. It was filled with fresh corn and many items from the land. When it was completed it resembled a small village. Each one of us put sixty prayers into the despacho. Each prayer, a K'intu, was offered up in the form of a fan made of three perfect coca leaves. After the despacho was created, Jose and several of the medicine people and fire keepers carried the despacho to the sacred fire. In the ancient tradition, the medicine people and the fire keepers are the only people allowed to lay a despacho on the fire. We were asked to return to the base camp. The prayers and love that were put into that gift were then lifted up by the flames of the fire and sent to the Apus.

The next morning there was a lot of snow on the ground and I asked Jose if the Apus were happy. He joyfully answered, "Oh, yes! They are very happy! Now we will have water to fill the lagoons and reservoirs and water for irrigation!" The snow was a gift from the Apus and Mother Nature. Incredible!

After three days in the mountains, we returned to the Sacred Valley. I certainly was not the same person who had walked up the mountain three days earlier. I had witnessed a direct communication with Spirit, and in so doing, I became part of the landscape.

When we were back in the Sacred Valley, Jose organized a ceremony to call in the mountain spirits. Jose sat with an alto mesayoq and together they called in the Apus. Sitting in the sacred darkness and hearing them come and talk to Jose in either Spanish or Quechua, the ancient language of Peru, was astounding, especially when Ausangate spoke to us during this ceremony. Jose would translate for me so I could understand what was being said. I was allowed to ask questions. The answers I received were enlightening and affirmed that on I was on the right path of learning shamanism. This was another aha moment for me.

During the ceremony, the Apus asked us to sing for them. We didn't know what to sing and then decided to sing "Amazing Grace." They said they didn't understand what we were singing, but they liked the sound of our voices.

Peru was a gift to me, including the information and teaching I received every day, and it helped confirm to me that shamanism needs to be a part of my life. In Peru, the Apus were a miracle that I actually witnessed. I traveled to the Source and I communicated with Spirit. The rituals and ceremonies that were taught to me during these shamanic studies made even more sense when I participated in them directly. (I realized I had experienced some of them in meditation before traveling to Peru.) In these ceremonies, energy is gathered, which opens up the heart and the soul and gives access to the inner truth and to the Creator. The people of Peru live their lives according to these ceremonies and rituals. The despachos are gifts to the mountain spirits and the Pachamama. The sacred fires are for cleansing and to deliver the love and respect of the despacho as it is laid on the fire.

It is difficult to explain shamanism because it is an experience. For me it has changed my life in a way that has allowed me to embrace myself as I embrace Mother Earth. We are all one. Spirit is in everything and everyone. According to Chief Seattle, "This we know: The earth does not belong to man. Man belongs to the earth. All things are connected like the blood that unites one family. Man did not weave the web of life; he is merely a strand in it. Whatever he does to the web he does to himself."

The shamanic practice is now my reality, and as such, it is a daily reminder of the gentleness of Spirit, the power of ritual and prayer, the restoration of stillness, and the healing of the breath.

❖ ❖ ❖ ❖

MICHELE GIESELMAN has worked as an intuitive healer and bodywork practitioner since 1998. Her interest in Earth-based medicine led her to pursue the shamanic teachings of the Inca tradition, sourced from the medicine people of Peru. In 2002 Michele completed the medicine wheel and is a full mesa carrier. She has since pursued master-level teachings with Jose Luis Herrera. She has over twenty years of experience in the field of health and wellness. Michele began her interest in the well-being of the body as a fitness instructor, Middle Eastern dance instructor, and personal trainer. She received her personal trainer certification from the British Columbia Recreation and Parks Association and has a tourism diploma from Thompson Rivers University. She assists her clients in working toward achieving balance and personal well-being.

42

The Calling

Michael Drake

Editor's note: This article is an excerpt from the book *Shamanic Drumming: Calling the Spirits,* by Michael Drake (Talking Drum Publications, 2012).

The spirits called me to a path of shamanism. I do not know why I was chosen. I ceased making such queries long ago. Over the years, I learned to just go with the flow. The how and why of my circumstances became less important to me than the lessons that I was learning along the way. As time passed, I began to see how my life experiences honed me into the artist I am today.

For as long as I can remember, I have been an explorer—pushing beyond familiar territory to investigate the unknown. As a child, I had a near-drowning, out-of-body experience that opened my eyes to the hidden dimensions of life and propelled my explorations. Like everyone, I was trying to find myself. I was also searching for something that resonated with me—anything that evoked a shared emotion or belief. I identified with people whose words were congruent with their actions. My inner self was most nourished when I was immersed in Nature. Being introverted and eccentric, I often felt a closer kinship to Nature than I did to people.

My birthplace was Oklahoma, but Topeka, Kansas, became my home at the age of five until I moved away at age twenty-three. I was raised in a conservative Southern Baptist Church, which shaped my personal ethics and early life. I had my first ecstatic experience as a youth at a church revival, an evangelistic meeting intended to reawaken interest in religion. This state of rapture and trancelike elation inspired my spiritual quest. For much of my youth, I had aspirations of attending seminary to prepare for some form of ministry. I met my wife, Elisia, at a church function. We were wed by our pastor in a church wedding in 1976.

After I graduated from college in 1977, I felt a great pull to "Go West." I mailed résumés to employers up and down the Pacific Coast. As fate would have it, I was offered a job with the Glidden Paint Company in Portland, Oregon. Elisia and I promptly sold our house and moved to Oregon. As a couple, that is how we often did things and that is how we still do things, after thirty-five years of marriage. We decide to do something, and then we just do it. Elisia and I have learned to trust and follow our inner yearnings. One of the things we learned working with spirits is that they often prompt us, through urges, to do one thing or another.

Upon our arrival in Portland, we soon found a house to rent. After settling in, we spent most of our free time hiking and exploring. Enamored with my new home, I began studying the geology and ecology of the Pacific Northwest. What I began to understand is that Nature sustains us and everything around us through an interdependent web of life. There is no separateness. We are all one consciousness.

In early 1980, I lost my retail managerial job. I was ready for a change, and with so much free time, I took up reading full-time. One of the influential books that I read was *The Dharma Bums,* a 1958 novel by Beat Generation author Jack Kerouac. Kerouac's semifictional accounts of hiking and hitchhiking through the West inspired me to embark, with my wife's blessing, on a backpacking/gold prospecting adventure to northern California. After all, in 1980 the price of gold hit a then record of $873 an ounce.

In May of 1980, my journey began with a bus ride to Yreka,

California. From Yreka, I planned to hike and hitch my way about fifty-three miles over a mountain pass to Sawyers Bar, California. I stepped off the bus in Yreka, shouldered my heavy pack, and started walking south on State Route 3. After I had walked a few miles, a local farrier in a pickup offered me a ride to the small town of Etna. I spent an uneventful night camped in the Etna City Park.

On day two, I arose early and continued my trek. After a few hours of steep climbing, I hitched another ride to Idlewild Campground, a forest service recreation area on the North Fork Salmon River six miles from Sawyers Bar, California. Idlewild became my base camp for prospecting and further explorations in the surrounding area.

After a few days of unsuccessful gold-panning, I decided to backpack into nearby Marble Mountain Wilderness. I walked up Mule Bridge Road along the scenic North Fork Salmon River until I reached the wilderness trailhead. From the trailhead, I hiked the North Fork Trail deep into Marble Mountain Wilderness.

I met no one along the trail. I was alone in the wilderness. Late in the afternoon, I came upon the skeletal remains of a large bear along the trail. It was one of the most peculiar sights I have ever beheld. The skeletal paws of the bear resembled human hands and the massive skull was quite intimidating. I later learned that a local bear hunter had reportedly shot a dangerous nuisance bear but had not killed it outright. The wounded bear had then escaped, but it eventually died next to the trail.

I dropped my pack and walked a short distance down the trail to a river crossing. The North Fork Salmon River was swollen with spring snowmelt, making it unsafe to cross. It began to drizzle again; it had been raining off and on all day. I had no choice but to turn around and look for a suitable place to camp for the night. Wouldn't you know it; the only level campsite was only a short distance from the bear skeleton.

I certainly was in bear country. There were tracks in the sand and mud all along the riverbank. I came across a bear footprint so large that I could step into it with my size 12 Vibram-soled boots. It wasn't a fresh track, but it was at the base of an ancient cedar in the very grove of trees where I was going to have to camp for the night. All of the large cedar trees in the area bore the claw marks of a bear marking its territory. The claw marks were so high on the tree trunks that I could barely touch them with my fingertips when standing on the tips of my toes. This was a very large bear and I was going to have to spend the night in its territory in a dark grove of trees along a raging river. I took some comfort in the fact that the tracks and markings might have been made by the bear that I discovered along the trail before it died.

I was nervous, to say the least. I am always on my guard when trekking through bear country. After setting up my tent, I fired up my camp stove and cooked a hot meal. To minimize odors that might attract bears, I hung my nylon food bag from a high tree limb some distance away from the camp. I then gathered up as much firewood as I could find for the long night ahead. I found some cedar bark, which is useful for getting a campfire started under soggy conditions. Once the fire was going, I stacked damp wood around the perimeter of the fire pit so that it would slowly dry. Heat from the flames warmed my face and hands and the warm glow perked up my spirits. As long as the fire burned, I felt relatively safe. I tended the flames late into the night until I finally ran out of wood.

Without the comfort of a warming fire, I had no choice but to crawl into my tent and try to get some sleep. I lay awake in my sleeping bag for a long time, listening to the night sounds. I focused intently on every strange noise I heard outside my tent. To get to sleep, I focused my attention on the current rushing over the river rocks. At times, the river made haunting sounds as it rolled big rocks along its course. At some point, I fell into a deep sleep.

Then it started; the most terrifying experience of my life. I was awakened by a mysterious roar. It resembled the sound of a helicopter hovering directly over my tent. The previous day, before entering the wilderness, I had heard the "whop-whop-whop" sound of a dual-rotor logging helicopter in the distance. Helicopters, like all motorized vehicles, are prohibited in designated wilderness areas. Rationally, I knew it was highly unlikely that the sound was emanating from a helicopter hovering over my tent, yet a whirling wind-like howl filled my ears in the predawn darkness. I have never been so frightened in all my life. I had spent countless nights camping in wilderness areas across the West and never had I experienced anything like *this*.

As I opened my eyes, I realized that I couldn't move, or I was too afraid to move. I was virtually paralyzed. I lay rigid inside my sleeping bag and prayed that whatever was outside my tent would just go away. My heart pounded like a drum. My panicked mind was reeling as I struggled to classify what I was experiencing. Frenzied thoughts of UFOs, alien abductions, and even Sasquatch raced through my mind. I don't know how long the mind-bending experience lasted. It was all so surreal. I started to hyperventilate. Death seemed imminent.

Suddenly, the eerie moaning stopped and the bizarre incident ceased, almost as abruptly as it had begun. I could hear the roaring river again, along with the pitter-patter of raindrops bouncing off the top of my nylon tent.

The paralysis ended immediately and I gasped in a lungful of air. I finally managed to sit up in my sleeping bag, my body trembling in shock. I sat motionless, lost in my thoughts, wondering what had just happened to me. The entire experience was much too real to have been a nightmare. As I relived the terrifying event in my mind again and again, the first light of dawn illuminated my tent.

I arose, hastily packed my gear, and then marched out of there as fast as I could. I retreated from the wilderness, returning to Idlewild Campground—back to familiar territory. Upon my arrival on May 18 (1980), I learned from a fellow camper that Mount St. Helens had erupted earlier that day at 8:32 a.m., killing fifty-seven people. The destructive power and devastation of the eruption served to distract me from my disturbing predawn experience. Though I prefer the isolation and quietude of the wilderness, I spent the remaining two weeks of my vacation camped in this developed campground, never venturing back into Marble Mountain Wilderness.

During my stay in this idyllic area, I made many new friends. I met mountain climbers, backpackers, gold prospectors, miners, kayakers, a hermit, and a colorful assortment of local hippies living on gold-mining claims and growing weed. All in all, it was an epic adventure for me. I will never forget it. Idlewild Campground became a restful sanctuary for me at that moment in time. Where the North Fork Salmon River wrapped around my camp, the soothing sound of the water lulled me into a peaceful sleep every night.

Many years later I began to understand the significance of my anomalous Marble Mountain experience, although I realize that I will never understand it fully. I have come to accept that there will always be that which is unknown to me—that which is "the Great Mystery."

I now also know that the eerie howl that aroused me on that fateful night resembled that of a bullroarer. A bullroarer is a thin, feathershaped piece of wood that, when whirled in the air by means of an attached string, makes a loud humming or roaring sound. Bullroarers produce a range of infrasonics, extremely low-frequency sound waves that are picked up by the cochlea (labyrinth) of the ear, stimulating a wide array of euphoric trance states. The bullroarer dates back to the Stone Age and is probably the most widespread among all sacred instruments. With over sixty names, it is universally linked to thunder and spirit beings in the sky.

These roaring sticks are used in certain ceremonial dances in the desert Southwest to invoke wind and rain. In some areas of the world, the instrument played a role in certain rites of passage. The sound of the bullroarer's spiral-shaped movement is widely considered to be the voice of an ancestor, a spirit, or a deity.

The first time I actually heard a bullroarer was in December of 1991. Elisia and I were traveling through New Mexico on a crosscountry tour, promoting my newly released book, *The Shamanic Drum*. By chance we happened upon the annual Shalako festival, which is a series of dances and ceremonies conducted by the Zuni people near the winter solstice in which they celebrate the return of the sun and pray for rain, growth, and fertility. Shalako is named for its masked dancers, who embody kachinas or ancestral spirits. Kachinas mediate between humanity and the gods of rain and prosperity in a sacred ritual performance that ensures the transformation of winter's death into spring's rebirth. Standing ten feet tall and resembling birds, the colorful Shalako kachinas dance rhythmically, clacking their long beaks together. They come to the human realm to collect the people's prayers and take them back to the spirit realm.

On the day of the Shalako ceremony, the six kachinas, one for each of the four cardinal directions plus zenith and nadir, entered Zuni Pueblo at dusk. Each Shalako deity was escorted by a group of singers and an attendant whirling a bullroarer over his head. As the first procession filed into the plaza, the sound of the bullroarer elicited an intense feeling of déjà vu, triggering memories of my traumatic experience in Marble Mountain Wilderness. Reflecting on my ordeal created anew the conditions for revelation, learning, and reintegration. I finally realized what had transpired on that life-altering night in 1980. Although I didn't know it back then, my guardian or tutelary spirit was "calling" me. Having been chosen by the spirit of a bear, my shamanic initiation had begun, and like a sluggish bear emerging from the slumber of winter hibernation, I gradually awakened to the knowing of my true self.

I have since had other initiation experiences, such as a shamanic death and rebirth. However, none of these subsequent experiences have impacted me as much as my Marble Mountain experience did in 1980.

That mystical encounter with Spirit shattered my ego, cracking me wide open. Shamanic initiation functions as a transformer—it causes a radical change in the initiate forever. It is typically the final step in becoming a shamanic healer, a process that is facilitated by the aspirant's shamanic teachers as part of a training program. However, initiation may also be spontaneous, set in motion by Spirit's intervention into the initiate's life. It is probably the most powerful and least understood of all forms of spiritual awakening.

Michael Drake is an internationally respected writer, teacher, and recording artist. He is the author of *The Shamanic Drum, Shamanic Drumming, I Ching: The Tao of Drumming,* and *Shamanic Drumming Circles Guide.* His musical albums include *Shamanic Journey Drumming, Power Animal Drumming,* and *Shaman's Drums.* His articles have been featured in numerous publications, including *Awareness, Sacred Hoop,* and *Mother Earth News.* He has been practicing and teaching shamanism for over twenty-five years. He has devoted himself to teaching and promoting drumming as a vehicle for healing, consciousness expansion, and community building. He facilitates shamanic drum circles and hands-on experiential workshops nationwide. His mission is to foster an empowered global shamanic community for the welfare of the planet and our future generations. His website is ShamanicDrumming.com.

43

The Gifts of Shamanism

Pamela Albee

My mother was a troubled woman who felt held down by her three children. After I was born she had a mental break, which today the medical community would classify as postpartum depression. While suffering from this, she tried to drown me in a sink of water; luckily my father pulled me out.

After she died forty years later, I came to learn that her passion was science and, when young, she had wanted to be a research scientist—but along we came and she felt stuck. As time went by, she increasingly exhibited bouts of rage that came out of nowhere. These were unprovoked and quite terrifying. I discovered that when she was sick, I almost always became sick as well.

As a child, I loved playing with insects and talking to plants. I had some kind of intuitive connection with them and many other things around me; it seemed as though we could understand each other's thoughts and feelings. I was like a sponge, intuiting information from the air and hyperaware of sounds, smells, and negative energies around me.

Growing up, we lived down the street from one of the oldest and largest funeral homes in town. My child-mind remembers it as a one-story brick building with ivy that crawled up the walls, covering pink-tinted windows. I felt the building held untold stories of the dead. My older siblings would tease me nightly, saying that the creaks and groans of our old home were actually dead bodies from the funeral home getting loose, walking around our house and hitting their bones on the furniture. I was always terrified. I'd run and tell my mom but her only response was, "Don't be stupid!" However, she never denied what my siblings said, so I waited and watched—always hypervigilant.

I never dared to venture near the funeral home because I was fearful of what might happen if I did. I had conjured up quite vivid, ghoulish imageries of the walking dead; they looked like characters from Michael Jackson's "Thriller" video. And while I never actually saw them, I could sure feel some type of hair-raising energy on the back of my neck and arms when I thought about them.

Not long after I was married, my husband's cousin was murdered by Ted Bundy. The only remnants of his evil were her skull fragments. Her memorial service was to be held at a Catholic church. However, by the time my husband and I had driven the three hundred miles to his aunt's house, the plans had changed and his cousin's service had been moved to a local funeral home. At this I became panicky, bargaining with my husband, trying to get out of having to attend the funeral. Embarrassed, he demanded that I attend, shaming me to "grow up." I had never been so frightened in my life and vowed never to go to another funeral, no matter what.

I skirted funerals for the next eleven years. Then my father was diagnosed with terminal cancer. My father was my champion; he had saved me from another near-drowning when I was seven years old. I couldn't miss honoring his memory and celebrating his life. I worked hard with a therapist during the months before his life slipped away, just to be able to attend his funeral. Although I was wide-eyed and frightened I did attend my father's funeral. I was extremely aware of every little nuance in the room. My mind was spinning with "what ifs" . . . what if some dead bodies got loose during my father's celebration and decided to bother me?

I went to Galway, Ireland, to visit my sister in 1994, and while there, we went out to collect turf from a peat bog. The bog was comprised of dense, decaying soil, soaked with continuous moisture, and as such, it had been thousands of years in the making. For centuries the spongy terrain in Connemara had been cut with a two-sided shovel into square blocks that, when dried, create a source of firewood called "turf." However, a new way of cutting turf had been developed since I was there in 1970. It retained the topography of the land and removed slices of earth with a machine, more or less like a core sampler would do. Once the machine had sliced down and extracted its turf, a deep eight-foot slice was left before the earth would fold back together again. Not aware of these unseen openings, I fell into one. As I began wiggling around in it, it sucked me in deeper, like quicksand.

I was lucky that some nearby lads managed to pull me out. After they did so, they gave me a firm warning to get the bog's earthy, oily-smelling liquid off me as soon as I could. We were ninety minutes from the village of Oughterard, and by the time we got back, I had to scrape the brown substance from my skin with my fingernails.

The next day I was deathly ill.

I came back to America very, very sick—consuming numerous prescriptions of antibiotics without relief. My lungs became incredibly reactive. I was diagnosed with asthma and for the next two and a half years experienced breathing problems and took more antibiotics, anti-inflammatory medications, and steroids. I had to make three trips to the emergency room, frustrated, with a defiant attitude, finally telling my asthma doctor: "Whatever is happening to me *is not mine!*" I remember my asthma doctor patting my leg and telling me I would be on meds for the rest of my life. I was devastated, yet more determined than ever to find a way to get better.

In 1997, not too long after my doctor's dire prognosis, a therapist friend of mine went to a seminar where she heard a presentation about shamanic extraction and depossession. She called me, excited and thrilled, to share the news, for she felt that perhaps this could help me. She also shared her view that I "probably had someone *dead* inside me!" I about had a coronary and almost hung up on her—fearing that perhaps one of those dead bodies that got loose from the funeral home actually *had* done something to me. After I got over my initial shock, however, something of what she said rang true. So I called the shaman she had recommended and gave her permission to perform a "remote spirit release" on me, without telling her anything more than I was suffering from asthma.

I was desperate to get this asthma out of me and met with the woman a few days later. She declared that she had removed the *spirit of an Irish woman* from inside of me, which had represented a block in my lungs. I never told her I had been in Ireland. I didn't tell her anything about myself, other than I had asthma. However, she told me lots about myself she couldn't possibly have known beforehand. I was intrigued. Then she asked me what I did. I told her I was a dental technician and made teeth.

"No, no," she said. "What do you *do?*" Her blue eyes fixed on mine. I mumbled something again about making teeth, but it came out as a question. Then she looked deeply into my eyes and asked one more time what I did. I suddenly blurted out my confession: that I "took on other people's illness so they could get well." I apparently had done this initially with my mother, and then with various friends and family along the way. In my early forties I had a friend I adored who was diagnosed with breast cancer. It was fast growing and it terrified her. She was working on a book and I felt she needed to be around to finish the book. The book was an amazing journey of helping others and I knew the world needed the book. So I asked (into the air) to take her cancer so she would live. Within days I began to have slight pain in my breast and within a few more weeks developed a large lump. In the meantime my friend went to another more prestigious breast cancer doctor for a second opinion. He ordered new tests and when he received the results he demanded to know why she was wasting his time—there was nothing there. I finally went to my doctor as the pain in my breast became more intense. I had a mammogram, ultrasound, and then an aspiration with biopsy of the fluids. The fluid was just edema and the rest disappeared as did the pain. I got very lucky—and my friend lived. As I explained these happenings to the shaman, she then asked me what happened when I did that. I told her I often got quite sick but the sick person I was interacting with always got well. Her eyes continued to look deep into my soul and she remarked, "That's a good way to die!"

I spent the rest of the afternoon picking her brain and then enrolled in a year's apprenticeship in something called Cross-Cultural Shamanism.

By the end of the three-hundred-hour course and hundreds of spiritual journeys, along with making and taking plant tinctures, practicing soul retrieval, dismemberment, extraction, and depossession, understanding psychopomp, and learning the basics of Plant Spirit Medicine, I was completely free of all asthma symptoms and took no further medications. I will be forever grateful to my first shamanic teacher and for the practice of shamanism, for it enabled me to regain my health and energy. But . . . the best was yet to come!

When undergoing my first few journeys, I felt like I was finally home in my own skin at the age of forty-five. However, I was still unnerved by death and dead bodies. Finally I enrolled in a course titled Death, Dying, and Beyond in Salt Lake City, Utah. It was being hosted by Michael Harner's Foundation for Shamanic Studies. I could have waited to find a course that was closer to my home and one that I could have attended with friends. But the point is, I wanted to enroll in a course where I *wouldn't* have access to the security of my friends. I needed to do this quest for myself . . . *by* myself. I also wanted my destination to be one that I could only reach by plane. That way I couldn't get in the car and just drive home if I got too scared. So off I went, and when I arrived, I got a room by myself.

I felt like I was finally going to get to the bottom of my dead body and funeral fears that weekend, as each part of the course proved to be sacred, and many of my fears began to dissipate. The last journey of the weekend began with a dialogue designed to assist the dead with crossing into the Light, which is a process called psychopomp. But all of a sudden, my fears suddenly sprang back up like the clown in a jack-in-the-box. Panic grew as I looked around for someone or something to rescue me, but I had made myself so self-reliant that there was no one. Shit! Now what was I going to do?

Our intention was to psychopomp someone who had died abruptly or traumatically. We didn't necessarily need to know them; they could even be someone we had read about in the newspaper. I decided to journey to my hometown where for over six years our community had been haunted and terrified by a serial killer murdering prostitutes. He was finally caught, but not before he had killed thirteen women. My intention was to ask my helping spirits to take me to one of the murdered prostitutes and to teach me how to help her transition into the Light.

As the drumming started we (my helping spirits and I) found ourselves walking down a dark L-shaped alley. Rounding the corner of the building, we found all thirteen prostitutes huddled in a corner together. I had only intended to help one! Now what? One hard-looking, very aggressive woman quickly braced herself in front of the other girls, arms outstretched for their protection. She made it clear that I was going to have to go through her to get to the others.

A couple of the others stood, wanting to know who I was and why I was there. I explained that I wasn't there to hurt any of them, and then I explained who I was. I told them I knew that Robert Yates had murdered them all. At this, one woman elbowed another and remarked, "See, I told you we were dead!" One by one the girls came out from behind the aggressive one, wanting to talk. We sat on the ground and my helping spirits built a fire as I told them all I knew about Yates: his arrest, conviction, and multiple life sentences. I assured them that he would never be released and would never be able to hurt any more women. When they heard this they began to sob, holding one another and cheering wildly.

I next asked them to look up to see what they could see. One by one they saw a light that grew brighter and brighter. The women began to transform, becoming clean, attractive, and sweetly dressed. I asked for any family members already in the Light who knew and loved the women to come and reveal themselves. It was incredibly emotional as loved ones hugged and cried and collected each of the women before escorting her into the Light. I could feel tears soaking my eye covering as I watched each woman ascend, except for one . . . the hard-looking, protective, aggressive one. She jumped up off the ground, ranting that, just as expected, no one had come for her. She said she had known for a very long time she was "unloved—and unlovable."

I tried to calm her as she continued to work up an intense disgust for herself, reviewing how many men had used and abused her since childhood. She didn't trust men and felt certain that no one would come for her. I told her I knew of one man that she could count on, no matter what she had done. I told her I felt that He loved her. But she quickly got in my face—ready to argue and fight with me.

Suddenly an intense bright Light beamed down from the heavens and an image of a male began to take form. He was dressed in white and had scruffy brown hair. I quickly recognized who He was, and I was so humbled that He had come to help that more tears filled my eyes, soaking my eye covering. The aggressive one got a bit unnerved by His presence and demanded to know, "Who's that?" I told her He was Jesus, the man who loved her. Back in my face, she screamed, "I'm unlovable! No one has *ever* loved me! I am a prostitute who has done horrible things." My heart ached for the pain she must have endured as she confessed her sins.

Ever so gently, Jesus held out his hand to her, but she recoiled with alarm. I whispered to her that this was the man who loved her—who had always loved her. That no matter what she had done during her life, or what had been done to her, she had always been loved by Jesus. He held firm with his outstretched hand, radiating kindness and compassion. She tentatively edged closer to Him, still not sure what to do. I coaxed her to touch the tip of one of his fingers. As soon as she did so, she began to transform into a beautiful young woman, and the years of abuse and struggle melted away. A smile appeared on her face as she took Jesus's hand; love poured out of her eyes as she looked my way, tears flowing down her cheeks. I believe she had just experienced the feeling of love for the first time in her life—with no demands for anything in return.

Jesus smiled at her, then quickly winked at me, and together they ascended into the Light. It was the most magnificent journey I have ever experienced in my life. I broke into choking sobs as the callback to consensus reality came. My classmates weren't quite sure what to think of me until we shared our journeys; then there wasn't a dry eye in the house. My fears of death and dying have completely disappeared.

My life has been rather difficult, and more often than not conventional medicine and the mental health care system have fallen very short in terms of being able to help me. There has been a light inside me, however, that has kept me striving to find ways to heal my own soul wounds as well as a persistence to stay here, move forward, and keep learning and sharing the stories of change, growth, and healing that the practice of shamanism can offer.

In 2004, Pamela Albee, CL, CCHT, CHI (certified counselor, certified clinical hypnotherapist, certified hypnotherapy instructor), and shamanic practitioner left a thirty-two-year career in the dental field and opened a private counseling practice, which includes clinical hypnotherapy and shamanic services. She also began teaching a variety of classes in shamanism. In 2008 she became a certified hypnotherapy instructor and director of Stepping Stones Education, and she designed various courses incorporating shamanism in a clinical setting. They include Nourishing Your Soul (introductory to cross-cultural shamanism), Therapy for the Fragmented Soul (soul retrieval), and Energetic and Spiritual Soul-Clearing (extraction and depossession) for health care providers. Today she offers classes and continuing education courses for health care professionals. Pam also offers telephone coaching for mental health care professionals wanting to blend and integrate shamanic interventions into their practice. Her website is www.steppingstoneseducation.com.

44

The Story of a Bear

Leon Sproule

My relationship with Bear began when I went to Portland, Oregon, to take the Foundation for Shamanic Studies' two-week program in February of 2002. I was apprehensive about my journeying skills, but I wanted to be in the program to meet Michael Harner (who runs the foundation) and to experience the course, which its catalog description deemed to be life-changing. My life *was* changing. I had retired from my job and my dad was dying of cancer. I wanted to feel some real connection to Spirit. I remember the first session on Sunday evening as a kind of get-acquainted-with-your-neighbor journey but not much happened. I started fearing for the worst and I began to have doubts about my being able to journey well enough to help other people.

The first Monday-morning session included a journey to the lower world to meet a local ancestral spirit, whom we were to ask, "How can I help your descendants?" I started out without much going on visually, but suddenly I realized that I was looking at a Native shaman with a mask and headdress that was large and impressive. He showed me his Bear and said, "We are brothers in the Bear. You should treat me and my descendants as brothers and not judge or criticize. Open your heart. Be thankful for the opportunities that they give you." I felt as if he had spoken directly to me, as I have been critical of Native Americans in the past. I vowed to change that as a result of this journey.

We then spent time beginning to learn extraction-type healing work for the rest of the day. That night was my first introduction to the power dance. After the method was explained and the drummers began, I watched in awe as people began getting up and singing a song as they danced around the circle. I kept wanting to get up but no song came into my mind. Each time the drums came around past me the feelings were intense. I wanted to do something. I had to move! "Sit still," I told myself, "you don't have a song." This feeling of wanting to get up kept building but I wasn't going to get up unless I had a song to sing. I was going to follow the instructions.

The next time the drummers passed right in front of me, they hit the drums. My body quivered and shook and a roar came out of me that was not human. I stood up, roaring and shaking my rattle. The drummers circled around me but no one could hear my small rattle. I heard Michael say, "Someone give him a rattle." A rattle appeared in front of me and I began to shake it and move around, growling and roaring as I did so. At one point the drummers got too close and I turned on them, roaring even louder. They began drumming intensely and I turned away. I felt that the drums were trying to drive me away from where I wanted to be. I kept roaring and growling in protest.

I don't know how many times I went around the room but I was consumed by Bear. I was Bear, in all of the ferocity and power and glory that is Bear. When I collapsed back into my place in the circle, I was shaking and trying to catch my breath. I think that a couple more people got up but I didn't notice anything until I finally calmed down.

That night and the next day, people kept coming up to me and thanking me for what I had done. I felt very sheepish knowing that I hadn't really done anything and that I was just as awed by what had happened as everyone else was. During the morning session, Michael ran a question-and-answer session in which the power dance was discussed. I was asked what I had experienced when I was dancing my dance. My true feelings were that I really had been a bear and that the villagers were trying to drive me away from the village with their drums. I couldn't explain it any other way.

That began my relationship with Bear. During the two-week program, I was in over my head but my bear never let me down. He was always there. When we learned about doing soul retrievals, I was sure that I couldn't possibly do that, but when I asked for help I was told to trust Bear. I did and was able to bring a very healing part back to the person I was working with. The rest of the training went similarly. I trusted the power of Bear and got what I needed to work with the lessons and help other people. Our group became very close over the two weeks and many of us planned to continue the learning with the three-year program, which meets two weeks a year for three years in a row.

After this program ended and before the next one began, I did many healings on family and friends. Most of the journeys I undertook were nonvisual journeys in which I felt various things and received flashes of insight, which helped me to figure out what was going on with the person I was working on. I was very dependent on Bear throughout all of these healings.

The three-year program began with its own set of experiences that were sudden, powerful, physical, and emotional, and at times seemed life-threatening. Bear was with me all of the time in everything we did. I then began doing some of the exercises with other power animals. Some of these required that I use my upper-world teacher, but when I needed to do a healing that I really cared about, I relied on my Bear.

After the first session of the three-year program, I was given a bear leg bone by a friend who knew I did shamanic work. I journeyed to ask my Bear about the bone. The message came through that this was a very powerful object and could in fact be a deadly weapon. I was told to wrap it up and put it away. I would be told when and how to use it. The interesting part of that journey was when my Bear stated that the bone was "Her" bone. I came to understand that he meant the Great Bear, Ursa Major, the true mother of all bears. I learned that while my Bear was a large male grizzly, the true power of Bear was female and all-encompassing. I began to recognize that many people had Bear as a power animal.

One day as I started to do a journey as part of a long-distance healing for a friend, I was surprised to see a Native American on horseback. I asked who he was and what was he doing in my journey. His reply was that he was the shaman who had introduced me to Bear and that he was going to help me with this healing. In this journey we actually went to the person and did the healing, traveling in a middle-world journey to where the person lived. The Native American instructed that I use the bone as an eraser to remove spots from the person's chest. Later it was revealed that this person we had worked on together did not have lung cancer, as had been previously suspected. After that, I began including the bear shaman in my journeywork.

The time came in the three-year program when I needed to make a costume, including a mask of one of my lower-world spirit helpers. I decided to make the mask and costume that I had first seen the bear shaman wearing. I began a series of journeys in which I asked for specific instructions on what to do. When I was told to carve the mask from a large hunk of cedar, I was shown that the side pieces were separate and was reminded that I had a piece of cedar behind the barn that I'd been saving.

It was true. Fifteen years ago, I had tossed aside a big hunk of cedar because it was too large to go into my woodstove. I would look at it from time to time, thinking that something could be made of it, but I never did anything with it. Eventually the piece of wood got stored in the back of the barn with the rest of the junk and scrap that I was always going to do something with.

I went and dug out the hunk of cedar but I couldn't see how it was going to work for my purposes. There was a branch that was in the middle of the wood that would hamper whatever I tried to do. When I journeyed again to ask how to do this, I was told to just start.

I began splitting parts off from the chunk, trying to figure out a way to get around the part with the branch. Soon, at each step of the process, I seemed to know just what to do. After splitting off the big pieces, I cut the ends off on my band saw. I began to see how the face would fit on the wood, but the branch had left twisted wood right in the middle of the left side.

I began carving with wood-carving chisels that had been sharpened by my friend Ken, who is an excellent wood carver. I have never carved anything before. I began learning how to cut the wood. The cedar had a tendency to split if it was carved in the wrong direction. I soon learned that the direction changed as I moved through the piece of wood. I struggled where the grain was bent and twisted on the left side. I would carve until I didn't know what to do and then quit. The next day in my journey, I would see more of what I was supposed to do and work some more.

One day, as I was struggling with the twisted grain around the branch, which had to be removed to get to where the form was that I saw in my mind, I kept thinking, *Why am I doing this? What is this about? Why do I have to have this right in the middle of the mask that I am trying to make?*

I remembered that Michael had talked about how the Natives who wanted to be a bear shaman would actually go and live with the bears. All at once I saw the story in my mind. The person whom I had been calling the bear shaman had once been a young man and had desired to be a shaman. He found the den of a mother grizzly and began crawling into the den and spending time there while she hibernated. When her male cub was born, the young man continued to crawl into the den and visit and play with the cub. When spring came, he followed them around the meadows and continued to play with the cub. The mother tolerated him because she had become accustomed to his smell. She treated him almost like a second cub.

This went on for some time until one day, when the cub was about two-thirds grown, a large male grizzly appeared. He went after the young man in a fit of rage because he had interpreted this person to be a rival for the attentions of the mother. When the male grizzly charged, the cub ran between him and the man. With one quick swat of his huge right paw the grizzly smashed the cub across the face, ripping open a large wound on the left side of the cub's face and breaking the cub's nose. The cub went down and the male grizzly left with the mother bear. He drove her away from the cub, and the man was left with the severely wounded cub. He was able to nurse the bear back to health, but hunting for enough food for the cub was a full-time job. The nose was never straight and a large scar formed on the left side of the cub's face.

When the cub healed, he and the young man were inseparable. The young man became well known as a shaman for his healing abilities and the people knew the bear as the shaman's bear. No person dared to harm the shaman's bear, which was known as Scar Face or Broken Nose. The bear came and went as he wished.

This was fine until the bear became older and older and was no longer able to hunt as easily for his own food. He became a village pest and would help himself to racks of drying fish as he wandered through the camp. The people were annoyed but not annoyed enough to risk the wrath of the shaman. They began using their drums to drive the bear from the village. Each time the bear would appear and start feeding at the drying racks, the villagers would quickly assemble and get their drums. They would drum and follow him around until he left.

When this story came to me, I immediately understood. The wood was the way it was because that was how it would reveal the true story of the bear and the shaman who had introduced me to the power of the bear. I now knew the source of the feelings that had come to me when I first met Bear in the power dance. The emotions swept through me and I felt the need to share this incredible story of Spirit and how things came together over time and space to be what they were meant to be.

LEON SPROULE, PE, is an engineer, shaman, gardener, and retired person who enjoys working with and talking about Spirit. Leon was born in Wyoming and spent his early years wandering in the natural world in the Black Hills of South Dakota. Graduating with a degree in mechanical engineering, he worked for Westinghouse, where he installed the generators at Grand Coulee Dam Third Powerhouse, among other projects. Then Leon was the hydroelectric superintendent for the Spokane Water Department in charge of Upriver Dam. After leaving the city, he obtained his license as a professional engineer (PE) and taught at Gonzaga University as an adjunct instructor in addition to his work for clients. Looking for healing, Leon began studying with Michael Harner and the Foundation for Shamanic Studies in 1999 to learn about Spirit.

45

The Soul Union Community

Johanna Lor Rain Parry

Her dark, piercing eyes locked into mine. "Slowly," she said. "Slowly." Her electric gaze chilled me to my spine. I could feel the word "slowly" vibrating through my pores.

I am a forty-something, white middle-class American woman. I was born in a very small town in the redwoods of California. Redwood City is where Sequoia Hospital is. My parents took me home to La Honda. We lived on Laguna Drive, across from the lake.

My life had been typical of my social group. My parents had a nasty divorce when I was around seven; my sister had severe emotional problems. I married a bit too young, had three boys, and worked for nonprofit organizations. My marriage outlasted my parents' ten-year marriage by two years. I am now on my second marriage; my father is on his third. My mother died in a car wreck when I was twenty-one.

Like most of my high-school contemporaries of the 1970s, I leaned toward open-minded thinking, liberal politics, and activism around the important issues. After an exploration of vegetarianism, meditation, and popular New Age trends, I found what worked for me. These were, you know, the basics: integrity, honesty, surrender to the higher power, and cultivating peace within by seeking to release any negative "stuff" that might keep me from my happiness. I did my best to be a good mom, not yell, keep the house clean, and put food on the table.

A lot of my friends were involved with things like network marketing and chain letters. Everyone I knew had more than one revenue stream as income, and on top of this, they were trying to find time for "their art" or "their meditation" or "their life work." Really, though, we were all driving our kids to baseball practice, getting tired of the drag of the day, and wondering how the world would turn out, given all of its chemical spills, environmental devastation, and urban sprawl. "What in the world will our kids' lives be like, anyway?" we wondered collectively.

When I was about thirty-one, something unusual began to happen to me. I began to have experiences that could only be called "spiritual emergences." Like most folks I know, I had had unusual experiences before. Everyone has a ghost story, or has sensed a visitation, or has in some way interacted with the paranormal forms of the spiritual dimensions. But these spiritual emergences were different in that they were quite electrical in nature, being often accompanied by unusual body movements, altered states of consciousness, and radical shifts in perspective. Some call a spiritual emergence the beginning of an awakening process.

Many people my age also began to have these experiences, and because of the extreme nature and length of my own experiences of this sort, I began to do emergency phone counseling for others who were going through similar events.

The commonality and frequency of the experiences and the sheer number of people I met who were reporting them made me feel something very unusual was beginning to happen, and this alarmed me. All of this was taking place sometime around 1995.

I soon discovered a community of people who were all going through these experiences on some level. I would come to call it a spiritual emergence network, and I became an extended member of it. It had been formed by psychologists, mental health professionals, and some professors from a leading psychological institute from the Bay Area. The program later became known as Star Gate, which over time morphed into a school for spiritual unfolding that utilized age-old, time-tested spiritual practices to promote emotional balance and psychological health. Star Gate is now a growing spiritual community called Kayumari.

I was connected to the work of the leading experts on the electrical energetic emergence, which some call "kundalini awakening." Others call it "being visited by the Holy Ghost" or "being grabbed by God." Regardless, the phenomenon was increasing at a startling rate, with no real official body of observers tracking it in a clear way. My years as an administrator in nonprofit organizations had taught me the value of statistics and some part of me felt that the abnormal experiences we were all going through cried out for objective documentation.

Yet the parties involved were too busy to attend to this. Or they were too distracted, for one of the symptoms of the emergence experience is a radical change in perspective. Due to this, many experiencers found themselves trying desperately to change lifestyles, relationships, and careers. This created an unbelievable amount of chaos and left entire communities of people feeling like there just wasn't enough time for *life*.

Then it happened.

I went to a public talk with my friend Michael. We arrived at the dojo of the Institute for Transpersonal Psychology in Menlo Park to hear an East Indian yoga teacher talk about hamsa yoga. We have all heard of the yogis from the Himalayas. Many of my friends had read Paramahansa Yogananda's book, *Autobiography of a Yogi*. For me it had served as a pivotal text when I was in my late teens; it had influenced many of the decisions I had made regarding religion and spirituality. Those that didn't get through that autobiography definitely made it through Carlos Castaneda's *Don Juan*, or Richard Bach's *Illusions*, or *Siddhartha* by Herman Hesse.

Everyone I know still craves the kind of magic that these novels pronounced as fact, including my lawyer friend, Michael.

The teacher whom we would hear that night claimed to be the spiritual successor to Shri Yuketeshwar, having trained in the Himalayas during his youth with the same nath yogis who had been known to interact with the immortal Babji. According to him, he had interacted with the being Shiv Babaji Gorakshanath, who descended directly out of the sun, primarily in the Himalayas; he occasionally takes a mortal form at will. This was the pitch, anyway, that had gotten us through the door.

I sat in a semicircle comprised of a group of about thirty people. I was seated on cushions that were about four feet from a thick, floor-length, insulated glass window. The yogi, whom everyone called Gurunath, meaning "teacher or light bringer nath," was seated on a dais at the head of the room. He was short and stalky, with vividly dark eyes. Light glistened from the glassy intensity of his gaze. His curly silver hair, combed straight back, was almost to his shoulders. The energy in the room was palpably thick.

Gurunath also called himself a master of Sufiism, kriya yoga, and what we know as indigenous shamanic traditions. He began his presentation by talking about science and the electromagnetic nature of the universe. He went on to describe the location of the human soul in the body. He talked about sacred geometry and the gradual stages of evolving consciousness as one begins the process of reabsorption by the universal divine. Then he told us he would show us what it was like to be breathed by the Divine Indweller. He told us that if we could relax and become like a child of five, he would enter our breath and make it longer, richer, and deeper. He told us that everyone in the room would feel the experience of being breathed by God.

To do this, he needed to "set the energy" of the room. He adjusted himself and asked us to look only at his eyes. Then he clapped his hands together sharply.

I immediately flew backward and hit the glass window, slid down onto the floor, and lay there having electric spasms until he waved his hand my way. My body suddenly relaxed. No one else had flown backward. I felt self-conscious about the interruption as I readjusted myself. The room was so still. Then I felt it. My breath became longer, beginning down at the base of my spine, coming all the way up through my spine, and continuing slowly into my third eye center, then to go back down again. It felt very rich, like a nourishing deep draft of mountain air.

The yogi was breathing through me.

He asked the group to raise their hand if they had experienced all three qualities of longer, deeper, and richer breath moving up and down the spine. Three-quarters of the group raised their hands. By the end of the evening, everyone had experienced this. As well, we had observed his aura change colors, and then we saw him literally dissipate into white light and then reappear. There were thirty of us in the room and each individual witnessed this, but to a different degree. Thirty hands were in the air: thirty witnesses.

"Look around," Gurunath encouraged everyone. "Why would anyone here not be honest about what they see?" We then witnessed his face change from that of one great prophet to another. Again there was a show of hands, and again, every hand was up: another unified experience. We also experienced our breathing generating heat, vibration, and light in our spinal column. "You are generating electromagnetic energy for use in spiritual evolution," he told us. "Eventually, this will allow you to be reabsorbed by God, and it can happen while you are still in your physical body. You can literally become the light."

He then gave all of us the experience of one mind. Everyone in the room stopped thinking at the same time, and we were suspended in a no-thought state until he released us with a hand wave. Again there were raised hands. He repeated this Siddha, or demonstration of God unity, until all thirty people in the room had raised their hand. "You have just experienced the no-mind state of unified God consciousness," he stated simply. "All true yogis keep their mind at zero point. Now that you have experienced it, you know what you are striving for." His light, playful manner created such an ease in the room that no one seemed shocked or surprised at what had just taken place.

Now I want to tell you the most amazing part of my story, which involves an ancient prophecy. I hesitate because it is so significant and I am not sure I can communicate it effectively. This information rocked the foundation of my world, and I am still readjusting as a result. To be really honest, I will never be the same again.

All of us, my generation, your generation, we as collective Americans, know of this prophecy for our time in history right now. If you are a

Christian, the story holds a different form than if you are Jewish, or Muslim, or Buddhist, or Sufi, or Bahai. It doesn't really matter. The Hopi have a prophecy that carries the same story that the Christian prophecy holds, as does the Jewish prophecy and every religion that has chosen to publicly announce the details of the "end times" or "purification," or what I prefer to call the time of "revelation."

The essence of the prophecy is this: In the days of the revelation someone will come to us who will bring the light of salvation to us all. We will come to "realize our true nature as the light and love of God." All those willing to believe this will be saved from darkness and suffering.

We humans can interpret this in many ways, just as you will want different interpretations of the next part of this story. Eventually we will hear them all, I am sure. Once this story becomes public knowledge, things will become very interesting.

As you've learned, everything I witnessed in the presence of this yogi had also been witnessed by a large group, meaning that I definitely was not the first person to hear this astounding news. I am, however, the first one to write about it publicly.

I also want to impart some additional information about this yogi who shared his knowledge with us. He receives great respect in his mother country of India, in his resident city of Pune, and from everyone who interacts with him. He was born into the ancient Siddhanath tradition through a royal premier family from Gwalior. (The Siddhanath tradition predates Buddhism by thousands of years.)

This is not a person with an ego problem. At his birth the great nath yogis appeared at his door, much to the dismay of his mother, who feared they would take him away with them. This is not an uncommon occurrence when a yogi is born fully realized. These "wise men" came bearing gifts for the newly born householder yogi, who would later be given a world mission, not unlike other prophets born into our world.

According to Gurunath, now a self-proclaimed leader of the Nath Sampradaya, Padhma Sambhava received his spiritual initiations from the "white brotherhood of nath yogis" and then took these teachings to Tibet. Also according to Gurunath, a few of the transformational techniques such as how to dissipate the physical body into pure light were witheld because humanity was not yet ready for the information.

This is one of the many stories that Gurunath tells. "I was having a wonderful dream one night. I was walking with the Lord Jesus Christ, talking and enjoying. When we came to the end of our walk, he turned to say goodbye. As I lay back down on my bed, still dreaming, he reached down and placed his hand on my forehead. Suddenly, I woke with a start. Looking up, I saw that it *was* the man Jesus. Standing over me in my bed, with his hand still on my forehead. His eyes were blazingly dark. His long hair flowing around him."

He sometimes follows this story by stating that Jesus of Nazareth was a Siddhanath yogi known in southern India as Ishwarnath. His master's name was Chettannath. Chettannath recorded in his memoirs his student who came from afar, Jesus of Nazareth, to whom he gave the spiritual name of Ishwarnath, once he became fully realized.

What needs to be understood here is that in the nath tradition, these titles reflect states of achieved expanded consciousness. Jesus, viewed through this tradition, was an Avadhoot yogi who transformed himself through the use of his breath into the light and love of God. He was working to become an avatar, the highest level of consciousness available to a human soul, when he was crucified. Upon resurrecting himself (not an uncommon ability for a nath yogi), he packed up his family and returned to India, where today certain villagers are fully aware of his place of burial.

This same process was used by Siddhartha, another nath yogi who became the Buddha by transforming himself into an avatar being, a fully reabsorbed soul.

Gurunath clearly states that he is an Avadhoot yogi, working to transform himself into an avatar. My understanding is that if this takes place, and he chooses to remain in this realm, the consciousness of all of humanity will also be transformed.

This is an incredible story, given that this is the same man who for years was exposed to physically abusive Catholic boarding-school reeducation attempts, which innumerable Native people in our history have endured at the hands of well-meaning priests from various imperialistic nations.

After hearing this story, I spent several years working to integrate it. Since then I have been paying much closer attention to the "spiritual emergence" that many of my contemporaries are going through. I have gained a deep spiritual understanding, which I had always thought would not be available to a woman such as myself. This is not an exaggeration. What I have learned is that our Creator him/herself is constantly in the active process of enacting evolution. We can never be done discovering ourselves, and because of this, because of my desire to continue to evolve spiritually, I have been practicing the art of breathing.

I also learned a most important lesson: how in God's name could I ever, ever, ever have thought that the Creator of the entire universe didn't have everything in perfect balance? This includes what happens here on this pitifully tiny planet in a vastly remote corner of only one of the seven universes of the cosmos. Regardless of how I may interpret things, the truth remains. Perfection is constant; it is only our interpretation of it that changes. Peace is constant; it is only our rippling in the mind of forgetfulness that changes.

After I began to integrate all of the information made available to me by this most powerful being, I became incredibly impatient for the world to be free of suffering and I began to feel feverish about getting people to come hear him speak. I figured that if he had done so much for me, and if I could comprehend his message and who he really was, then anyone could. Certainly he was saying and revealing the same information to everyone. Why, then, weren't people forming lines around the block to see him?

I finally realized that people weren't interested in yet another guru from India. In fact, many of my peers who had heard Gurunath talk, as I had, then talked themselves *out* of believing what he had to say. So strong is our belief in the absence of miracles that I watched seeker after seeker allow their mind to completely forget the experience they had had in the room. They literally did not remember the power of the moment, nor the nonlogical nature of what the collective group had experienced and verified in front of each other. Even those I deemed to be spiritually advanced in some way forgot the magic that we had all witnessed. The veil of the negative mind swallowed them within several hours of their having left the session and none of them have mentioned him or it to me since.

After the 9/11 tragedy I decided to work harder to determine how this could be so. In desperation I turned to my mother, she whom I have always surrendered to. But this time, it was she in the form of Gurunath's wife, Shivangini. Her long black hair frames a glowing, cherubic face and she occupies a still, quiet space at her husband's every *satsang* (a community gathering of truth seekers), typically standing at the back of the room, speaking up in Hindu only when he gets a story a little incorrect. He then graciously acknowledges her correction, and re-explains.

I slid up beside her after a satsang one evening. Like a child, I blurted out my desperate confusion. "How is this possible?" I complained, waving my hands in the air like an Italian mime. "If he is who he says he is, where are all the people?" I wanted to know. I looked at her expectantly. I then remembered that Jesus had only twelve disciples; the masses were not really interested in consciously living in the light and love of God. That was why Jesus was killed. There was no organized media campaign to give him the protection of the people. When I read the Bible, I see references to the breath of union process everywhere.

"How on Earth is this revelation supposed to take place if no one recognizes who he is?" I mumbled.

Her dark, piercing eyes locked into mine. "Slowly," she said. "Slowly." Her electric gaze pierced and seared into my spine.

I could feel the word "slowly" vibrating through my pores. Her electric gaze held me. *The revelation of all humanity will be that we are all one soul. Full realization of this is available to everyone. It begins with our breath,* I heard in my mind.

Today there is a growing community called Hamsa Yoga Sangh. Loosely translated, it means "soul union community." This community of people is dedicated to establishing Earth peace through the reunion of the soul with the one conscious mind within all of Creation. Their master periodically comes from India to make presentations; spiritual initiations and energetic empowerment sessions are typical components of them. They also spend a small amount of time each day doing the breathing practices that are the key to expanded, still-mind awareness, which is germane to changing the energetic vibration of our atoms and molecules. It is the key to burning away all of our negative karma, or stores of negative energy, which are locked into the pranic chakra centers located along our spinal channel. This is the very same negatively charged, heavy energy that prevents humans from rising above the harmful thought patterns of the human mind.

Once the electric kundalini energy is in motion, burning off the negative charges of energy ("purification"), and we are vibrating at the same rate as the fabric of our known and unknown universe, we will certainly be reabsorbed into the eternal, Divine Light.

In the words of Yogi Raj Sat Gurunath, "If we are to herald the dawn of a new age, we must all realize that humanity is one's only religion, breath one's only prayer, and consciousness one's only God."

❖❖❖❖

JOHANNA LOR RAIN PARRY is a student of ceremony, Vedanta, and pure spirituality. She has apprenticed in lineages that span unbroken for over five thousand years. She worked to bring earth-building methods back to Native nations and showcase how local communities and townships can change local laws and permitting processes to heal the profoundly destructive "neighborhood" development process that is currently erasing our natural landscape. The organization at www.natural-villages.org outlines much of this. Johanna helped end the spraying of a chemical, highly toxic to invertebrates, that was being dumped over hundreds of thousands of contiguous acres of national forest, which effectively mutated frogs and invertebrates. She is also an artist, a graduate of the Art Institute of Seattle, and a writer who earned certifications in journalism and fiction from the Writers' Institute of New York. A grandmother with three grown sons, she spends her time writing, serving elders, and remembering.

46

The Slow Build
of a Shamanic Path

Lewis Mehl-Madrona

We all have moments of change. Some are profound, others less so. In various stories shamans have moments of epiphany in which the world shifts and everything looks different. My story is not like that. I have worked at cultivating relationships with the spirits for years, and it has been a slow process. I would have wished for an expressway to them, but my path was a footpath. Each experience led me further along the journey. I want to tell some of these experiences.

I grew up in southeastern Kentucky, raised by traditional Cherokee grandparents and not knowing that most people in the United States didn't converse with spirits. I discovered this when my mother finally succeeded in raising the money to move us to Ohio and I began high school there. What a shock! I learned to keep quiet relatively quickly.

My great-grandmother was a healer and my grandmother talked to spirits. She put out coffee and tobacco for them every morning. She was relieved when they took the coffee. My mother tried to convince her that the coffee had disappeared due to evaporation but my grandmother replied that she didn't believe in evaporation. My grandfather took me fishing as an excuse to learn how to pray. We sat on the bank, smoking tobacco, and throwing all the fish back. Only much later did I realize that we were there to pray instead of to fish.

In college, I studied biophysics. I fell into that because it seemed the most spiritual discipline at Indiana University. Sir John Eccles, a Nobel Laureate, was in residence, and he taught a course on the neurophysiology of the soul. I remember sitting in pubs with him, debating the interrelationships of soul and matter. In the psychology department, B. F. Skinner was experimenting with pigeons. I wanted to be a healer because my grandmother was one, and so I decided to go on to medical school.

Because of my work on magnetic resonance imaging, I was admitted to Harvard, Yale, and Stanford, but not to any of my state schools. I happily went to Stanford, where I discovered there was no course on healing whatsoever. I remember the moment when I decided to study traditional healing seriously. I was sitting in pharmacology class, and the professor looked at us from high on the lecture podium, saying, "Boys, life is a relentless progression toward death, disease, and decay. The physician's job is to slow the rate of decline." I was shocked. My great-grandmother, the healer, would have turned over in her grave.

I ran over to the Stanford Indian Center and found a Cherokee healer to call. By the next weekend, I had gone to Kidla's home for a visit. I eventually found another healer, Grandfather Roberts. Between these two men, I learned much. I embarked upon my alternative education in spiritual healing while studying conventional medicine at the same time.

My first moment of doing a ceremony without a teacher occurred about fourteen years after I started studying with healers. I was working as a general practitioner in San Francisco, but I was exploring as many alternative healing modalities as I could. I learned acupuncture. I learned Cherokee bodywork—a form of osteopathic healing. I practiced guided imagery and visualization. I realized that what I had absorbed from my grandmother and great-grandmother was really hypnosis and/or storytelling by others, and I was pursuing both of those practices vigorously. I was learning homeopathy and was immersed, as were many of us in those days, in nutrition and the study of micronutrients.

One day a woman hobbled into my office on crutches. She had been diagnosed with rheumatoid arthritis by specialists at the University of California at San Francisco Medical Center. She was from a higher socioeconomic status than what I was accustomed to seeing. I wondered why she had come.

She told me that she had received the best possible treatment that conventional medicine had to offer for rheumatoid arthritis, but she hadn't improved. The doctors had little else to offer her. She had heard of me and knew that I performed ceremonies. She had decided that a ceremony would cure her and wanted me to do one for her. "If you do a ceremony, it will make me well," she said.

I was taken aback. I had never had such a request before. I took all of her information and told her I would call my teacher for guidance and get back to her. That evening I finally reached Kidla. I could hear the coyotes howling behind his house. I told him everything she'd said.

"Fool," he said. "Just do a ceremony and she will be well. She's already told you that."

"But what do I do?" I asked.

"Anything," he said. "Anything will work. She's already told you so."

"Anything?" I asked.

"Anything," he replied.

"But what *specifically* should I do?" I asked.

"Just pretend you are me," he said. "Do what I would do. You've been studying with me for years. Just make it up. Be me. Perform me. Do *me.*"

So I did just that. When she returned, hobbling on crutches into my office on Sacramento Street, I welcomed her and laid out my sacred objects for doing a ceremony just as I imagined Kidla would do. I sang the songs he would have sung. I prayed in the way he would have prayed. I doctored her in the way he would have doctored her. I ended the ceremony with a pipe shared between us. I put my heart into this ceremony with the intent for her to receive what she wished. I asked the spirits to intervene.

One week later, this woman returned to my office without crutches.

She could walk freely. "Your ceremony worked," she said. "I can walk on my own." Strangely, I was amazed. I didn't really expect that it would be so dramatic. I just did what I imagined Kidla would do, and as he had predicted, she and the spirits did the rest. I excitedly called Kidla to tell him the news.

"Oh, ye of little faith," he lovingly mocked. "I told you so. We are here to make the performance so that people and spirits can act on their faith. You did your calling. You performed the ceremony. It was perfect because the spirits liked it and did what they do and she is better. That's how it works."

That was my graduation of sorts, for at that point, I was ready to do my own ceremonies for people. It had only been a fourteen-year apprenticeship and there were more to come. In addition to studying with Kidla, I was studying with another healer, Marilyn, who was Arikara-Hidatsu (the Arikara-Hidatsu were indigenous peoples of the Dakotas) and performed the ceremonies of her people. I was carrying stones for her for sweat lodge ceremonies and generally serving as her assistant. She lived south of Santa Cruz and I visited her on many weekends. I was learning the Black Elk family style of purification lodge. I carried stones for Marilyn and assisted her for ten years, overlapping my fourteen years of study, before I did my first ceremony. I had amazing experiences with Marilyn. Spirits came to her fire, to her lodges, to her healings. I saw those spirits and marveled. I spoke with them and sometimes, to my excitement, they spoke back to me.

After ten years of carrying stones, I got my chance to lead a purification ceremony in a sweat lodge. This is where we heat stones outside of the lodge, which is a dome-shaped structure made of willow saplings and covered with tarps and blankets. We bring the stones inside the structure and pour water over them. This produces steam, which we call *inipi*, the breath of life. This heals us.

I was doing a workshop in Nashville, Tennessee, and was invited to go to a purification ceremony at a spiritual community in Tennessee. I'd never miss a purification lodge, so off I went with five other people from the workshop. We drove the two hours to Somerville and showed up just in time. We found the site for the ceremony, and to my chagrin, I discovered that, instead of tobacco, marijuana would be used in the ceremonial pipe.

I argued with the people who had made this decision. "This isn't traditional!" I exclaimed. I began talking to the locals about what I understood to be appropriate and inappropriate during purification ceremonies. Apparently I really annoyed them.

"If you're so sacred," they said, "do it yourself. We're out of here." The heavily bearded, denim-clad locals marched away in a huff. What was I to do? The stones were hot. The lodge was there. Water was in the buckets. I had brought five people.

"Let's do it," I said. I pretended to be Marilyn. I imagined doing what she would have done. I loaded the pipe in the way she would have done, praying with the others over sage and putting tobacco into the pipe for each of the seven directions. I apologized to the spirits for any mistakes I might make, telling them that it was my first time and that I was leading the lodge due to unexpected circumstances.

During the ceremony, I did make mistakes. I sang some songs out of sequence and I reversed a couple directions. However, the intent was right. My heart was in the right place, and therefore it was a wonderful ceremony. The small mistakes didn't matter. I felt tolerated by the spirits, for my efforts were heartfelt.

After this, I continued to lead purification lodges. That was my initiation and approval.

During this time, I was also looking for my father, who was Lakota. The best I could do was find his best friend, who had married my mother after my father's relationship with my mother had ended—having lasted only a matter of days. My father had sworn his best friend to secrecy about him, so all I could learn was that he was Lakota and Métis (French indigenous Canadian) from Wounded Knee, South Dakota, and that he hadn't wanted to ever be found by me. His friend for whom I was named—Lewis Eugene McKinley Jr.—would tell me no more except that my father had died in a car accident in South Dakota after returning from the Korean War.

Although I didn't find my father, what I *did* find was Lakota spirituality and Sonny Richards, who became my teacher. Sonny introduced me to the vision quest (*hanbleciya*) and the sun dance. In the hanbleciya, we sit in Nature for four days and nights and "cry for a vision." I asked for assistance in becoming better at working with people to help them recover. In my most memorable hanbleciya, Sitting Bull appeared and asked me to pull buffalo skulls* for him in the sun dance. Since then I have pulled buffalo skulls around the sun dance ring every year as homage to Sitting Bull and as a request that he use his power to help others. I say to Sitting Bull, "If I do this, will you come and help the people I see?"

He says, "Yes."

I have danced the sun dance now for fifteen years. I am a late starter in that I came to the Lakota ways later in life compared to some. In each of these dances, I imagine the sick and the wounded and ask myself to suffer for them, to dance for them so that they might heal. I have amazing experiences of the Tree of Life speaking to me and seeing her spirit in her leaves. And while that is wonderful, it's really all about deepening relationships with the spirits and not necessarily experiencing the epiphany that some people describe.

It is now 2012 and I have more spirit friends than ever, although it has taken me forty years to build them. These spirits tell me who they want me to believe they are. I have contact with the five men who taught healing to Walker in the late nineteenth century. Or do I? They say that's who they are, but are they? I don't know. I just accept what they say. I also have contact with Charles Eastman, the first Lakota physician.

Whenever I am trying to help someone, I call upon these spirits and anyone else who will come and I ask them to come whether we are in ceremony or not. I ask them to come for the most ordinary medical appointments and to do what they can for the people I'm treating.

---

*Pulling buffalo skulls is a traditional practice in which skewers tied to buffalo skulls are pierced into a man's back. The man then drags the skulls around the circle as he dances. It is a form of self-sacrifice.

I think spiritual healing is about many small encounters with the spirits over many years, not about a grand epiphany in which everything changes. It's these many small encounters that build relationships in the spirit world that give us the capacity to help others. To me, that's what really matters.

Lewis Mehl-Madrona, M.D., Ph.D., graduated from Stanford University School of Medicine and trained in family medicine, psychiatry, and clinical psychology. He has been on the faculties of several medical schools, most recently as associate professor of family medicine at the University of Saskatchewan College of Medicine. He is the author of several books and has been studying traditional healing and healers since his early days, writing about their work and the process of healing. His primary focus has been on Cherokee and Lakota traditions, although he has also explored other Plains cultures and those of northeastern North America. His goal is to bring the healing wisdom of indigenous peoples into mainstream medicine and to transform medicine and psychology through this wisdom, coupled with European narrative traditions. His website is www.mehl-madrona.com.

47

Northern Lights

Lynn Andrews

Since my earliest memories, I have seen lights around people, an aura of color—green, blue, orange, red—that seems to emanate from their very bodies. As a child, I had no idea what those lights were and it never occurred to me to ask. As is the way with children, I was certain that my parents saw the same thing even though they never talked about it. It didn't occur to me that not everyone saw these lights.

My parents were both highly educated and it was important to them that I learn about the beautiful things of life. When it was time for bed, my mother would take out books on the lives of great artists, like Picasso and Beethoven, Schubert and Modigliani, and read me to sleep with exotic visions swirling through my head. My father, a member of the Nobel family and educated in Norway in childhood, used to talk to me about people he considered to be heroes and heroines, books, music, and the papers he enjoyed reading so much—everything but the lights.

I spent my early childhood on a little ranch outside of Spokane, Washington. I was an only child who was alone much of the time (until I got old enough to begin school). But even though I was alone, I never felt lonely. For as long as I could remember, I had felt the presence of a great being of light around me, a golden white glow that I could actually see fill up a room when I was concentrating on something. I had no idea what it was; it seemed just an aura of existence, a kindness and a goodness—very subtle.

Although my father talked to me about God, we didn't attend church. We also never talked about this beautiful glowing light I saw, which I did not associate with God until I was much older. I just accepted it and knew that it was always with me.

Because there were no other children nearby, my father made sure I had a horse and a dog, and as I got older I was allowed to saddle up my horse and ride out into the wilderness. Even though I was still young to be going so far alone, I was never afraid because I knew that my wonderful being of light was with me. I would talk to it as I rode out, not as a "little friend," just as a presence that made me feel very secure.

After I started Catholic school, I met a Native American girl named Bev who was my age. We used to ride our horses to school together. We also spent whole days riding through the wilderness and the great open spaces and we became good friends. Bev's father, however, was an alcoholic who could get very violent, and he was quite abusive to all of his children.

One morning in second grade, as Bev rode up on her chestnut mare, Rainbow, I could tell that something really bad had happened because there was a deep red light that surrounded her; it emanated from her. I sensed, from the intensity of that light, that she was very angry and very hurt. I remember thinking as I got on my small painted pony, Sugar, that Bev seemed to be trying very hard to act normal. In light of the pain that I could so obviously see in her, I wanted to comfort her and thus asked, "Beverly, what happened? I can see by the red lights around you that there was some trouble this morning."

And she looked at me with a look that could scorch stone.

"I'm fine," she said abruptly, tracking her fingers through her long black hair and looking away. "Everything's fine. It was just a hard morning because I was sleepy and didn't want to get up."

She wouldn't look at me, so I rode close to her and put my arm around her shoulder. She jerked away from me, so angry, and asked, "What are you doing?" Again she said, "I'm fine. And what do you mean, you see 'red' all around me? I don't see red, anywhere."

No further words were spoken the entire ride to school. After we tied up our horses and walked into the schoolyard, I said, "I am really sorry. I didn't mean to make you upset."

And Bev said, "Don't ever say anything like that again. I'm perfectly fine." She had a bruise on the back of her neck and she took a scarf out of her pocket and wrapped it around her throat to cover it.

I just stood there, wanting to say, "Everything's going to be okay." I knew she'd had a fight with her dad and been hurt. I understood that was what the red light around her was telling me. I also realized that it was very important to her that everything appear perfectly normal.

As if reading my thoughts, she turned to me, eyes blazing, and whispered, "Don't ever mention this to anyone."

I guess I invaded her space, I thought. And it occurred to me that she didn't want me to see the lights around her that allowed me to see so deeply into her. She had not asked me to do that, and although I didn't understand any of it, I decided that unless somebody asked me to see their lights, I should not mention them ever again. Mentioning it must be something that wasn't appropriate, although it seemed the most natural thing in the world to me.

Bev walked off and left me standing there, and I realized that I had nearly lost our friendship. She was my best friend, my only friend at that time really, but we would have been best friends even if there'd been other children around.

Later that night I told my father about the incident, but I didn't tell him how it started. I didn't tell him that I had seen the intense red lights around Bev and that they informed me that something was deeply wrong and I had asked her about it. My father said to me, "Don't have a best friend. Don't get too close to people because they may leave you and then who would you have? You'd have nobody."

As the days went by, I thought about how much my seeing the red lights around Bev had scared her and how I had almost lost our friendship because of it. I still didn't know that everybody didn't see lights around other people; I just decided that there must be something very wrong with talking about it. So for many years after that, whenever I would see things in people, see their pain and their need for healing and comfort, I would never tell them, or anybody else, for that matter. I kept things to myself. I went deeply inside myself and decided to hide my ability, whatever it was.

But I didn't feel good about hiding something that was so very important to me. It felt more like a burden I was carrying rather than something that could be used to help people. And yet I didn't want to experience the anger and rejection I had felt from Bev ever again. Because I didn't know where to find someone I could trust to ask about it, I never tried to find answers to why I could see these lights around people and understand the pain that was behind them. I just felt different, somehow, and more separate than ever.

Today it's curious to me that I never asked my paternal grandmother, Lala, about it. She was an accomplished musician in Europe and for many years we carried on a very dear correspondence. She was quite spiritual in her own way. She used to talk to me about her relationship with the "Little People," the sacred fairies, and she even told me that I was the only one she could speak with about such things. I felt honored, but I still didn't talk to her about the lights I saw.

I went to Catholic school and I loved it and the nuns who taught me to play the piano. I discovered that I really liked the study of classical musicians and the music they created, and the study of great art and great writers. The school had a beautiful place to pray, a chapel where I could go to be with the great being of light that I didn't feel safe describing to others. I was so afraid they would be angry with me, as Bev had been.

I didn't go to Bible school, but I was beginning to understand that the golden-white glow I saw was connected to the Creator of our exquisite life. I sensed, however, that my experience of this beautiful light was not analogous to the manner by which the nuns experienced Jesus or God, if that's what the light was. In any event, I so loved to sit in the chapel surrounded by this wonderful glow, feeling close to something very sacred. To me, the great artists I was studying had all been inspired by God. They had been given incredible insight and great talent, which they developed into extraordinary ability. I took what I was learning through the study of music and sat in the chapel with the light, talking about art and music. I wanted to understand the artists' inspiration— what had inspired Mozart to suddenly come up with his magical sonatas. It made me feel very close to Creation, and I gradually began to understand that I was really talking with God.

I had always wanted to study higher consciousness as I understood it to be. I had also wanted to teach, if only I could figure out what it was I was supposed to be teaching. I had hidden the sacred light I saw and my ability to see lights around people for so long that I'd begun to lose all concept of myself as an individual, even though I had long since realized that other people didn't see these lights.

As I got older, thankfully my outlook began to change. I had discovered that if someone had a headache or a sore neck, when I put my hands on them, their ache would go away. It was not something I ever spoke about with anyone. But the more this happened, the more I wanted answers, so I started asking others about "seeing lights around people," but I didn't tell them why I wanted to know. They, in turn, would usually look at me like I was out of my mind.

At that point, given the lack of answers, I started reading everything I could get my hands on. I read the Bible. I read the sacred texts of the Middle East. I discovered that there were many psychological works about healing, but nothing, really, about seeing lights around people and in those lights seeing their pain. I read everything from Carl Jung to Antoine de Saint-Exupéry, the author of the book *The Little Prince.*

As lives go, I think I moved from my teenage years into adulthood in a fairly typical manner. After college, I entered into a venture with R. Buckminster Fuller to develop environmentally sensitive toys that would give children a sense of their own power to influence the world around them, and I got involved in producing documentaries in both the United States and Europe.

But I still didn't talk about my ability to see lights around people, my ability to see and understand their pain. I didn't talk about the great being of light that could actually illuminate an entire room. I knew that I had been given wonderful gifts, but my childhood experience with Bev kept nipping at my heels and I was afraid I was doing something wrong. I felt I was not living up to the gifts I had been given, unlike the artists and musicians I had studied who had given me so much inspiration, and I didn't feel very good about being *me*.

Things changed for me when I met Agnes Whistling Elk and Ruby Plenty Chiefs, two female shamans from the far north of Canada, who took one look at me and knew exactly what I was seeing and how sacred it was, to them as well as to me. They are part of the great spiritual tradition of shamanism, which sees energy and understands energy and knows how to use energy to heal the spirit, mind, and body.

In the months before meeting them, I had been having very strange dreams, and the instant I met Agnes, I knew she was the woman I had been dreaming. All of a sudden, the pieces of my life fit together, all of them. In Agnes's kindness, beauty, and graciousness I found so much meaning and purpose in life, and I finally knew who I was.

Which was the greater epiphany, discovering my ability to see lights around people and to understand intuitively what those lights meant, or meeting the women who would make it all make sense to me and show me how to develop and use my ability to heal and teach others, as I had longed to do my entire life?

Perhaps the answer lies in sitting with the great Northern Lights of a summer's eve. We know intellectually where those lights come from, but in them there is such a sense of mystery and awe that it makes us want to know more, see more, and experience more of the wonder of life. Curiously, through the marvels of modern technology, we have developed the ability to actually photograph auras around people. Now all we have to do is learn, as a culture, to understand what the variations and nuances of those lights tell us about the energy blocks we create within ourselves that make us ill. We need to also learn how to use that same energy to heal, as Agnes and Ruby and their amazing circle of female shamans do—and taught me to do as well.

Try sitting with the Northern Lights or a beautiful sunset. Allow yourself to be moved into the great mystery and beauty of life and maybe you will hear the song lines of Creation that illuminate your soul, as I do. We all have gifts, which we can experience if we will sit still and listen to their call.

LYNN ANDREWS is the *New York Times* and internationally bestselling author of the Medicine Woman series, which chronicles her three decades of study and work with shaman healers on four continents. Her study of the way of the sacred feminine began with Agnes Whistling Elk and Ruby Plenty Chiefs, Native American healers in northern Canada. Her quest for spiritual discovery continued with a shaman curandera of the Mayan Yucatán, an Aboriginal woman of high degree in the Australian Outback, and a Nepalese healer in the foothills of the Himalayas. She is initiated as a member of the Sisterhood of the Shields, forty-four women who are healers from cultures as diverse as Panama, Guatemala, Australia, Nepal, North America, and the Yucatán. Today, Lynn is recognized worldwide as a leader in the fields of spiritual healing and personal empowerment. Her website is lynnandrews.com.

Back Where It All Began

Itzhak Beery

All I could share with the eager group of thirty strangers who were sitting on the floor in a big circle was, "I know my name, Itzhak, but I no longer know who I am and I'm no longer sure of what reality is." My throat was dry, and I was choosing my words carefully. I was in the first class of a shamanic workshop at the New York Open Center that was being run by Nan Moss and David Corbin. I took a big deep breath and shared with them that a few months prior I had returned from a trip to Ecuador, and that trip had challenged my whole identity and the beliefs I held about myself. No longer could I consider myself a "normal" person, artist, advertising man, and atheist. I confessed how deeply depressed I had become by these realizations I had arrived at in Ecuador, and how, as a result, I couldn't make sense of why I was here on this Earth. Nothing had prepared me for this upsetting turn of affairs, even though I had already taken a basic core shamanism course with Michael Harner and had participated in another shamanic workshop with John Perkins.

It all began in March 1997, after a week of visiting shamans in the high Andes Mountains of Ecuador, where I met for the first time the man with whom I would eventually apprentice, Yachak don Jose Joaquin Pineda. Our group of sixteen, from the Dream Change Coalition with John Perkins, had made our way east to Baños, a small and colorful town famous for its ancient thermal baths, towering waterfalls, and lots of sugarcane stands. Baños, a gateway to the jungle (known as the Orienté), is popular with many travelers seeking information and supplies before starting on their jungle adventures.

After a long wait, our bus was finally granted permission by the military forces that dutifully controlled the comings and goings of that oil-rich and indigenous-population territory in the early evening. In a long caravan of heavy trucks and old cars, we embarked on a snail's pace and dangerous ride down the Pastaza River. The twisted muddy road led us down the steep gorge. It was slippery and difficult to navigate. Periodically I prayed that our expert old driver would make the long grueling overnight trip. At sunrise, as fog still was covering the ground, we entered Shell, a tiny oil town with a small military airport where we were to board a six-seat Cessna that would take us beyond the Cutacu Mountain range to reach Miazal. This Shuar community of sparsely populated longhouses was our final destination. We came to participate in sacred plant medicine healing ceremonies and learn their way of life. The Shuar, as we were told by John beforehand, are also known as the Jivaro and the "headhunters" of the Amazon. They are fierce warriors who had never been occupied by the Spaniards and practiced head shrinking until the mid-1960s, when missionaries arrived to "save their souls." They used to spread out over a large part of the jungle, but eventually they escaped to this small area as Western civilization slowly crept deeper into their territory.

Streams of small waterfalls dug deep burrows in the rich, soft soil and washed over the dangerous, winding road. Looking through the dark glass windows two hundred feet into the dark canyon, from which emerged the roaring sound of gushing water, literally took my breath away. I remember thinking to myself, "What the hell am I doing here, leaving behind safe life, loving family, and familiar world? What if it all will vanish in a second with the bus falling off the cliff? Am I crazy? Why?" I felt that familiar ball of fear swirling in my stomach.

A few hours after sunrise, once we were airborne, a mesmerizing vision appeared beneath me. I could finally see for the first time the

Sacred Anaconda, the famous Amazon river, majestically surrounded by an infinite ocean of green jungle.

Cautious Shuar men, women, and children from the community, dressed in colorful shorts and T-shirts and adorned with beads, welcomed us as our plane touched down on the grassy landing strip. Some approached us with big smiles and proceeded to unload our belongings into the waiting canoes. We shook hands and piled into the canoes, and gliding down the tributary, we found ourselves in a small jungle encampment in less than an hour. We settled down in our small bamboo-walled rooms and then toured the area, adjusting to the jungle's hot and humid weather. I marveled at its plethora of plants, birds, and animals—and then I had my first encounter with the vicious red fire ants, which took advantage of my innocent bare feet. My feet ballooned in a few minutes to a size I never expected possible, and it was hard to shove them into my new rubber boots. As darkness fell we gathered in the improvised kitchen to eat our last dinner (not much) before the planned ceremony the next night and the hiking trip the next morning.

Waking up in this primary paradise the next day was a dream come true. I waited eagerly to meet the shaman and his wife, who, we were told, had walked for three days through the thick jungle to work with us. But we could not wait very long. To cleanse our digestive system and clear our mind we had to embark on a vigorous day of challenging hiking up to the twin sacred waterfalls. It was traditionally done to intensify the ayahuasca's effect and reduce our body's resistance to it.

Still in darkness that early morning, *uwishin* (shaman) Daniel Guatchapa had walked deep into the jungle to harvest those "plant teachers," a fresh bunch of chacruna leaves and *natém* vines (ayahuasca in Quechua), also called "vine of the dead." They are the plants of the ancestral spirits. And to retain the pure essence of their energy he had to pick them fresh before sunrise. It took him the better part of the day to clean them carefully, cut them, and then boil them slowly, until the plants became a thick brown drink. Throughout this process he chanted his *icaros*—the sacred prayer songs—asking his ancestors' spirits, the jungle spirits, and the plant spirits to come and help him during the healing he would perform that night.

As night finally fell, we gathered in the round community lodge, with its thatched palm-leaf roof. I could feel the tension building in the warm, heavy air. We sat quietly on the dugout canoe benches along the walls, looking into each other's eyes, whispering and making some small talk. We were truly nervous in anticipation of the unknown. Even the night creatures' cacophony began to sound sharper and more alarming than before. All of us were tired and hungry.

Daniel Guatchapa was sitting by his wife near the entrance. He was barefoot and clad only in shorts. Juan Gabriel, our Spanish-speaking guide, was sitting by them. By now the Shuar's traditional three-log fire was almost out, and Juan began to explain how the ceremony was going to be held and what to expect while we were under the influence of the mysterious drink. With prayer, Daniel poured himself a glass of the ayahuasca brew, consumed it, and began chanting to himself a long, beautiful, monotonous rhythm. When he felt ready, he motioned us one by one to come sit in front of him on a turtle-shaped stool and tell him our intentions for the healing. He then held the glass to his mouth and performed an individual chant to each glass.

I tried to come up with a "significant" question in my mind, afraid that I might waste this rare opportunity. I decided to ask: "What does the future hold for me before I reach my fiftieth birthday?" I shared my question with him and he then handed me the bitter, smelly drink. I gobbled it up, washed it with trago (sugarcane rum), sniffed wild tobacco water, and went back to my place.

I witnessed many amazing teachings and visions that night, but I do not wish to exhaust you with all the details. Some of them, however, are worth telling, as they really changed my life.

I lay on the hammock waiting. After a while my stomach was beginning to churn. I needed to purge. Held by my friend, we crossed the three-log fire in the center of the lodge, passed by the shaman, and went into the bushes in front of our communal lodge. I bent forward toward the bush's large leaves and a huge gas bomb blasted out of my mouth.

At that moment I heard the plant asking me, "Look deep inside me." I held its leaves in my hands, brought them closer to my eyes, and looked at them intently. To my true disbelief, I started to see from the inside of the leaf. I witnessed its internal composition. I saw every cell and every vein of it; they were radiating golden-green light, and darker shades of green veins ran through them. I felt how the sun's energy was being absorbed in it. I was surprised to see the intricate tube architecture and construction of the inner plant, to see the water drops flowing inside it, feeding every cell.

Each cell had thoughts and feelings and wanted to communicate them with me. I started to talk to the plant through my heart. I knew we understood each other on the deepest and most intimate level. "You humans don't recognize that we are also a complete living being with wisdom, thoughts, and feelings just like you humans," it said, and then added, "We are truly happy to be here on this Earth to serve you with all your needs. All humans have to do is to ask us for help properly." They went on by saying, "If you want you can always easily communicate with us directly by focusing your intentions and your vision deeply into our essence."

My wide-open eyes were hurting and I felt exhausted. I fell on my knees, bent over, and took in the rich smell of the jungle soil. I opened my eyes and there he was, a small moth on the dark ground, an inch away from my nose. I studied him carefully. He was brown and hairy, with two large gray-and-black eyes painted on his wings. In an instant, he grew huge and, to my surprise, I merged with him—becoming the moth itself.

Soon I was hovering silently above the jungle canopy. From above, I saw the jungle in full daylight, as if it were high noon. The jungle spirits continued to communicate with me. "Watch this view carefully, and take it in deeply." They went on, saying, "You came here to help protect the jungle and all the enormous life-forms it holds." And in urgency, "Time is running out, we need all the help you can give us." With tears in my eyes I promised to do all that I could possibly do to help. I felt a huge sense of personal responsibility, pain, and fear, which brought me back down to the jungle's dark soil. I stood up slowly and went back to my hammock, waiting to be summoned for my healing.

Soon I heard my name called. Visions were flooding my head and the act of walking, even with the help of my friend, was a very unstable task in the total darkness. I took my shirt off and, lying on my back, closed my eyes. At this point Daniel started whipping my body with a bunch of fresh green branches while chanting a rapid rhythmic icaro in his soft, melodic voice. "Bee, bee, bee, bee, dee, bee, dee, dee, bee, bee, bee . . ." he sang. I was fascinated by the geometrical shapes that I was now seeing and by his enchanting voice. With a loud gurgle he was now throwing his *tsentsak,* the magical dart, at different parts of my body, sucking out the bad energy from them and then spitting it out on the dirt floor with loud growling sounds.

To my astonishment my body responded by involuntarily pulling itself up every time he did this. Suddenly, I felt a big anaconda snake enter my anus and slowly crawl all through my intestines, making its way up my body. As it did so, my body began turning and twisting unwillingly with the force of the smooth snakelike movements.

When it reached my throat I stopped breathing. I opened my eyes in despair to see, to my left side, a jaguar peeking out from behind a large green bush. At first it appeared in a cartoon form and then it transformed into the real animal. Without hesitation, the jaguar leaped onto my face, and at that precise moment I released a dark cloud of garbage from my mouth and he swallowed it whole. The anaconda pushed the same blocked bad energy out of my body. I let go and relaxed onto the bench, at the same time noticing that I was totally at peace with all these happenings.

The shaman then put his mouth on mine and softly blew his spirit and breath into my mouth. Then he put his mouth over my chest and sucked all traces of the ayahuasca from my body. To my amazement my head cleared instantly in a miraculous way. I felt tired and at the same time energized and stunned.

Swinging lightly on my hammock, I closed my eyes and relaxed. Listening intently to the night's sounds, the millions of cicadas, the croaking frogs, the soft wind brushing the leaves, the river murmuring below, the hypnotic icaro chants, and the people who were throwing up in the bushes, it all became one big harmony, a magical symphony of Nature.

As I opened my eyes again I noticed that the trees in front of me had shapeshifted into three huge well-sculptured Shuar warriors, like the presidents' faces carved on Mount Rushmore. They looked straight at me, talking, winking, and having fun amongst themselves. I was in awe. "We trees also have individual faces and distinct personalities, just like you," they told me before I drifted into a light sleep.

The next day, after the long-awaited breakfast, I sat again in front of Daniel Guatchapa on the turtle-shaped wooden stool and described to him what I had seen and experienced the previous night. I asked him to explain to me what it all meant. His narrowed and intent black eyes lightened and he laughed wholeheartedly. He said that he had seen it all too and as a matter of fact, he had been responsible for introducing the anaconda and the jaguar to me. They were his power animals and had done his bidding very well. When he told me this, I felt both thankful and disoriented.

"The plane is arriving; hurry up before the storm comes," we were told. We packed quickly, said goodbye to our new friends, and started our hike back to the grassy airstrip through the rain forest's winding path. I walked hurriedly, deep in thought, trying to recount the previous night's experiences one by one as overhead I heard the sound of the Cessna plane approaching.

I realized that I could not rely on logic to explain the events of the previous night; it just wouldn't work. This confused me. "How can this ceremony manifest in the material world?" I wondered. I could not deny my experience. "What is real? Who is real? How can I now live in a world that has no clear definitions, nothing to hold on to?" I sure knew that the anaconda and the jaguar were real, but were they really? In what dimension? In my analytical mind I knew that the shaman had sucked the ayahuasca right off my chest because I had felt it; my brain had been cleared. But how could this be?

I also knew that when I had looked at the bush, I knew its feelings and was able to communicate with it. But I could not explain why this was so. I also knew, deep inside myself, that if we don't do everything we can to save this jungle and these incredible possessors of knowledge, we won't be able to explain that either.

Back in New York, I didn't have anyone to share my experiences and thoughts with. I decided to meet similar people by joining a shamanic workshop at the New York Open Center, and, together with a group of participants, we founded the New York Shamanic Circle, which now hosts almost sixty events a year. I also founded Shaman Portal, a website that promotes traditions of shamanic activities and teachings around the world. I did this in order to keep my promise to the spirit of the moth and the jungle.

Through my teachings and healings I hope to spread the shamanic message around the world. This book is part of that message. I hope it will encourage you to spread your own shamanic wings and fly.

✧ ✧ ✧ ✧

ITZHAK BEERY is an internationally recognized shamanic healer, teacher, and author. He was initiated into the Circle of Twenty-Four Yachaks by his Quechua teacher in Ecuador and by Amazonian Kanamari Pagè. He has also trained intensively with other elders from South and North America. The founder of ShamanPortal.org and cofounder of the New York Shamanic Circle, he is on the faculty of the New York Open Center. His work has been featured in the *New York Times*, films, TV, and webinars. An accomplished visual artist and owner of an award-winning advertising agency, he grew up on Kibbutz Beit Alfa in Israel and lives in New York. Itzhak's book *The Gift of Shamanism: Visionary Power, Ayahuasca Dreams, and Journeys to Other Realms* was published by Inner Traditions. His website is www.itzhakbeery.com.